ON LOSS

AND LIVING

ONWARD

Published by Familius LLC, www. familius. com

Familius books are available at special discounts for bulk purchases for sales promotions, family or corporate use. Special editions, including personalized covers, excerpts of existing books, or books with corporate logos, can be created in large quantities for special needs. For more information, contact Premium Sales at 559-876-2170 or email specialmarkets@familius. com

Library of Congress Catalog-in-Publication Data

2014935341

pISBN 978-1-938301-92-6
eISBN 978-1-938301-69-8

Printed in the United States of America

Portions of essays have been published previously on the author's blog "Melissa Writes of Passage"

Versions of "Wilkommen in Oktoberfest" and "Schooling Grief" have been previously published in Melissa Dalton-Bradford's *Global Mom*

"Bridge to Elysium" was previously published under the title "Irreantum" in the *Journal of the Association for Mormon Letters.*

Edited by Ashley Isaacson Woolley, Maggie Wickes, Aimee Hancock, and Michele Preisendorf. Special assistance from Jessie Christensen and Sharlee Mullins Glenn.

Cover design by David Miles

Book design by David Miles and Maggie Wickes

Author photo by Michelle Lehnardt

10 9 8 7 6 5 4 3 2 1

First Edition

ON LOSS

AND LIVING

ONWARD

COLLECTED VOICES

for the Grieving and Those

Who Would Mourn with Them

MELISSA DALTON-BRADFORD

EARLY HARVEST

Midsummer. Eventide. Live waters.

You: broad-backed bundle of golden sheaves

hewn down,

washed,

rushed

headlong through death's threshing current.

You: pre-ripe, holy harvest

wrested from these, your people;

gathered to those, your people

who attend from iridescent pastures.

You: Firstborn son,

First fruits of my womb,

Firstling of our flock,

First raised of our labors . . .

Enfolded now in the arms of the

First raised from the dead,

First lover of the flock,

First fruits of the tomb,

Firstborn Son . . .

O, Son!

Sweet, sacrificial fruit of my flesh,

Preserved in spirit

'Til that first morn when you, our first reborn,

Shoot forth

'Mid spring.   'Mid song.

For Parker Fairbourne Bradford, February 20, 1989–July 21, 2007

OH, THAT MY words were now written! oh that they were printed in a book! That they were graven with an iron pen and lead in the rock for ever!

For I know that my redeemer liveth, and that he shall stand at the latter day upon the earth:

And though after my skin worms destroy this body, yet in my flesh shall I see God:

Whom I shall see for myself, and mine eyes shall behold.

—Job 19:23–27

CONTENTS

INTRODUCTION

IT WAS A Wednesday when Parker and I stood together under midsummer heat in a parking lot in front of his first college apartment. Just a week earlier, this firstborn of ours had begun a program called Freshman Academy and was already so settled and at ease, so optimistic and brimming with contentment, he was radiant. With characteristic gusto, he bounded around his apartment complex, introducing me to a bunch of his new friends, giving me the rundown of every class and professor, and raving about how great everything was. He said he had been learning at "turbo speed," and now felt he had made the right choice to come to this school for one semester before leaving in the winter to serve as a missionary for our church. He was, as he announced confidently, exactly where he should be.

Although I tried to act nonchalant and give him space, I was all awriggle inside as I took in every square inch of my son and his new surroundings. Heart churning with maternal pride at such a son and friend, I remember inhaling slowly, gratefully. *We've launched our eldest*, I thought. *Look at him. Beautiful boy.*

"Okay, Mom, forget food, chocolate, money, whatever," he'd said, shrugging, hands hooked loosely on the edge of his jean pockets. "Next package, just send lots more family pictures, all right?"

"Pictures? I'm on it."

Reluctantly feeling my way into having him start a life apart from us, I was secretly tickled to know my grown son just wanted more of *us*. Flattered, actually, that family trumped a crate of Butterfingers.

"Hey, when you guys come again, bring everyone with their swimsuits, 'kay?"

He had already sent daily emails, a couple with pictures of the canals and swimming holes to which the locals had directed the newly arrived students, places they went after class to keep cool and have fun. For Parker, who'd spent the first half of his life on a small, closely patrolled island in Norway and the second half of his life in the heart of Paris, this rural world of southeastern Idaho with its unmarked, open irrigation canals and meandering rivers was more than a novelty to him. It was downright exotic. He'd never seen the likes of this before.

"Swimming suits? You're serious?" I chuckled, knowing he was completely serious. "All right, just promise you'll take care of yourself and"—here came the thing mothers feel, and it went right to my spine, tightening it like a rope of twisting metal cables—"don't take any risks. Please stay safe."

Before I could finish speaking, he was shaking his head, one eyebrow cocked.

"*Risks*? Come *on*. The standards at this school are like . . . " he held his hand to gesture above his six-foot-two height, ". . . like way up *here*."

I tried to lighten up and laughed with him.

"No, but Parker," I added, planting my palm flat on his chest. "Risks with *you*. I'm talking *physical* safety. It's Mom talking. Don't take any risks."

Tilting his head, he squinted, released a barely audible puff of air through his lips and waved off my concern. Though confident and energetic, he had no history of dangerous behavior, and we both knew that. No extreme sports. No pranks. He had never gotten as much as a parking ticket. In fact, he didn't have a driver's license yet. Having spent his adolescence in Paris, the closest thing to a license he had was his subway pass, which he'd used to effortlessly navigate the city he'd called home. "Risky" was jumping onto a public bus without a stamped ticket. And that, well, he *had* done.

Still, for some reason I did not understand, I could not uncoil that constricting metal cable that now felt cold in my back.

"No, really, honey. I'm just say—" And for a fraction of a second I let myself lean into the words. "You mean *everything* to me."

So much for nonchalance.

He squirmed out from under my smooshy blanket of protection and we hugged firmly, kissed each other on the cheek, and said our see yas and love yous.

Those were our parting words. I have replayed the conversation at least a thousand times in my head.

I planned on seeing him again in just three days, so this was no heart-wrenching good-bye. I was now focused on getting out of the late afternoon heat, into air conditioning, and back on the road to Utah Valley—a five-hour drive south. Parker, I could tell, was focused on getting back to his friends. There had been talk about a water activity that night or the next.

Slipping into the driver's seat, I wasted no time switching the air to full blast. How hilarious would that be, I thought—some makeshift irrigation canal beach party with the mom, the dad, the three younger siblings, Parker, his band of new college buddies, an inflatable volleyball, and a chorus line of oblivious cows chomping alfalfa in the background. I caught my own reflection smiling back at me as I glanced in the rearview mirror for a parting look at my boy.

Over my shoulder, casually, accompanied by some banal stream of consciousness about sweat or seat belts, captured in a mirrored rendition and through smoked glass, I saw him. It is a peculiar, fleeting, but endlessly-repeated film clip which has worn its frames into my memory: daylight saturates the royal blue of his T-shirt, the edges of his shoulder blades move beneath the taut stretch of fabric, the arms swing easily, those busy, mitt-like hands tap a happy, trilling little beat on his thigh. All that anticipatory energy under all that movement—the hops down some steps, the back that appears to me suddenly so broad, so capable, and the heartbreaking promise of it all. And that blue color changing as it passes from full daylight into the shadows of a doorway.

Before I turned from the parking lot to the street, I looked back to catch a glimpse of him again. But he had already ducked into his apartment and was gone from view.

I drove away.

The next night, in an ICU at the Port Neuf Regional Medical center in Pocatello, Idaho, I saw those same shoulders again. They were just as ample and perfectly formed, but they lay as motionless as stone. There was no blue T-shirt, nor any shirt for that matter. His body was stripped naked and draped from the waist down with a white sheet and laid facedown on a gurney to drain fluid from his lungs while they contracted and expanded with the ventilator. Like a toppled Greek statue of polished, gray-veined marble, my exuberant man-child lay in a deep coma. Life support shooshed in-and-out its feeble tide. A nurse avoided making eye contact with me, but told me, as she busied herself with the machinery snaking in and out of my child's body, that I had a "gorgeous hero son." She told me that he had repeatedly tried to save a drowning fellow student, that the two had been sucked into and pinned underwater in "one of those darned hidden undercurrents" under a small bridge in "one of those darned irrigation canals," and that the fellow student had survived.

In spite of every possible scientific and spiritual intervention, Parker would not survive. Nothing caused matter to defy gravity. Not even my own faith, which thundered and churned inwardly like the massive engines of the sinking Titanic.

On the morning of Saturday, July 21, sixty-five hours after feeling his heart beat against my own in a hug under the summer sun as bright and vital as he was, Parker Fairbourne Bradford was pronounced brain-dead. His life support was removed and his lungs released a final sigh of this earth's air. That scant whisper gouged vengefully into the V space where my ribs meet. Then a rip—swift, sweeping, lethal—tore all the way through me.

———————

"RESURRECTION IS FOR those on both sides of the tomb," writes minister Laura Mendenhall, in a eulogy given at the funeral of an infant girl. Of that truth, I am living proof. When your most beloved dies—when your profoundly bonded flesh and blood dies—you die too. It seems the inviolable law of nature. My "death" manifested itself physically—the heart palpitations, the anvil on my chest for months on end, the weakness, the fatigue, the overwhelming longing for endless, blue-black drifts of oceanic sleep. My child's death also marked the zero point, or meridian, of my life; everything I know is measured as *before* and *after* that split.

Resurrection—the metaphorical one—takes both a staggering amount of effort and a continuance of God's life-giving grace over a very long period of time. It takes much more work and far more grace and many more years than anyone uninitiated in traumatic loss seems to fully realize.

Like a literal resurrection, our family's resurrection began from underground. We were buried in sorrow, entombed in grief. Our family had been in the middle of a move from Paris to Munich, Germany when we lost Parker—we entered a new geographic world at the same moment we entered the alien land of loss—which translated into an extreme kind of isolation. Isolation complicated our grief. But it offered us solitude as well, which we needed. Our souls instinctively needed darkness and retreat—a wilderness place apart—a certain protection from the glaring and blaring invasion of the world at large. This first inclination, though we didn't know it at the time, had an ancient name: *avelut.*

Avelut is a prescribed course of grief that has its roots in centuries of Jewish tradition. I stumbled upon that term somewhere on a deep midwinter morning close to that soul-chilling first Christmas without Parker. Throughout the year of avelut, those who mourn (particularly parents grieving the loss of children and children the loss of parents) remove themselves from normal celebrations, entertainments, or other distractions. They do not listen to, watch, or read anything that is "this-worldly" or frivolous. For the earnest *avel,* as my husband Randall and I unwittingly became, that meant no television or movies, no magazines or newspapers, no casual Internet surfing, no mall hopping, no iPod jogging playlists or similar music, no German Fussball games, and (thankfully) no Oktoberfest.

Avelut sounds extreme, I know. But it was what our souls naturally hungered for. And in case I make it or us sound all too holy, all I can say is that nothing felt quite holy enough. We hungered to stay close to the reverence we had experienced those first few days, close to where we always felt that the Spirit and its strength and light—and Parker—were accessible. We did what we could, both together and individually, to hold on to that holiness. This meant holing up. As a result, that first year was about as close to monastic living as any married couple could get.

As they withdraw socially, avels enter an intense journey of meditation and study. For the Jew, this study is of the Torah; for us, it was of all holy scriptures and literally dozens of the best books on the subjects of loss, grief, spirituality, and the reality of eternal life. Never having read a grief memoir in my life, I was now amassing my own library of them. During my first year of avelut, every morning when the children left for school and Randall left for the office or for the airport, I turned to my daily pattern of digging and searching amid piles of books spread about me in a circular mountain range. I sat cross-legged on the floor with sometimes twenty books open at once: Testaments, both Old and New and other scriptures of my faith; a poetry anthology; a modern French novel; a German lyric; a prophet's or pioneer's personal journal; a Norwegian memoir; a commentary on the book of Job; a stack of professional journals on parental grief; collected talks from great spiritual leaders past and present and from the East to the West; discourses from Plutarch and Plato; my *Riverside Shakespeare*; accounts of Holocaust survivors, 9/11 survivors, tsunami survivors; and Parker's own words, which we have treasured in his journals, poetry, school essays, letters, and lyrics.

Oh. And my laptop.

For hours to months on end, I went spelunking through others' words. When someone's words hit the bedrock of the Spirit, I knew it in half a breath. There were revelatory moments when a correct insight stunned me to immediate tears or, more often, head-to-toe stillness. At times my heart would leap a hurdle or my eyes would stretch wide open; other times I would hold my breath or exhale audibly in gratitude. Whatever my physical and intellectual response, every time a writer *got it*, I'd quickly type those words into my files.

Unswerving, I kept at it—mining, sifting, cataloging; grieving, mourning, learning, writing; adapting. While I never found the *one* book that for me addressed the desperate underside of grief as well as the magnificent promise of the loving bond that endures and evolves despite physical separation, I was (to my surprise) on my way to writing one.

And today—almost seven years after Parker was taken in an early harvest that plowed our souls right open—I finished this book. I lovingly pass it on to you.

Its essays recount our family's intimate experience with major, obliterating loss and our life's road as it has rolled on before us with both its potholes and its landmarks of bright-burning, spiritual significance. Its quotes are like the flecks of gold I have finally brought to the surface after mining for so long at the center of the earth. It is, however, only an outward token of our family's grief and a tangible proof of my avelut, because what I can't pass on and what can't be sampled vicariously is the experience of this journey itself. Our descent into the necessary weight and waiting that are part of being instantly buried alive and then slowly resurrected have revealed much to us. We have felt on our very chests the suffocating tonnage of the grave and of grave realities. We have felt detached from life "up there" on the surface. We have felt at times terrified and often quite alone. We have even walked hunched over, like we'd lived forever in underground tunnels or were just creeping out of our own graves.

But what the tomb teaches! In its isolation and obscurity you see and sense what is hardly visible or palpable in broad daylight. Somewhere there, as you wait on the Lord—as you lie flat, motionless, arms wrapped over your shredded heart, holding your breath or weeping aloud—you feel the hint and muted hum of light reverberating within that tomb, within your soul, a vibration coming from a source nearby. Of course, it was there all along, that lucent presence, that light-that-shineth-in-darkness. But you couldn't comprehend it. In your agony and desperate disorientation, you couldn't comprehend it.

In silence, in retreat, in your necessary entombment, your soul gradually reorients itself and, with a slow turn, you see the source of that soft vibration. You realize He was seated next to you in that darkness, quietly waiting, His eyes mellow and steadying, His hands resting calmly on your head, emitting real heat.

There, touched by God's incandescent grace, your grave is transformed into a bed of rebirth. Your cold body is warmed to new life. Noiselessly, He stands. And you, drawn by ardor, follow as He rolls away the stone with an outstretched finger. Just one glance and you understand that He is asking that you reenter the world with its sometimes blinding sunlight and frequent neon facsimiles. He is asking that you follow Him from death to a new life, which you gratefully give back to Him.

And so once again—raising us from either grave sin, grave sorrow, or from the grave itself—Christ has conquered death.

While Christ offers life and love without measure, I can but offer hope and vision in generous shovelful after shovelful of all the printed compassion I can possibly deposit at a grieving person's feet. A single volume cannot be comprehensive of all I have studied, collected, and experienced. It might, however, be the beginnings of solace, solidarity, and strength. I write expressly for parents who have faced the unthinkable brutality of burying their child. But I write also for anyone who has felt the despair of losing a beloved anyone—for all whose hearts have been rent by death.

And I write generally for those of us—and it will be every last one of us before our lives here are finally there—who will be called on both to mourn and to mourn with. For you who are uninitiated to the topography of the land of loss and are faced with another's grief, you might be in need of a guide or many guides, a single someone who has traversed the terrain herself or many who have had this peculiar soil underfoot. May you find in these diverse quotes and my personal essays voices that share how to lovingly accompany your bereaved friends with inspiration and reverence.

It is a sacred charge, all this necessary grieving, mourning and comforting, a delicate and divine calling. Because grieving, mourning, and comforting are what make us most human and most godly. This shared burden can even seal us together as a human/divine family, because "the closest bonds we will ever know," writes Cormac McCarthy, "are bonds of grief. The deepest community one of sorrow." My belief is that from such bonds of grief arise also the most resilient and resplendent bonds of joy.

Above all, Parker, I write for you. Wheresoever and by whomsoever this book's contents will be shared, may this be told as a memorial of you.

Melissa Dalton-Bradford
Prangins, Switzerland
February 20, 2013

PART I

LIFE AT DEATH

PLUNGED

AT 5 P.M. on Thursday, February 20, Willie died. Minutes later, Lincoln burst into [his secretary, Nicolay's] office. "Well, Nicolay," he said, "my boy is gone—he is actually gone!" He began to sob. According to Elizabeth Keckley, when Lincoln came back into the room after Willie's body had been washed and dressed, he "buried his head in his hands, and his tall frame was convulsed with emotion." Though Keckley had observed Lincoln more intimately than most, she "did not dream that his rugged nature could be so moved. . . ." "This is the hardest trial of my life," he said. "Why is it? Oh, why is it? . . ." Despite his relentless duties, he suffered an excruciating sense of loss. On the Thursday after his son died, and for several Thursdays thereafter, he closed himself off in the Green Room and gave way to his terrible grief. "That blow overwhelmed me," he told a White House visitor; "it showed me my weakness as I had never felt it before."

—Doris Kearns Goodwin, *Team of Rivals*

THE CALL CAME at 3:30 on that Sunday afternoon, a bright sunny day. We had just sent a younger brother off to the plane to be with him for the summer.

"Mr. Wolterstorff?"

"Yes."

"Is this Eric's father?"

"Yes. . . ."

". . . I must tell you, Eric is dead. Mr. Wolterstorff, are you there? You must come at once! Mr. Wolterstorff, Eric is dead."

For three seconds I felt the peace of resignation: limp son in hand, peacefully offering him to someone—Someone. Then the pain—cold burning pain.

—Nicholas Wolterstorff, *Lament for a Son*

———————

"NO! IT'S NOT true." Those were the words I blurted out when I'd reached [my husband] Olav on the telephone at home that evening from my hotel room in Brussels. There'd been a message that I should call home as soon as possible. Fear pierced me like a knife. . . . Could an accident have happened involving someone in my own family, just as I had feared my whole life? Was something wrong with [my youngest son] Jørgen? . . . The worst moment of my life. The worst night. The worst morning—the horrible flight home. And there were to be more.

—Gro Harlem Brundtland, *Dramatiske År* (Dramatic Years)

———————

O MY DAUGHTER! I aspire to the shadow where you are resting, since my heart is dead.

—Victor Hugo "Veni, Vidi, Vixi; I came, I saw, I lived"

———————

WHEN I SAW him lying there like a sleeping prince, his beautiful full lips tinged blue, I knew. I knew when I pulled up his eyelids and saw his huge brown eyes fixed and staring, I knew when I screamed for his father and watched him give CPR. And when he said, "Call nine-one-one," I knew. My son was wearing his T-shirt that read "*Anime fiammagente*"—souls aflame.

Jesse's small flame had joined the many.

—Marianne Leone, *Knowing Jesse*

———————

WHAT GREATER GRIEF can there be for mortals than to see their children dead?

—Euripedes, quoted in *Great Thoughts from Classic Authors*

───────

HAVE YOU EVER heard the sound of a mother screaming for her son?
The torrential rains of a mother's weeping will never be done.
They call him a hero, you should be glad that he's one, but
Have you ever heard the sound of a mother screaming for her son?

—Carly Sheehan, "A Nation Rocked to Sleep," quoted in *Stop the Next War Now*

───────

A VOICE WAS heard in Ramah, lamentation, and great weeping: Rahel weeping for her children refused to be comforted for her children, because they were not.

—Jeremiah 31:15

───────

THOSE TWO HOURS between the accident and our arrival at the hospital became the most vivid, sobering, memorable moments of reflection I have ever had or will ever have. I was lifted momentarily out of space and time as I knew it and was suspended somehow between two worlds.

One was this world of my past, so wonderful to me, which was now lying in a tangle of metal on the side of the road; the other was the world of my future, which awaited me at the end of that long ride to the hospital as a vast and frightened unknown.... In that brief window of time I exhausted all possibilities except one. I realized that I would have to suffer and adjust; I could not avoid it or escape it. There was no way out but ahead, into the abyss.

—Gerald L. Sittser, *A Grace Disguised*

───────

FOR A HAPPY household, cared for and spared by Heaven for twenty years, I have God to thank; for a much longer pursuit of my vocation, accompanied by undeserved blessings; for great abundance of joys and sorrows, which, in my calling and as a sympathetic friend, I have lived through with others. Many a heavy cloud has passed over my life; yes what has come from without, faith has surmounted, and what from within, love has recompensed. But now, this one blow, the first of its kind, has shaken my life to its roots.

—Friedrich Schleiermacher, "Sermon on Nathanael's Grave,"
quoted in *This Incomplete One*

PAIN

WITH REALITY COMES pain, and the pain, when it comes, is stunning. The pain is actually physical, mostly in your stomach and chest. Your chest feels crushed and you can't seem to catch your breath. I remember feeling pinned like a butterfly, or somehow eviscerated. One woman drew an arc that started at her head and ended at her knees and said, "His death was cut out of *here*." The pain comes in waves—moves in, backs off, then in again. People try describing it with superlatives or metaphors, then give up the attempt. And no one wants to try too hard anyway; they'd much rather talk about how, with time, the waves of pain gradually become less frequent. "Now when I think of him," one woman said, "I don't get that *wrenching*, I don't know the word to use, that *wrenching*, feeling."

—Ann K. Finkbeiner, *After the Death of a Child*

I FELT A crushing weight sitting over my heart and felt my chest constrained by steel bands that prevented me from taking a deep breath. I can remember going out to take a walk one day and feeling such an ache in my chest that I thought I was coming down with the flu. As I walked, tears began to wet my face and I started to sob but couldn't get enough air because of the tightness of those steel bands. I remember thinking as the spasm of grief subsided, "So, that's what the word heartache means."

—Judith R. Bernstein, *When the Bough Breaks*

HOW CAN YOU help families face tragedy such as ours, or those even more tragic, such as lingering deaths, multiple deaths, shootings, stabbings, suicides, burnings, or whatever?

First, you need to know how it feels. It hurts! It really hurts! It hurts each member of our family individually and together.

—Vern Albrecht, quoted in *Grieving: The Pain and the Promise*

WHAT MEANING DO [words] have for an afflicted heart? None! . . . How can I believe that Fahmy is really dead? How can you believe that Fahmy, who requested your approval just hours ago, when you were short with him—Fahmy who was full of health, good spirits, hope, and happiness when he left home this morning—is dead? Dead! I'll never see him again at home or anywhere else on the face of the earth? How can I have a home without him? How can I be a father if he is gone? What has become of all the hopes attached to him? The only hope left is patience. . . . Patience? Oh. . . . Do you feel the searing pain? This is really pain. You were mistaken previously when you occasionally claimed to be in pain. No, before today you've never known pain. This is pain.

—Naguib Mahfouz, *Palace Walk*

MY BOWELS BOILED, and rested not: the days of affliction prevented me. . . .
My harp is tuned to mourning, and my organ into the voice of them that weep.

—Job 30:27, 31

EARLY IN THE journey, pain and anguish are our constant companions. Hurt permeates every waking moment and casts the world around us in darkness. Virtually all of our physical and social surroundings and daily routines arouse pain and anguish when we meet them for the first time after loss. First encounters are among our most difficult experiences—they cluster and fill the early days of our grieving.

Pain and anguish hold center stage, no matter where we turn. We often feel desperate and tortured by the least little thing. Sometimes our early agony is so great, our pain and anguish so preoccupying, that it seems we are nothing but the hurt we feel. No wonder we fear there will be no end to it.

—Thomas Attig, *The Heart of Grief*

PAIN INSISTS UPON being attended to. God whispers to us in our pleasures, speaks in our consciences, but shouts in our pains. It is his megaphone to rouse a deaf world.

—C.S. Lewis, *The Problem of Pain*

SENSATIONS OF SOMATIC distress occurring in waves lasting from twenty minutes to an hour at a time, a feeling of tightness in the throat, choking with shortness of breath, need for sighing, and an empty feeling in the abdomen, lack of muscular power, and an intense subjective distress described as tension or mental pain.

—Erich Lindemann, "Symptomatology and Management of Acute Grief," in *The American Journal of Psychiatry*

PEOPLE WHO HAVE experienced grief will testify that it is felt in the heart, like a weight of cold pain.

—Doris Lessing, "Grief like a weight of cold pain"

IT WAS DIFFICULT to swallow food and I lost too much weight. It seemed as though my muscles had collapsed. My acute vision suffered. The shock to the physical body is very real. I was told that whenever I see a new doctor, I should tell him or her that I am a bereaved mother. It is part of my medical history.

—Barbara, bereaved mother interviewed in *Beyond Tears*

I DIDN'T WANT to see this
Oh my eyes can hardly bear the sight.
I didn't want to know this
Oh my heart can hardly bear the weight.
These little bones
Washed by the rain
Worn by the wind
Whitened by the sun.
These tiny bones
They'll never grow
I'll never know
What you could have become.

—Mairead Hannan and Paul Kelly, "Little Bones"

RANDALL & CO.

OUR HANDSOME BOY had not grown cold in Room #2 of an Idaho ICU by the time news of his passing had reached every end of our community in Paris.

Michel, Randall's work colleague and tennis partner, was the first to call.

Michel's low, slow words came from Paris through Randall's cell phone. "It's not true, Randall!" Michel repeated over and over again, "Oh, my dear Randall!"

Unable to sleep more than five minutes at a stretch, Randall and I had been out walking all night through our childhood neighborhoods. It was now after 3:00 a.m. The previous afternoon, we'd left Parker's body at Portneuf Regional Medical Center in Idaho and had driven the nearly five hours southward to be with family where we both grew up, in a small town in Utah.

Michel and his family loved us very much, Michel cried. "We hold you all close."

With the green glow of his cell screen casting death onto his face, my husband listened silently as Michel, an understated Frenchman, choked on sobs as he said goodbye. The confluence of sorrow and sympathy worked its way down to Randall's knees, and they gave way. His legs folded under his body right on the spot. There he sat in his pajamas, barefoot and curled like a beggar beneath a street light on the sidewalk. He cradled his head in his hands. Peak heat season in the desert west, but all day long his body had quaked as if it were midwinter.

Now Per was calling from Norway, and Randall put the cell on speaker. There under the aloof moon, Randall's lifelong career mentor reassured us with solemn but straightforward affection: he and his wife loved us.

The next call was from Munich. It was Stefan, Randall's boss—a big guy, a big presence, but I could hear that he felt reduced by his own total defenselessness. His small, broken cries teetered toward me where I now crouched next to Randall in the darkness.

Then came the whispers, "I'm in the Vatican, lighting a candle for Parker." That was Stefano, a work colleague from Rome.

A week later, on the sweltering afternoon of the funeral, there stood other work colleagues who had flown in from all over: Zaki representing all Randall's associates from Scandinavia; Franck from France; Lothar and Stefan from Germany; Stefano from Italy; Russ from Japan.

And a week after the funeral, jet-lagged and grief-loaded, Randall was required to be sitting in his office. It was the day after we had landed in Munich. Work colleagues met him as he came through the sliding glass doors. Everyone there *knew*. Phone calls and emails, which had flown back and forth between the US, France, and Germany during the days surrounding and following the accident, had kept Randall's company aware of our family's situation.

One German—towering, burly, a legendary connoisseur of lager and cigars—took Randall in his arms and then muffled his own quaking moans by burying his head in his American colleague's shoulder. On Randall's desk, two small handwritten notes already lay, penned in German: "Your pain is our pain," and "We can only pray to God for your healing." Day upon day, there were flowers, soft eyes, the touch on the shoulder, and respectful requests to "do anything to lessen your work burden, Randall."

For the first time in his two-decade career, work *was* a burden, a considerable one. Although some find work a welcome distraction from pain and loneliness, this was not the case for my husband. The idea of "business as usual" was repulsive to him on every level, and discussions of head-count reductions and a new operating model rang with sickening hollowness in the gutted-out space between his head and his feet.

"I want to be a postal worker. Or a cowboy on the range," he pled with me many times through his own tears that awakened him every morning. "It's not the scrutiny, or some fear of people seeing me weak, watching me be so broken. That's not it. It's the superficiality. I don't have the heart for it. None of this company stuff matters compared to what I now know . . ."

And I couldn't blame him. Together, we had undergone a seismic shift. Randall had seen, felt, heard, and in turn learned things of a spiritual nature that altered understanding of the world. Much of what had been of relative value a month earlier—the temporal, the material, the commercial, the superficial—didn't matter *at all* anymore. All of that paled in comparison to what he now knew regarding love and loss, life and death, and that fragile silken strand from which all existence hangs.

Moreover, grief had drained his energy. Standing up in the morning was work enough.

During those first weeks back in the office, the predictable routine did steady Randall somewhat, but only enough to fool him into thinking he was "on the mend." Because of course he was not.

In the middle of an intense discussion about the implementation of the new commercial model, his secretary Patricia passed him an express delivery piece of mail: the bills from the air ambulance that had life-flighted Parker to the trauma center. With one glance, whatever was "sturdiness" folded in on itself like an old dime-store pocket umbrella. "Patricia," Randall whispered as he took her with him out into the hallway, holding the mail in a hand dropped heavily to his side, "Can you . . . will you please take care of this one for me?" She opened the papers with her boss standing there numbly, his eyes ice-blue pits of despair. And she dropped her head and broke down.

Less than a month from tragedy, and in the throes of an international conference call, an email notice popped up on Randall's laptop screen: the insurance company needed a scanned copy of *Parker Fairbourne Bradford's death certificate*. Mule kick to the gut. Macroshock. Fibrilation. The deadening plunge of the universe into the cranium. And racing to a window for air.

All the bracing against these waves of pain, all the acting as if unscathed (which is, after all, what competent people are expected to do, play The Impervious One), all that harnessing of anguish was physically exhausting for my husband. The lie of stoicism was almost physically impossible for him to keep up, at least for very long stretches.

"I need to retreat and be alone, to digest this, to go into the depths," he told me. He knew he couldn't be alone for long with a leadership role at work. So he went underground—literally.

There was something in the building's underground parking lot—the isolation, the darkness, the hermetic seal of the car doors as he shut himself into the driver's seat—that liberated and soothed him. There, in his car, he could weep as loudly as he needed to for his lunch break and again for a few minutes in the late afternoon. A lightless car. A lightless subterranean garage. A lightless grave.

But these retreats were brief, ending every time with the *ping!* of a timer he had set.

A major restructuring initiative was taking place within his company, and Randall knew that if he were not present—and energetically so—many of his colleagues' jobs (and livelihoods and families' futures) would be jeopardized. He couldn't care less about that all-important corporate bottom line; he could, however, care about the human story above that bottom line.

Two weeks back at work (near the one-month marker of our son's death, and on what happened to be Randall's birthday) a large group of his colleagues from around Europe who had not seen him since learning of Parker's passing were convening for an important meeting in the Munich offices.

"How am I supposed to keep up some steely façade for hours of back-to-back meetings and a board presentation?" Randall had asked me that morning, eyes already red from weeping since predawn. "How am I supposed to lead? And with energy? I can hardly dredge up sincerity."

He'd aged, it seemed, a good twenty years in a month. And by this time I was beginning to wonder if this man in front of me who suddenly looked like a hospice patient would in fact be able to manage the major, visible, and relentless demands of his position. Was this the same man who, just over a month ago, had managed the demands like he'd managed our early morning 12ks: sprinting and racing and laughing all the way through the last 3k, high-fiving me and throwing his sweaty head to the skies: "Don't get much better 'an dat, does it, babe?!" And I'd slap him on his derrière.

Now I pitied him, pitied what he had to do. All I could do to help was promise I'd be on my knees for him that day. All. Day. Long.

"You call me, hon. Call me any time. Any time. Just make it through this one day, okay? You must. You can."

I kissed his eyelids as he pulled on Parker's leather bomber jacket. "Parker will be there with you," I said. "He knows it's your birthday."

Beneath the crushing chest press of sorrow and absence, Randall found his way through the soundless corridors of his company's building to an empty conference room in an untrafficked corner. Alone there, he knelt to pray. With one foot wedged against a door so no one would enter, he wrestled with fear and longing and confusion so suffocating, he had to raise his head so he wouldn't pass out. Through the floor and down from the ceiling, he then felt warmth surround and seep into him. It spread its light through his body and he felt, as if from nowhere, a physical reinforcement. "Like love," he told me later.

What happened next was a personal and a professional triumph. Not a triumph for my husband's profession, but a triumph for the nature of professionalism across the board and across the world. On that day in some steel-and-stone antiseptically sterile regional office outside of Munich, Germany, something quiet but spectacularly human happened.

Randall rose from his knees and returned to his office where he and his colleague Craig were at a computer screen preparing documents for Randall's presentation on the company's major restructuring initiative. Craig knew about Parker. In fact, Craig had received the first phone call after Randall had gotten The Call from me at 7:00 a.m. Munich time: "Honey, come now. To Idaho. Come to Idaho right now." It was Craig who'd scrambled anxiously, plotting Randall's emergency flight from southern Germany to southeast Idaho so he could have those last sacred hours with his comatose child. It was this same Craig who'd been Randall's right-hand man ever since.

Now the two tried to focus on their computer screen while person after person tapped gently on the door, entered, and silently looked straight into Randall's eyes as he rose to greet them. Then they took him into their arms.

Kari from Finland. José Luis from Spain. Hans from northern Germany. Chris from the U.K. Lars from Norway. Antonio from Italy. Michel from France. Colleague after colleague from two decades of work. It was as if in bodily form the whole panorama of Randall's career was streaming through his door. From embrace to embrace, Randall wiped his tears, turned back to Craig (who was from Wisconsin, by the way, and was also wiping tears), and the two then cleared their throats and tried to focus on that computer screen again.

Computer screen. Tap-tap. Eyes. Embrace. Tears.

Computer screen. Tap-tap. Eyes. Embrace. Tears.

The sequence went on for hours.

When Randall did have to stand at the end of that day to present in front of all these colleagues, was his heart still constricted with anguish? Was he unable to face their scrutiny? Intimidated? Destabilized? Helpless?

No. No, because he had already looked into their eyes, and there he'd seen injury, vulnerability. He'd seen humanness, intimations of which he'd observed throughout years of interaction, but which had been mostly hidden behind what is called professionalism. Hidden behind titles and door plaques on corner offices, distorted by a razor thin but magnetic bottom line.

Now he felt their humanness resonating from their faces, which mirrored their generous, human presence. Breaking down or falling silent for a second or two didn't faze him, and it didn't faze them either. So he simply did what he needed to do, all the time watching closely the eyes of those before him.

Their eyes (maybe this will make no sense) allowed Randall to present with tremendous emotion—hands trembling and heart skittering—about that blessed corporate bottom line. For that day, at least, everyone in that room knew *it* was not the bottom line at all.

At the end of that memorable birthday, Randall received one last knock on his door. It was Craig. From Wisconsin. He stood there a moment, his GQ square jaw and outdoorsy good looks uncharacteristically stiff, locked mid-breath. Craig gripped the doorknob, holding the door a bit ajar, neither completely entering nor leaving the room.

First, he searched with his eyes out the window. Then he looked at the floor. Then he looked right at Randall.

"I . . . I, ah . . . Randall, I just want . . ." His throat was tight, his voice seemed to go a pitch or so higher than usual.

"I just want to say . . . I don't know . . . I just don't know, Randall, how you made it through this day."

Shaking his head once, Craig caught himself. But not in time. Randall's colleague broke into one open sob. Then he excused himself and walked out the door.

DROWNING

[GRIEF IS] A tidal wave that overtakes you, smashes down upon you with unimaginable force, sweeps you up into its darkness, where you tumble and crash against unidentifiable surfaces, only to be thrown out on an unknown beach, bruised, reshaped.

—Stephanie Ericsson, *Companion Through the Darkness*

⎯⎯⎯⎯⎯⎯⎯⎯⎯

I'M IN THE middle of a hurricane, in a tiny life raft. My raft's leaking badly; some days I'm sure I'll go down.

—Elaine, interviewed in *The Worst Loss*

⎯⎯⎯⎯⎯⎯⎯⎯⎯

WORST OF ALL, far worse than lying awake all night, were the mornings. There seems to be daily a brief period shortly after I opened my eyes when I completely forgot Robby was dead. Then, like a tidal wave, remembrance would come and engulf me and make me feel as if I were drowning. I had to fight my way out of bed every day—and I mean every day. This went on for several months and was probably my toughest battle.

—Harriet Sarnoff Schiff, *The Bereaved Parent*

⎯⎯⎯⎯⎯⎯⎯⎯⎯

SORROW COMES IN great waves . . . but rolls over us, and though it may almost smother us, it leaves us. And we know that if it is strong, we are stronger, inasmuch as it passes and we remain.

—Henry James, "Letter to Grace Norton," *Henry James: Selected Letters*

I WAKE AND feel the fell of dark, not day.

—Gerard Manly Hopkins, *Gerard Manley Hopkins*

O LORD GOD of my salvation, I have cried day and night before thee: Let my prayer come before thee: incline thine ear unto my cry; For my soul is full of troubles: and my life draweth nigh unto the grave. I am counted with them that go down into the pit: I am as a man that hath no strength: Free among the dead, like the slain that lie in the grave, whom thou rememberest no more: and they are cut off from thy hand. Thou hast laid me in the lowest pit, in darkness, in the deeps. Thy wrath lieth hard upon me. And thou hast afflicted me with all thy waves.

—Psalms 88:1–6

I AM FULL of confusion; therefore see thou mine affliction; for it increaseth. . . . A land of darkness, as darkness itself; and of the shadow of death, without any order, and where the light is as darkness.

—Job 10:15–16, 22

I'D FALL ASLEEP and wake up with a jolt. I'd wake up five or six times, and each time it kept coming back to me as a brand-new shock, it would always be new. . . . I'd have panic attacks in the supermarket whenever something triggered a thought of [my son] when I wasn't expecting it. [I thought I was] going crazy. [I was] bombarded with feelings [I] couldn't even name.

—Rita, bereaved mother interviewed in *Beyond Tears*

I WAS SO bewildered that I was unable to voice questions or think rationally. I felt wild with fear and agitation, as if I was being stalked by some deranged killer from whom I could not escape. I could not stop crying. I could not silence the deafening noise of crunching metal, screaming sirens, and wailing children. I could not rid my eyes of the vision of violence, of shattering glass and shattered bones. All I wanted was to be dead. Only the sense of responsibility for my three surviving children and the habit of living for forty years kept me alive.

—Gerald L. Sittser, *A Grace Disguised*

MASTER, WITH ANGUISH of spirit
I bow in my grief today;
The depths of my sad heart are troubled—
Oh, waken and save, I pray!
Torrents of sin and of anguish
Sweep o'er my sinking soul;
And I perish! I perish! dear Master—
Oh, hasten, and take control.

—Mary L. Baker, "Master the Tempest is Raging," *Hymns*

GRIEF TEACHES THE steadiest minds to waver.

—Sophocles, quoted in *Grief: Contemporary Theory and the Practice of Ministry*

SUFFERING IS ONE very long moment. We cannot divide it by seasons. We can only record its moods, and chronicle their return. With us time itself does not progress. It revolves. It seems to circle round one centre of pain. . . . For us there is only one season, the season of sorrow.

—Oscar Wilde, *De Profundis*

WHEN THROUGH THE deep waters I call thee to go,
The rivers of sorrow shall not overflow;
For I will be with thee thy trouble to bless,
And sanctify to thee thy deepest distress.

—John Keith, "How Firm a Foundation," *Hymns*

HOW A SOUL thus struck is likely to wail,
how I could curse,
and cast my cries at you like a child
throwing stones in the sea!
Consider how one doubts, O God! when one suffers,
how the eye that weeps too much is blinded,
how a being plunged by grief into the blackest pit,
seeing you no more, cannot contemplate you.

—Victor Hugo, "I will see that instant until I die"

SAVE ME, O god; for the waters are come in unto my soul. I sink deep in the mire, where there is no standing: I am come into deep waters, where the floods overflow me. I am weary of my crying: my throat is dried.

—Psalms 69:1–3

SUPPRESSED GRIEF SUFFOCATES, it rages within the breast, and is forced to multiply its strength.

—Ovid, quoted in *The Routledge Dictionary of Latin Quotations*

—————

WHAT MADNESS, TO love a man as something more than human! What folly, to grumble at the lot man has to bear! I lived in a fever, convulsed with tears and sighs that allowed me neither rest nor peace of mind. My soul was a burden bruised and bleeding. It was tired of the man who carried it, but I found no place to set it down to rest. . . . The grief I felt for the loss of my friend had struck so easily into my inmost heart simply because I had poured out my soul upon him, like water upon sand, loving a man who was mortal as though he were never to die.

—Saint Augustine, "I wondered that other men should live when he was dead"

—————

FOR HE BREAKETH me with a tempest, and multiplieth my wounds without cause.

—Job 9:17

—————

MY APPREHENSIONS COME in crowds;
I dread the rustling of the grass;
The very shadows of the clouds
Have power to shake me as they pass:
I question things and do not find
One that will answer to my mind;
And all the world appears unkind.
Beyond participation lie
My troubles, and beyond relief:
If any chance to heave a sigh
They pity me, and not my grief.
Then come to me, my Son, or send

Some tidings that my woes may end;
I have no other earthly friend!

—William Wordsworth, "The Affliction of Margaret,"
in *The Complete Poetical Works of William Wordsworth*

———————

TOO SAD IS the grief in my heart! down my cheeks run salt streams. I have lost my Ellen of the hue of fair weather, my brightfbraided merry daughter. . . .

Orphaned is her father, with a crushing wound in his pierced and broken heart, in inconsolable distress—how well I know, bound down with my yearning for her!

Since I lost my neat slender girl, all the time I mourn her sadly and ponder on her ways. When I think of her, anguish springs up and wretched affliction in my breast, my heart is faint for her and broken because of her; it is a pang to speak of her, my trim daughter, of the dear gentle words she uttered, and of her delicate pale white hands.

Farewell, my soul, my joyful gay princess, farewell again, my Nelly, pure of heart, farewell my pretty little merry daughter, my angel, resting in the midst of the grave-yard at Walton.

—Goronwy Owen, "Elegy for his daughter Ellen"

———————

FAREWELL, THOU CHILD of my right hand, and joy;
My sinne was too much hope of thee, lov'd boy,
Seven yeares tho' wert lent to me, and I thee pay,
Exacted by fate, on the just day.
O, could I loose all father, now. For why
Will man lament the state he should envie?
To have so soone scap'd worlds, and fleshes rage,
And, if no other miserie, yet age?
Rest in soft peace, and ask'd, say here doth lye
Ben. Jonson his best piece of poetrie.

—Ben Jonson, "On my first Sonne," *The Broadview Anthology of Poetry*

APART

ONE IN PAIN is removed from the surface of the world and has to withdraw into his own being. The theme of spiritual growth is one of withdrawal followed by return. But the person who returns after the harrowing withdrawal that follows suffering is changed, and in turn brings that change to the world around him.

—Martin Israel, quoted in *Grieving*

AFTER THE DEATHS of their husbands, the women sank into separate wells of grief, unsure about how they would live, how they would raise their children alone. "For the first month, I didn't leave the house," says Breitweiser.

"I was scared to death," Van Auken recalls. "I wasn't eating. I dropped 12 lbs, pronto. I was barely breathing. You felt like you had a big hole right in your gut."

And they found it hard to communicate with people who hadn't lost family members on September 11. "We were in comas," Kleinberg says. "Everybody was an earthling, and now we were from Pluto. You needed to go to a support group and call someone so you could talk Plutonian."

—Francine Prose, "Hell's Angels" in *Live Your Best Life*

WHEN JESUS HEARD of it [John the Baptist's death], he departed thence by ship into a desert place apart. . . . And when he had sent the multitudes away, he went up into a mountain apart to pray; and when the evening was come, he was there alone.

—Matthew 14:13, 23

I AM FEEBLE and sore broken: I have roared by reason of the disquietness of my heart. Lord, all my desire is before thee; and my groaning is not hid from thee. My heart panteth, my strength faileth me: as for the light of mine eyes, it also is gone from me. My lovers and my friends stand aloof from my sore; and my kinsmen stand afar off.

—Psalms 38:8–11

DON'T THEY KNOW that the world has changed forever? It's as if everyone has gone on with business as usual, and I'm just standing here looking on. The parade, so to speak, has gone on without our family. People are continuing to laugh and clap at the new floats and have forgotten about our float, which is wrecked and ruined on the side. It's incomprehensible to me that things could continue on as if nothing had happened. Doesn't everyone know that the brightest light has been stolen away? Shouldn't there be ceaseless mourning? Shouldn't you be talked about everywhere I go? Everyone should stop what they are doing and be sad and hurt like me. How can they so effortlessly continue on with their lives? How can they be happy and joke and talk about the weather?

—Ellen Knell, *Letters to Erica*

STOP ALL THE clocks, cut off the telephone,
Prevent the dog from barking with a juicy bone,
Silence the pianos and with muffled drum
Bring out the coffin, let the mourners come.

Let aeroplanes circle moaning overhead
Scribbling on the sky the message He Is Dead,
Put crêpe bows round the white necks of the public doves,
Let the traffic policemen wear black cotton gloves.

He was my North, my South, my East and West,
My working week and my Sunday rest,
My noon, my midnight, my talk, my song;
I thought that love would last forever: I was wrong.

The stars are not wanted now: put out every one;
Pack up the moon and dismantle the sun;
Pour away the ocean and sweep up the wood,
For nothing now can ever come to any good.

—W. H. Auden, *W. H. Auden: Collected Poems*

I WALKED INTO a store. The ordinariness of what I saw repelled me. . . . How could everybody be going about their ordinary business when these were no longer ordinary times? . . .

I tried to jog and could not. It was too life-affirming. I rode along with friends to go swimming and found myself paralyzed. I tried music. . . . Is there no music that *fits* our brokenness? . . . Is there no broken music? . . .

There are those who plunge immediately back into work. I honor them. But I could not do it. And even if I could, I would not. Plunging back at once into the ordinary and the life-affirming could not be my way of honoring my son. It could not be my way of remembering him. It could not be my way of living with faith and authenticity in his absence.

—Nicholas Wolterstorff, *Lament for a Son*

PEOPLE WHO HAVE recently lost someone have a certain look, recognizable maybe only to those who have seen that look on their own faces. I have noticed it on my own face and I notice it now on others. The look is one of extreme vulnerability, nakedness, openness. It is the look of someone who walks from the ophthalmologist's office into the bright daylight with dilated eyes, or of someone who wears glasses and is suddenly made to take them off. These people who have lost someone look naked because they think themselves invisible. I myself felt invisible for a period of time, incorporeal. I seemed to have crossed one of those legendary rivers that divide the living from the dead, entered a place in which I could be seen only by those who were themselves recently bereaved. . . .

. . . . I think about people I know who have lost a husband or wife or child. I think particularly about how these people looked when I saw them unexpectedly—on the street, say, or entering a room—during the year or so after the death. What struck me in each instance was how exposed they seemed, how raw.

How fragile. . . .

How unstable.

—Joan Didion, *The Year of Magical Thinking*

I NEED TO be alone. I need to ponder my shame and my despair in seclusion; I need the sunshine and the paving stones of the streets without companions, without conversation, face to face with myself, with only the music of my heart for company.

—Henry Miller, *Tropic of Cancer*

HAVE MERCY ON me, O Lord, for I am in trouble: mine eye is consumed with grief, yea, my soul and my belly. . . . I was a reproach among all mine enemies, but especially among my neighbours, and a fear to mine acquaintance: they that did see me without fled from me.

—Psalms 31:9, 11–12

SPEAKING OF THE UNSPEAKABLE

EARLY OCTOBER. TWO months and two weeks after burying Parker. The shock of major loss has crash-landed our family on an island of pain. We've also literally landed in a foreign country: just days after the funeral, we've moved with our three surviving children, catatonic with grief, to Germany. We're doubly shipwrecked.

And still we've had no word from Grandma and Grandpa.

No phone calls. No emails. No messages in a bottle. Nothing.

I need my parents now more than ever. But do I call them?

No.

Why not?

Because I'm overwhelmed with sadness. I'm soaked through with our three children's sadness and with my husband's sadness, which sad saturation is compounded by the demands of an international move managed under extreme physical and psychological impairment. The vacuum of no familiar anything or anyone is gaining suction with each day that passes.

And because I'm afraid.

I'm afraid that family and friends are done now. Done with grief. They've moved on to brighter things, lighter things. And the trailing question strangles me: Is that what I'm expected to do, too? Be *done*? Am I supposed to "get over it"? Get to work? Get myself together, get a grip? Get on with life, get a life? I've never done this before, this incomprehensible and inescapable pain, so I don't know the rules. I do know, however, that I'm doing really well just *getting up*.

I'm afraid of other things, too. I'm afraid of what might happen as soon as I open my mouth, afraid of the inadequacies of language to transmit the borderlessness of anguish that I barely understand myself. I'm afraid that if I call on anyone, including my own parents, such a call will be misperceived as a plea for pity. I'm afraid that if compassion has to be prompted out of others, it's not the compassion I want.

And I'm afraid that if no one talks to me about my son he'll slip from my grasp. He will disappear into oblivion. I recoil at a quote I find from Russian author Alexander Pushkin: "Oblivion is the natural lot of anyone not present. It's horrible, but true."

So this, fear instructs me, *is how you'll lose your child a second time.*

Confused and overwhelmed with pain and fear, I find myself existentially cut off from the horizontal world and yearning for the vertical. In prayer, I reach upward, and in all other ways I dig downward. Deeper and deeper within myself, I'm trying to get to bedrock, digging into this island of grief I've been shipwrecked on. I climb down into this crater I've holed out with my nails in the middle of the night—all those soot black hours I spend on my knees, scraping at the hallway floor, pounding on the kitchen floor, rocking on the bathroom floor. And I crouch there in that hole. I go very, very quiet. And maybe a bit crazy.

And I wait. I crouch. I wait. I watch. I wait.

And wait.

It's the last week of October and gunmetal gray presses down on the Isar river outside our apartment window. The leaf-shedding trees I've been watching daily, hourly, are emaciated, stripped to bark nakedness. It's mid-afternoon and I'm in my bathrobe. The phone rings. It's my parents, together on speaker phone. Their voices are slightly unnatural, and remind me of pastel taffy. Sugary softness wrapped in wax with tight twists at both ends.

"Our whole California trip was just wonderful, Melissa. Very enjoyable and relaxing."

Pause.

". . . Mm-hmm."

Pause.

"Yes. Mom and I thought the hotels were comfortable, and the weather, well, what did you think, Donna?"

"Very comfortable. Unseasonably warm . . . even balmy . . .'"

Pause.

"...Mm-hmm."

Pause.

"And then there was the hotel swimming pool. Kidney shaped. Too cold, but deep aqua tiles. Pretty to look at."

Pause.

"...Mm-hmm."

When we hang up, I drop the phone on the bed. I'm immobile with exhaustion. I can't lift my head. From one half-opened eye I see on the bedspread that I've left a dark blue tear-print as big as a tile-lined kidney-shaped swimming pool.

Alone in this claustrophobic, dim bedroom I feel all my cells collapsing and my bones turning to syrup and my torso cramping and my neck muscles tensing. Then I hear an animal in me growling through gritted teeth and a clenched jaw, and the moan builds—swells, opens to a long, low yowl.

And I fall majorly apart. Who knows how long it lasts.

At some point I pull myself together, gather my wits, blow my nose, pray out loud, cry a few words to Parker, and call back my parents.

My voice is dulled and groggy as I stammer like I'm coming out from under anesthesia.

"Mom?"

"Oh, it's you again, honey. Good, good! Did we forget something?"

"I . . . I need . . ." I have been lying on my side, but now I sit up to assume my erect, well-planted persona. This way I can breathe and project better. "I am going to say something now . . ."

"Melissa? Did we do something? You sound . . . Wha—did we say the wrong thing? . . . Sweetheart?"

("*David, come back. Hurry. She's on the phone.*")

"Mom? . . . I need . . . what I want is . . ." I close my eyes. "Can we just talk . . . talk about . . . about *what matters*?"

By now my dad, who's turned off the speakerphone, has the receiver close to his lips. His voice vibrates in its lowest register. I know this voice: panic-control mode.

"Melissa? Now tell us please, honey. What do you need to talk to us about?"

I try to speak, but it's too physically demanding to push words ahead of the crying that is surging, it seems, upwards from the floor of my gut, so I make some incomprehensibly muffled sounds. My parents wait on their end of the line as I begin filling up that kidney-shaped pool with the tears of a child.

Infantilized. I'm six years old again, needing my mommy and daddy, I think while I keep fighting for breath between gasps and whimpers, scrambling to find my mind, find myself. *I don't know how to control any of this. How can this be happening?* This forty-something someone, the one who not long ago was resourceful and commanding enough to referee several major international moves, plucky and outspoken enough to lecture before hundreds, a turbo-charged joie de vivre Type A type . . . That someone is replaced by a mucus-drooling amoeba, a formless heap of swollen-eyed sweaty-stale bathrobed-ness that can't form a single pronounceable shape in her rubber-slobbery mouth.

"Melissa?" My dad's now whispering.

"Oh, Melissa, dear, what did Dad and I do? Was it the *pool* honey? Oh, darling . . ." My mother's voice is cracking. "That's it, David. I *knew* it. Oh, I . . . Should we, should we not have said the word *pool*? . . . David, you see? I just knew we'd say something wrong—"

"No! NO, Mom." I drill a fist into the mattress. "No! I . . . I just—" I catch myself, pulling down my pitch, which suddenly reminds me of a hurt and angry child. I purse my lips and lift my head, sucking in swift courage. "I need to talk . . . but . . . I can *not* talk about just anything. I have to talk about *Parker*. About him. I need us to talk about *Par*—"

The dam ruptures. The floodgates smash. Deluge. Tides of tears. From both sides of the Atlantic.

Remorse.

Apologies.

Love.

My parents hurriedly explain that they've intentionally not called for so long to give us "room." They didn't want to "open any wounds," they say. They didn't want to "remind us of our loss."

"The longer we didn't make contact," my mom's voice is twisted with pain, "the more awkward we felt about calling."

"You hadn't been calling *us*," my dad interjects softly, "so we reasoned that you must have been doing well . . . enough."

Which they knew was probably unlikely, they say, but they had at least hoped. . . . And in the worst-case scenario, if in fact we weren't doing well, we probably wanted to be left alone.

"Were we wrong?" my dad asks.

"Besides all of that," my mom cuts in, "we've been traveling, you know, and lecturing," which I know is their way of finding a practical distraction from heavy things. My dad, during those days around the funeral, had been discreetly clenching his chest. I didn't know how much of the weight of grief his aging heart could bear. He probably needed reprieve. "Death, like the sun," wrote La Rochefoucauld, "is not to be looked at steadily."

They explain to me how hard it was to decide to finally call, that before they dared pick up the phone, they'd agreed on a game plan. No mention of anything even remotely associated with Parker. And by all means keep the tone upbeat and frothy—light, feathery talk.

I find no words. I wrap a moist, shredding tissue in and around my fingers, which are stone cold.

"Melissa, sweet daughter," my mom's voice is loosening as if massaged with oil. "We love you, honey, and we're so utterly brokenhearted about Parker we can hardly . . ." There is silence. I hear the unfamiliar sound of my mom trying to talk through tears.

"What your mother's trying to say," my dad steps in, "is that we can hardly breathe."

Now I hear the far more unfamiliar sound of my dad struggling through tears.

"We are *sorry*." Mom has the voice of a young girl.

"And," Dad clears his throat, "we're deeply, deeply sad." He speaks so softly that if I close my eyes, I could swear he and my mom are sitting on the edge of my bed, as they sometimes did when I was young. "We are *mournful*," he adds like he's dragging those last two syllables, freighted and ancient as a rusted tanker hull, along a gravel riverbed.

"This is all so new to us," my mother speaks softly, "and we don't know how to do this well."

"But we can change this, can't we?" There is such smallness in Dad's voice. "Can we change this and stay in this horrible thing together?" he adds, deepening his tone. "Please?"

Every blessed day from that moment on and for months on end, at 3:00 a.m. Mountain Standard Time, my parents, unable to sleep for their own suffocating sorrow at losing their eldest grandchild, call Munich.

═══════════

It's impossible to "remind" someone of the One Thing that is splitting the seams of their heart and mind day and night. Buttoning a collar, folding gym socks, frying an egg, putting a key in the ignition, sitting and staring and feeling one's own heart beat—all of it is hot-throbbing with thoughts of loss and of the loved one. If co-mourners think it's their job to avoid acknowledging the One Thing—if they go away or go silent, or if they do show up yet fill their conversations with distracting chatter and quick-fix platitudes—they misunderstand grief and their role in mourning and com-forting. They can add injury to agony.

The bereaved can become desperate and/or angry and/or resentful if friends avoid them in their time of dire need. If fear, discomfort, self-con-sciousness or self-absorption drive observers of grief to silence or to a literal detour away from their grieving friends (and down another aisle in the grocery store, for example), the bereaved will probably interpret this as a tacit disregard of their loss. Friends needn't ambush them with attention or crush them with affection. But if they disassociate themselves, waiting at a distance for the bereaved to "get over it," they not only lose the great bless-ing—for both sides—of mourning together, but they risk disappearing from that relationship altogether.

If friends disengage—especially in those early months of grief—what happens when they return to their broken friends much too late offering explanations like the following? (These are actual quotes with good people's faces behind them):

"I couldn't speak to you. Your story kind of intimidated me."

"I didn't want to get you worked up about the past."

"Your pain frightened me. You looked too sad to approach."

"I felt totally helpless. I kept trying to find something original to say. But I guess I never found that thing."

"You were so sad for so long, and I was worried. I thought the Gospel was supposed to fix these things."

"We didn't know how to help you find closure."

"I've been an awful friend. Honestly, I've been so distracted with other things in my life."

"We thought we'd wait a few weeks until you looked like you were over the worst part, until you were healed. Then it seems the weeks passed so quickly and, well . . ."

"A parent's worst nightmare. I hope you'll forgive me, but I just didn't dare get close to it, to you."

The process of mourning is by nature constant, constantly changing and communal; it is not something distanced friends can later "catch up" on. Fortunately, the impasse I experienced with my parents lasted only a few weeks. We were able to repair any damage to our otherwise loving lifelong relationship. There were other relationships, however, that did not recover from the silence so promptly or so smoothly.

In studying bereavement, I have been stunned to learn that on top of losing a loved one to death, the bereaved often lose friendships and family due to their grief. As one bereaved woman wrote to me:

"The deadliest silence for me has been the silence in my own family—my many brothers and their wives. What keeps them silent and unable (or un-willing?) to reach into my mourning and comfort me? What keeps any of us silent? As I contemplate past (and passed up) opportunities to comfort the mourning, I wonder if it is simply lack of awareness. Busy-ness. Selfishness."

Or as another person recounted:

"My mother died when I was in high school, and I still clearly recall the pain of being shut out from my friends with a wall of silence. I thought then that young people could not be expected to understand such grief, but even older people struggle to understand one another's grief."

Grief has the power to test every person, every age, and every relationship;

it will stretch the understanding, patience, long-suffering, and forgiveness of mourners and co-mourners alike.

Very often, co-mourners feel helpless and uncertain about what to do, and they may expect the bereaved to coach them on how to help. But you can no more expect the grief-stricken to coach you on how to mourn with them than you can expect the freshly amputated to offer tips on how to administer first aid. After Parker died, we were battling the enormous physiological and psychological demands of acute grief; with our limbs torn off, the last thing we had energy for was persuading our closest confidantes that we were bleeding to death, and needed someone to pinch the artery. Either they saw it—and felt it with us—or they did not.

And that is precisely it. The grief-stricken need others to feel it with them.

But what if others do not feel it with you, what then? What do you do when your parents haven't called? When certain family, friends, neighbors, and church members have backed away, or conversely, bombarded you with empty chattery platitudes—if they in other words have been incapable of engaging in your life drenched with mourning? When a friend disappears, it seems, from off the face of the earth? Or another has judged or rushed or minimized your grief? When instead of "I am here, I will not leave you, I'm with you in this," you hear the post-air raid drone of silence?

And you suddenly smell the unfamiliar stench of a saucepan of resentment simmering on your red-hot frontal lobe? When your heart has begun feeling a bit dried out, then brittle, then crusty from anger, curling up around the edges under a low grade fuming, toasting under the grill of indignation, despair, isolation, blistering beneath the scorch of compounded pain?

What then?

The Old Testament tells of Job, who loses everything, including the support of his friends and family: "He hath put my brethren far from me, and mine acquaintances are verily estranged from me. My kinsfolk have failed, and my familiar friends have forgotten me." Job is stripped of glory, ground into the dust, mocked, misjudged, condemned, and abandoned. Yet God reveals that Job will only be an acceptable High Priest when he "prays for his friends"—the very people who have added to his misery. Job, who has nothing left to give, offers up a precious intangible. He offers forgiveness.

I'm no modern-day Job. No perfect saint. No loser of absolutely everything and everyone. No victim of a community-wide boycott. My family and I were lavished with love from all sides, many times from surprising sides. And I was also able to look into the kind and moist eyes of my parents and see that their silence had been due not to malice, but to innocent ignorance. When, in December, we walked into my parents' home for Christmas and glimpsed each other face-to-face for the first time since the funeral, our instinct was to fall into each other's arms and then to our knees. There, hands clasped and tears streaming with relief, pain and bittersweet joy, we prayed aloud *with* and *for* each other.

It is one thing to pray *with* and *for* those who are apologetic and eager to learn to comfort the grief-stricken. It is something else to pray for those who either never come at all, or who come, it seems, not to feel our sorrow or even to encourage us as we flail, but to diminish or disallow our grief or, as bad, to inspect us. Who rather than encircling us, circle us, as did Job's friends, critiquing, minimizing, rushing, and judging the nature of our grief. Who told Job that he had better *not feel sorry for himself.* (My answer to them? You are far less likely to feel sorry *for* yourself if you are not left to feel sorrow *by* yourself.)

Praying as Job did—for a heart that forgives malicious, misguided, or just plain "miserable comforters," as Job calls his friends—is not just a good way to keep our cool. Praying is the only way to turn down the killing sizzle of indignation and make way for the enlivening warmth of the Spirit. Only when we are free from anger and resentment can we receive the love that is waiting to rescue us from that isle of grief where, without love, we would remain stranded, parched, starving to death, captive in our grief.

"And the Lord turned the captivity of Job when he prayed for his friends."

What might that prayer have been, the one Job spoke on behalf of his friends? I suspect it would have prefigured another prayer uttered by the only true and great High Priest:

"Father, forgive us all for we know not what we do."

TEARSPEAK

TEARS ARE THE silent language of grief.

—Voltaire, *The Works of Voltaire*

THERE IS A sacredness in tears. They are not the mark of weakness, but of power. They speak more eloquently than ten thousand tongues. They are messengers of overwhelming grief . . . and of unspeakable love.

—Washington Irving, quoted in *Grieving God's Way*

HEAVEN KNOWS WE need never be ashamed of our tears, for they are rain upon the blinding dust of earth, overlying our hard hearts. I was better after I had cried, than before—more sorry, more aware of my own ingratitude, more gentle.

—Charles Dickens, *Great Expectations*

THERE WAS PLENTY of suffering for us to get through. Therefore, it was necessary to face up to the full amount of suffering, trying to keep moments of weakness and furtive tears to a minimum. But there was no need to be ashamed of tears, for tears bore witness that a man had the greatest courage, the courage to suffer. Only very few realized that. Shamefacedly some confessed occasionally that they had wept, like a comrade who answered my question of how he had gotten over his edema, by confessing, "I have wept it out of my system."

—Viktor Frankl, *Man's Search For Meaning*

WHAT CANNOT BE said will get wept.

—Jim Harrison, "Pleasures of the Hard-Worn Life," *New York Times* online

THE TEARS CAME freely, and I did not attempt to refrain them when I was alone. Indeed, for over a year, there was no day I did not weep, and I did not find that tears cut me off from her. It was the tearless void that severed us at times.

—Sheldon Vanauken, *A Severe Mercy*

NO HOUR IS ever eternity, but it has its right to weep.

—Zora Neale Hurston, *Their Eyes Were Watching God*

TEARS ALONE WERE sweet to me, for in my heart's desire they had taken the place of my friend.

—Saint Augustine, "I wondered that other men should live when he was dead,"

I WASN'T WEARING a black armband when I went to China, and I'm sure a lot of people just thought I was unstable. From the shop clerks, to the security people, to the airline employees, I was having a difficult time. I was always in tears and not very coherent. Once on the plane, I sat between two very nice middle-aged men, who had no idea what they were in for. I cried most of the way over, and when I wasn't crying, I showed them your pictures and told them about you. The flight was 12 hours long, and I know that about half an hour into it they were wishing for a seat change.

Once I arrived in Xi'an, I was told by the professor who picked me up that they were sorry you had died, but I needed to stop crying and get on with things. That was the last time you were mentioned.

—Ellen Knell, *Letters to Erica*

JESUS WEPT.

—John 11:35

BUT I HAVE
That honorable grief lodg'd here which burns
Worse than tears drown.

—William Shakespeare, *The Winter's Tale*, in *The Riverside Shakespeare*

BUT WHY CELEBRATE stoic tearlessness? Why insist on never outwarding the inward, when that inward is bleeding? Does enduring while crying not require as much strength as never crying? Must we always mask our suffering? May we not sometimes allow people to see and enter it? I mean, may *men* not do this?

And why is it so important to act strong? I have been graced with the strength to endure. But I have been assaulted, and in the assault wounded, grievously wounded. Am I to pretend otherwise? Wounds are ugly, I know. They repel. But must they always be swathed?

I shall look at the world through tears. Perhaps I shall see things that dry-eyed I could not see.

—Nicholas Wolterstorff, *Lament for a Son*

BUT THERE ARE other griefs within,
and tears that at their fountain freeze;
For by the hearth the children sit
Cold in that atmosphere of Death,
And scarce endure to draw the breath,

. . . To see the vacant chair, and think,
"How good! how kind! and he is gone."

—Alfred, Lord Tennyson, "In Memoriam," *The Poetical Works of Alfred Lord Tennyson*

TO WEEP IS to make less the depth of grief.

—William Shakespeare, *3 Henry VI, The Riverside Shakespeare*

WEEP WITH THEM that weep.

—Romans 12:15

A PEDANT WHO beheld Solon weeping for the death of a son said to him, "Why do you weep thus, if weeping avails nothing?" And the sage answered him, "Precisely for that reason—because it does not avail."

—Miguel de Unamuno, *Tragic Sense of Life*

COMPASSION WILL MELT where this virtue is felt,
And its dew is diffused in a Tear.

—Lord Byron, "The Tear," *The Poetical Works of Lord Byron*

THE STOICS OF antiquity said: Be calm. Disengage yourself. Neither laugh nor weep. Jesus says: Be open to the wounds of the world. Mourn humanity's mourning, weep over humanity's weeping, be wounded by humanity's wounds, be in agony over humanity's agony. But do so in the good cheer that a day of peace is coming.

—Nicholas Wolterstorff, *Lament for a Son*

MY GRIEF LIES all within,
And these external [manners] of laments
Are merely shadows to the unseen grief
That swells with silence in the tortur'd soul.

—William Shakespeare, *King Richard II, The Riverside Shakespeare*

SOBS, HEAVY, HOARSE and loud, shook the chairs, and great tears fell through his fingers on the floor—just such tears, sir, as you dropped into the coffin where lay your first-born son; such tears, woman, as you shed when you heard the cries of your dying babe; for, sir, he was a man, and you are but another man; and, woman, though dressed in silk and jewels, you are but a woman, and, in life's great straits and mighty griefs, ye feel but one sorrow!

—Harriet Beecher Stowe, *Uncle Tom's Cabin*

BUT A MERMAID has no tears, and therefore she suffers so much more.

—Hans Christian Andersen, *The Little Mermaid*

PERSONS WHO GRIEVE have a whole jungle of emotions in their guts which need to be expressed in some way. Sometimes openly, sometimes by talking, sometimes by crying, sometimes poetically, sometimes through ritual: there are many ways, but people must have the opportunity to express real feelings because unresolved grief is a destructive horror. . . .

People need to be encouraged to talk about the person who died, to remember him, to share about him, yes, perhaps to even talk to the person who is now dead.

—Elizabeth Kübler-Ross, *Death: The Final Stage of Growth*

PAST TEARS ARE present strength.

—George MacDonald, *Phantastes*

I WAS TRYING to shop for groceries. I say "trying" because it was not going very well, since I had all three of you girls with me. . . . I must have looked exhausted and at the end of my rope because an older woman with iron grey, shoulder length hair came up to me and put her hand on my shoulder. She then said, "Treasure every minute with your children." As I looked at the woman in surprise, I saw that tears were streaming down her face. She didn't say anything else, but turned and walked away. I never saw her again, and I have often wondered what secret sorrow she must have been bearing. I wonder now if she had lost a child. I still have a strong impression of that woman, and since your death, I have found that I often want to approach a young mother and tell her the same thing: "Treasure every minute."

—Ellen Knell, *Letters to Erica*

THANK GOD, BLESS God, all ye who suffer not
More grief than ye can weep for. That is well—
That is light grieving!

—Elizabeth Barrett Browning, "Tears," *The Poetical Works of Elizabeth Barrett Browning*

ENGLISHMEN RARELY CRY, except under the pressure of the acutest grief; whereas in some parts of the Continent the men shed tears much more readily and freely.

—Charles Darwin, *The Expression of Emotion in Man and Animals*

SO RUNS MY dream: but what am I?
An infant crying in the night:
An infant crying for the light:
And with no language but a cry.

—Alfred, Lord Tennyson, "In Memoriam," *The Poetical Works of Alfred Lord Tennyson*

I WILL NOT say, do not weep, for not all tears are an evil.

—J. R. R. Tolkein, *The Return of the King*

THOSE WHO DO not weep, do not see.

Victor Hugo, *Les Misérables*

SILENCE, SPEAKING, LISTENING

THE MOST IMPORTANT things are the hardest things to say. They are the things you get ashamed of, because words diminish them—words shrink things that seemed limitless when they were in your head to no more than living size when they're brought out. But it's more than that isn't it? The most important things lie too close to wherever your secret heart is buried, like landmarks to a treasure your enemies would love to steal away. And you may make revelations that cost you dearly only to have people look at you in a funny way, not understanding what you've said at all, or why you thought it was so important that you almost cried as you were saying it. That's the worst, I think. When the secret stays locked within not for want of a teller but for want of an understanding ear.

—Stephen King, *Different Seasons*

WE HAVE TWO ears and only one tongue in order that we may hear more and speak less.

—Diogenes Laërtius

MAYBE WE DO not speak of it because death will mark all of us, sooner or later. Or maybe it is unspoken because grief is only the first part of it. After a time it becomes something less sharp but larger, too, a more enduring thing we call loss.

Perhaps that is why this is the least explored passage: because it has no end. The world loves closure, loves a thing that can, as they say, be gotten through. This is why it comes as a great surprise to find that loss is forever, that two decades after the event there are those occasions when something in you cries out at the continual presence of absence. . . . I write my obituaries carefully and think about how little the facts suffice, not only to describe the dead but to tell what they will mean to the living all the rest of our lives. We are defined by whom we have lost.

—Anna Quindlen, "Public & Private; Life After Death," *New York Times* online

SOMETIMES YOU TALK, sometimes you don't; it makes little difference. The words aren't the right ones; or rather, the right words don't exist. "Language is like a cracked kettle on which we beat out tunes for bears to dance to, while all the time we long to move the stars to pity." You talk, and you find the language of bereavement foolishly inadequate. You seem to be talking about other people's griefs.

—Julian Barnes, "Pure Story," *Flaubert's Parrot*

WERE IT POSSIBLE for us to see further than our knowledge reaches, and yet a little way beyond the outworks of our divinings, perhaps we would endure our sadnesses with greater confidence than our joys. For they are the moments when something new has entered into us, something unknown; our feelings grow mute in shy perplexity, everything in us withdraws, a stillness comes, and the new, which no one knows, stands in the midst of it and is silent.

—Rainer Maria Rilke, *Letters to a Young Poet*

AND WHEN [JOB'S three friends] lifted up their eyes afar off, and knew him not, they lifted up their voice, and wept; and they rent everyone his mantle. And sprinkled dust upon their heads toward heaven. So they sat down with him upon the ground seven days and seven nights, and none spake a word unto him: for they saw that his grief was very great.

—Job 2:12, 13

I WAS SITTING, torn by grief. Someone came and talked to me of God's dealings, of why it happened, of why my loved one had died, of hope beyond the grave. He talked constantly. He said things I knew were true. . . .

I was unmoved, except to wish he'd go away. He finally did.

Another came and sat beside me. He didn't talk. He didn't ask me leading questions. He just sat beside me for an hour and more, listening when I said something, answered briefly, prayed simply, left.

I was moved. I was comforted. I hated to see him go.

—Joyce and Dennis Ashton, *Jesus Wept*

IN THE "TALKING cure" of therapy, silence is usually associated with defensiveness, resistance, negativism, denial and shame. But silence may also be a mark of profound respect, a recognition that ordinary language is inadequate before certain vast and terrible realties. This taboo applies not only for what is forbidden, but to what is sacred, as well.

—Moishe Lang, quoted in *A Broken Heart Still Beats*

NOTHING IS MORE barren, to one in agony, than pat answers which seem the unfeeling evasions of a distant spectator who "never felt a wound."

—Truman Madsen, *Eternal Man*

WHEN A PERSON is born we rejoice, and when they're married we jubilate, but when they die we try to pretend nothing has happened.

—Margaret Mead, quoted in *A Promise in the Storm*

THERE IS NO grief like the grief which does not speak.

—Henry Wadsworth Longfellow, *The Works of Henry Wadsworth Longfellow*

AND IT HAS made me mute who was such a talker:
my heart has entered into such a great abyss
that I can find scarcely anyone to listen
with whom I can talk about this.

—Jacopone de Todi, "And It Made Me Silent"

BE SILENT OR let thy words be worth more than silence.

—Pythagoras

THOUGH I SPEAK, my grief is not assuaged.

—Job 16:6

IF YOU SUPPRESS grief too much, it can well redouble.

—Moliére, quoted in *Emotional Sobriety*

BREAK, BREAK, BREAK,
On thy cold gray stones, O Sea!
And I would that my tongue could utter
The thoughts that arise in me.

But O for the touch of a vanish'd hand,
And the sound of a voice that is still!

—Alfred, Lord Tennyson, "Break, Break, Break,"
The Poetical Works of Alfred Lord Tennyson

I SOMETIMES HOLD it half a sin
To put in words the grief I feel:
For words, like Nature, half reveal
And half conceal the Soul within.
But, for the unquiet heart and brain,
        A use in measured language lies;
        The sad mechanic exercise,
Like dull narcotics, numbing pain.
In words, like weeds, I'll wrap me o'er,
Like coarsest clothes against the cold:
But that large grief which these enfold
Is given outline and no more.

—Tennyson, "In Memoriam," *The Poetical Works of Alfred Lord Tennyson*

GIVE SORROW WORDS; the grief that does not speak
Whispers the o'er-fraught heart and bids it break.

—William Shakespeare, *Macbeth, The Riverside Shakespeare*

FOR THE DEPTHS,
Of what use is language?
A beast of the field moans a few times
When death takes its young.
And we are voiceless in the presence of realities —
We cannot speak.

If we who are in life cannot speak
Of profound experiences,
Why do you marvel that the dead
Do not tell you of death?

—Edgar Lee Masters, "Silence," *The Second Book of Modern Verse*

THE DOE CALLS in the moonlight
and cries till her eyes are melting:
her delicious little fawn
has disappeared in the brown night.
To tell her sad luck
to the forest of her forefathers,
the doe brays in the moonlight
and cries till her eyes are melting.
But no answer, none,
to her long anxious calls!
And with her neck stretched out to the skies,
mad with love and rancor,
the doe brays in the moonlight.

—Maurice Rollinat, "The doe mourns her fawn"

TALKING IS COMFORTING. Talking is comprehending. Talking is healing. Talking is remembering. This parents must do. This they will do. Anyone standing between these parents and their need to express themselves about the experience of their loss and their feelings relative to it will be deeply resented, and eventually, their friendship discarded or pushed aside.

—Ronald J. Knapp, *Beyond Endurance*

OUR SOCIETY HAS perpetrated a fraud. We are led to believe that the last thing bereaved parents want to do is to talk about the death of their child. The complete reverse is true. Parents want to talk and want someone to listen. Someone who can hear the crying of their soul.

—Katherine F. Donnelly, *When the Bough Breaks*

SOME SAY NOTHING because they find the topic too painful for themselves. They fear they will break down. So they put on a brave face and lid their feelings—never reflecting, I suppose, that this adds new pain to the sorrow of their suffering friends. Your tears are salve on our wound, your silence is salt.

—Nicholas Wolterstorff, *Lament for a Son*

WHEN PEOPLE OUTSIDE the immediate family are encountered who do not allow . . . expression of emotions and thoughts about the deceased children, it creates a resentment that is difficult to control. Subsequently, the time comes when parents begin to separate themselves from insensitive and uncaring people in their environments who insist on keeping channels of communication closed.

Many times a wedge is driven between those suffering the loss and very dear and close friends. We can refer to this as a "wedge of ignorance"—ignorance about the great importance of open . . . communication.

—Ronald J. Knapp, *Beyond Endurance*

THERE'S ONLY ONE thing worse than speaking ill of the dead—and that is not speaking of the dead at all.

—Anonymous

BUT I WOULD strengthen you with my mouth, and the moving of my lips should assuage your grief.

—Job 16:5

WILLKOMMEN ZUM OKTOBERFEST

ISABELLE, MY HUSBAND Randall's French work colleague, has asked to sit right next to him in one of Munich's big Oktoberfest tents.

Randall has done this sort of regional company dinner more times than he can count. But this time, our family's tragedy is only weeks into our history. Already, he's having to learn to survive these settings—the loudness that feels violent, the crudeness that makes his back hunch in discomfort, his shoulders bent over his thoughts so throbbing that his soul feels as if it has third degree burns.

As the revelry swirls around him, Randall looks vacantly at his watch, wondering just how long he needs to survive until he can offer some excuse—he needs to put more money in the parking meter; a client from Asia is texting with an emergency; he might be having an allergic reaction to the latex seat covers; *anything*—so that he can leave. He sits here doing what he has done so often, shoulder to shoulder with the joking and the jocular, his body feigning interest but his thoughts rocketing beyond a galaxy away.

Isabelle has taken the spot on the wooden banquet bench right next to Randall. She has placed her brown unstructured handbag between the two of them. The bag was a gift on her fortieth birthday from her children, whose photos she's slipped into the small plastic sleeves of her wallet, which weights the bottom of her bag. They are always there, those children's photographed faces, even if only in Isabelle's subconscious, giving ballast to her everyday. Isabelle has exchanged the pictures every year as her children have outgrown braces, eyeglasses, haircuts, or pug noses, and when she does take out the old and slips in the new, her round hazel eyes rest mindfully on their smiles. She sometimes smiles, too, before putting the pictures into collage frames she keeps at her bedside.

Right now, sitting next to her work colleague, she is not aware of it, but something of the weight of those photos is prompting her next move. She clears her throat. She smiles. She turns halfway toward Randall who smiles weakly in return, gesturing with raised eyebrows and a half nod, as if to ask, *Do you need me to scoot over, give you more room?*, and then slides away a few inches. Then, Isabelle reaches for her handbag, picks it up, placing it on her lap as she moves the one or two inches toward Randall. He stares ahead. She then looks at the floor, considering.

The beating heart of the Oktoberfest merrymaking momentarily moves to their table when two raucously breathless musicians plant themselves behind Randall. The first, a shiny accordion slung over his ample gut, is pumping his instrument so frantically that sweat drizzles down his jowls and into the folds of flesh around his corpulent neck, soaking to translucency the white peasant shirt he's wearing unbuttoned to show a slick patch of wiry chest hair. His flesh glistens like the surface of his worn-slick lederhosen, which have bright flowers embroidered up the suspenders. He grins broadly, exposing the ochre glint of tar-stained teeth. He oom-pah-pahs up and down with his knees, while his gray bristled eyebrows keep time—oom-PAH!-oom-PAH!-oom-PAH! Under those brows are eyes glassy from too many Pilsners, yet wide open to meet the gaze of every onlooker as if to dare them to try not to be jolly. The man jigs ever closer, and Isabelle and Randall are slapped in the face by a thick, sickly piquant stink of sweat and beer.

In the same instant, the glinting bell of a tuba nearly smacks Randall on the head as the second musician spins precariously close. The man's nose and cheeks are inflated, and lost in pleats of exerted smiling is the suggestion of two eyes between lamb chop sideburns in rusty red. Like a fat golden periscope, the tuba seems to peer intrusively over the crowd at the table.

Isabelle sees how Randall hardly reacts. Hands over his ears, eyes closed, he holds uncannily still as the oom-pah-pah and its accompanying laughter move away to another table.

Randall's hands fall instinctively from his ears; deep in his own thoughts, he holds one hand over his mouth. Isabelle rubs the back of her neck. They happen to turn and meet each other's glances, where they roll their eyes and wince, as if agreeing, *Pretty loud here, huh?* Randall motions to Isabelle's stein—*You enjoying your drink?*—and she makes an awkward grimace, her mouth drawn up to one side, conveying her indifference. They sit in silence.

Laughter erupts at the far end of the banquet table. Some coworkers, well into their fourth round of bratwurst and drinks, now start pounding the table in unison—faster, louder, barking a Bavarian drinking ballad.

Randall's shoulders hunch, and his head drops toward his chest, which he pulls ever more inward until his profile is practically concave. His bones, as if protecting his torn heart, take on the curve of a question mark. His suit jacket drapes a frame that has lost thirty pounds in only a few weeks—Isabelle notes how gaunt his face is.

The table banging and ballad barking end as abruptly as they began. Both Isabelle and Randall raise their heads, glance at each other, and heave a sigh of relief and solidarity. *Thank heavens that's over.*

The miming ends as Randall looks down into his stein filled with mineral water with its slice of lemon circling silently like a planet off-orbit, and Isabelle, leaning on one elbow, takes a breath so audible that Randall looks up to meet her glance.

"So," she begins in French while rearranging her cutlery, "have you . . . relocated to Munich?"

"Thanks for asking," he says, straining not to yell, although how else will she hear him? "Yes, I live here now."

Randall is polite, but inwardly confused. All his work colleagues knew he'd been promoted and had moved. *Had been moving*, in fact, the week the fatal accident happened. What was she getting at?

Isabelle purses her lips then asks, "And . . . has . . . your family moved with you?"

Randall, protecting himself from the threat of painful small talk, whispers a courteous but terse, "Of course."

He must spare his energy. He must spare himself.

Now, she pivots her whole body more directly to him. Slowly, she takes her handbag from her lap and puts it on the bench to her other side. Its heaviness now leans into her lower back.

"And your children are . . . they are . . . adjusting to . . . their new life?" she asks, her hand reaching for a table napkin, her eyebrows raised in hopeful but cautious anticipation.

"There are certain . . . There are a lot of challenges," he answers, looking at her just once, then focusing again into his hands clasped together and resting on the table. He has hardly been able to move them since he first sat down. His limbs are filled with lead.

A tuba squawks, laughter from a far corner bubbles across the sticky crowd and peters out as it reaches these two. She looks at the napkin she now notices she's been crumpling in her lap, then stretches it flat across her knees, lifts it up, laying it like a wrinkled tarp over her plate. Wiping one hand over her eyes, exhaling, she then props the weight of her whole upper body on one arm by planting the heel of her hand on her forehead between her brows. A moment, and her next sentence comes inchingly.

She lightly touches the sleeve of his jacket with her fingers. "Randall," her tone thickens, "I'm just trying . . . to ask you about your *son*."

The word. And his face transforms from stone to flesh.

She continues, "I am so sorry," his eyes, now meeting hers, have turned from opaque to open, "but can you . . . please—I hope this is not hurtful—but can you please *tell me about your son?*"

It feels as if an invisible glass dome has descended—*swoosh*—on this far corner of a noisy tent teeming with partiers. At the same overcrowded banquet table where bedlam is the first thing on the menu—only feet from the yodeling accordion player and the jaunty tuba player, right next to where the jaded waitress grunts under the pewter tray holding eight beer steins she hoists overhead, inches from where two men (already plastered) swat at her ruffled skirt, amid that whirl of chaos—madness recedes. For an hour, the world and its deafening excesses fade as two work colleagues sit elbow to elbow, talking and wiping tears at Oktoberfest.

PART II

LOVE AT DEATH

SEEKING SOLACE FROM STRANGERS

MUNICH WAS, BY no fault of its own, only full of strangers. It was full of people who had not known us all those years when we were a buoyant, energetic family of six. And no one knew us from two weeks earlier when we stood broken at the side of a grave of a beautiful boy named Parker.

Strangers, in their effort to no longer be strangers, ask questions. Harmless people—mothers at bus stops, shop owners behind cash registers, old couples walking dogs, jaunty mail deliverers, genteel neighbors, they all ask typical and supposedly harmless questions. "Are these *all* your children?" and "Do anything special during *your* summer vacation?" were such hurtful questions, they cut off blood flow to my head and ripped off my wits and emotional armor right there in front of the bakery. So I grew antisocial and panicky, felt geriatric and at the same time jittery with fear at the mere thought of doing something as simple as walking one block to the local grocer to buy a dozen eggs. Or taking my two youngest to the local park . . .

A young German mother is pushing her toddler in a swing next to the play structure where Dalton and Luc are letting off steam after school. Off-handedly, she asks if I have other children.

"Yes," I say, "Two."

"Younger? Older? Where are they?" she asks, pushing her blonde son by the soles of his shoes, squealing as she tickles his stomach each time the arch of the swing rushes him, laughing, to her arms. I am silently tallying how many hours and days and even months on end I had done the same with my tow-headed toddler Parker.

"One is sixteen, a daughter," I say. "And—" my blood heats up, "nine weeks ago I buried my firstborn, a gorgeous son, who was exactly eighteen years and five months old to the day."

A fraction of a second passes as I look right into this stranger's eyes. I am searching, holding my breath, hoping. She keeps pushing her little boy then shakes her head, as if to rattle its contents, blowing a puff of air to lift the bangs off her forehead. Not missing a beat, she sighs lightly, "Well, thank heavens you have three others."

I could never return to that park.

The next month I'm sitting in a pediatrician's examination room. Eleven-year-old Dalton has contracted a bad chest cold he just can't shake, and a starched-smock doctor I've known for twelve minutes takes notes as I recite Dalton's medical profile. I would like antibiotics. Frau Doktor would like a complete history. Dalton would like to get out of there. Sitting stripped to his underwear on the gray examination table, he appears disconnected from our conversation, which is in German, a language I incorrectly presume Dalton cannot yet understand.

"You know, Frau Bradford," she places her pen flat on her clipboard, "this boy seems depressed."

"Depressed?" I feign nonchalance. "Hmmm. You think? Well, maybe he *looks* sad." I act like I'm studying him. He does indeed look very sad. Mournful, even.

Weakly pulling at a string dangling from the leg of his underwear, he coughs that foamy, upholstered kind of cough, wiping his nose with the back of his hand. Frau Doktor's Kleenex reflex is snappy.

"And the reasons your son would be sad . . . ?" she asks, extending him a tissue. She then poises her pen to make the list: "I suppose your recent move from France? The new school? Losing friends?"

"Actually . . . those aren't the reasons," I say. "Well . . . except maybe the last one."

I sense where this is going, and I'm hoping I can escape without entering the holiest of all my holies and maybe breaking down. That would be bad, breaking down in front of my sad, stripped-down son, in front of this woman who peers at us like lab rats, clipboard and pen in hand.

I search for Dalton's eyes. They are the same eyes, peeled wide open with pain, during those very last minutes—just three and a half months earlier—in an Idaho ICU. Under this long, hot moment boils up in me a visceral craving to go back. I want to flee from this moment, to escape this language with its pointy hospital corners, devoid of condolence, barren. Childless.

Oh dearest Lord, I want to be back where we were all together. Take me back.

"Frau Bradford . . . ?" She clicks her pen and raises her eyebrows.

I adjust myself in my chair, fold my hands in my lap, breathe deeply. Then, like some reporter from the nightly news, I orate, "On July 19, in a canal on farmland in the western United States, there was a water activity organized by a group of university students, among whom was our oldest, our eighteen-year-old son. That night, he and another student were sucked up stream and pinned in a hidden undertow. Twice, my son got out. Twice he went back in trying to save the other boy. The other boy survived. But my son . . . "

I finish. The woman tucks her pen in her breast pocket. And with all the tenderness of a tongue depressor, says: "Ach, such strokes of fate. You had best not think about it. Best get on with your life."

She needn't offer me any tissue since I am drier than the cinders I feel reduced to.

———————

We're at church. This new, tiny congregation of well-meaning strangers is struggling to know what to do with us. I know this because from where our family sits in a sodden clump in the back pew, I watch as eyes flit from looking into ours. Smiles strain. Shoulders turn away to some sudden, nervous preoccupation. And behind my stock-still façade echo all the words I crave to hear—honest ones, simple ones like, "I know what happened, and I'm sorry." Sunday after Sunday, silence swells.

My gut winds itself into a knot as thick and bristly as ocean-liner rope. Is wanting someone to ache with me presumptuous? Is quietly weeping through the sacrament hymn ill-placed? Is my grief selfish? Self-indulgent? Self-pitying?

The knot groans.

And then one day in late autumn, a member of our church who hadn't spoken to us until that moment strides up to me, plants one hand on my shoulder, and with the other hand pumps mine, exclaiming, "Smile! It's such a *great day* to be alive!"

My scripture pages, the Book of Job, to be exact, still bear the little warped pockmarks from the tears I shed as I took refuge in our car.

———

Lars is straight from the cast of *The Sound of Music*: blonde, blue-eyed, with a bank of snow white teeth, as quick and light on his feet as a Bavarian leprechaun, perfectly proportioned, and perhaps thirty-one. Or nineteen. Ageless. He's murmuring along with Celine Dion (his German accent does wonders for her English), who's piped into the salon where I've arrived for a long-overdue trim. Lars tries to make small talk while admiring our mirrored reflection: me still and old in the chair, him elfin and nimble on his toes. I sense under my lips a polite smile trying to emerge from hibernation—I've not been able to smile since July, months ago—but I just don't have that kind of strength.

Lars hums and sections off hair, cooing, crooning, and combing. But I'm so clogged with anguish I sit frozen, fearing what will come out of my mouth if I open it. My mind scampers ahead, frenzied, trying to plot escape routes around the inevitable question about family and children. At the rate Lars is talking, we'll hit that question head on before he takes his first snip.

"Life's short," he says, stretching smooth a swath of my hair, scissors held at attention. "There's never enough time to love the people who matter the most to us."

My scampering panic stops like I've pinned its tail under my boot. My throat constricts.

"You're right, Lars,"—and where this came from, I'll never know—"I buried my oldest son four months ago today."

Scissors in his right hand frozen, length of my hair held taut in the left hand, neck craned forward and eyes narrowing, he asks,

"Wha-what . . . ?!" I repeat myself, whispering. But it costs me my composure. Lars drops hair, scissors, and both his arms, hangs his head in a slow side-to-side shake, turns from the mirror to me, tears welling up in his eyes, and with a scarcely audible groan, bends toward me to wrap my shoulders in a hug. "Oh, no, no. I am so sorry, *so sorry* . . ."

———

Not everyone can be a Lars. And because he was just so unusual and I was so vulnerable, I went back to him again and again, even when my hair didn't need a trim.

One day late in the spring, I found myself reclining in his salon chair, my hair a wad of suds, Lars working the scalp, when he asked me something truly bizarre, even inconceivable. "So, if you're a singer," he said, "why have you never sung anything for me?"

"Sung anything?" I hadn't been able to sing for anyone since Parker's funeral. "Like . . . *a song?*"

"A song, yes. Why not? You love to sing." He finished sudsing. "I want you to sing for me."

I closed my eyes and let Lars rinse warm water through my hair. As was always the case when I allowed myself to go a quarter inch beneath the surface in my thoughts, my mind went first to a dry, hot July and an ominous canal in Idaho. Behind my eyelids I felt the swift seep of tears.

"And . . . where should I sing? For you?" I held my eyes closed while salty memories drizzled down my temples and into the water spraying my hair. The soothing gush of Lars's rinse melted every taut, anxious, self-protective, and throbbing boundary of my spirit, and I was taken back to a warm laundry room in our first home "abroad" on an island in Norway where I was watching my own hands folding my children's clothing. Those small empty limbs of cotton tights. Those flattened undershirts. My hands stroking their fibers. Their feathery voices in the next room. And then my mind's eye looked out a window on the soft soundproofing of tumbling, eternal, harmless, and unharmed Norwegian snow.

"Where you should sing? Well, where else?" Lars laughed once. "*Here*, of course. And now."

I sputtered lightly, a tactic that should have deflected his request. But he didn't let this one go. He kept rinsing, now more slowly, tenderly, and gently stroked the last suds from my hairline. In my mind, I opened the small window, the one that looked out onto the gorge padded with a white comforter bolted in place with quiet, wise pines. I watched my hand open up that window. I felt my mouth open slowly, taking in the brisk Norwegian air, as warm water flushed a world of anguish out of my head and down the salon drain.

SACRED GROUND

THE TRUST OF those who grieve is a sacred trust, and we must respond with the best that is in us. It requires much prayer, study, and humility to respond to this great mission of comforting.

—DeAnna Edwards, *Grieving*

WHEN OTHERS HELP us heal, they too may suffer in some way. Suffering is the modest price of real friendship. Parents, leaders, and teachers who quietly pay this price day and night for their children and their charges are true friends.

—Wayne E. Brickey, *Making Sense of Suffering*

I'VE REALIZED SOMETHING since you died. The pain of grief is palpable and heavy, but it can be shared somewhat. When Isadora [Duncan] said that her friend grieved with her, I think she meant that her friend was willing to take on some of her pain. She was literally willing to share some of the pain by being willing to feel the hurt. I have felt a lightening of my heavy load when I am with someone who is willing to shoulder some of the burden. The only way to do this is for them to literally take some of my pain onto themselves by experiencing some of the hurt, but not everyone is capable of doing that.

—Ellen Knell, *Letters to Erica*

GRIEF AND SADNESS knits two hearts in closer bonds than happiness ever can; and common sufferings are far stronger than common joys.

—Alphonse de Lamartine, French Writer

YE OUGHT TO . . . comfort him, lest perhaps such a one should be swallowed up with overmuch sorrow. Wherefore I beseech you that ye would confirm your love toward him.

—2 Corinthians 2:7–8

THERE IS NO better exercise for the heart than reaching down and lifting people up.

—John Andrew Holmes, quoted in *A Broken Heart Still Beats*

EVERYBODY GRIEVES. I see grief in their faces. I do not need their letters to know it. I do not create their grief out of mine. To each his own. Their messages are brine-soaked. They wind up flotsam. No one reads them, not even in Atlantis. Everybody grieves. The faraway look. The bowed head and stooped walk. One could see life is nothing but grief. The brave procession in the street. The buried eyes. Bright buried eyes.

Into every heartbreak beauty intrudes.

Lilies in a potter's filed.

Everybody grieves.

—Roger Rosenblatt, *Kayak Morning*

EVERY BOND IS a bond to sorrow.

—James Joyce, *Dubliners*

IN THE COURSE of my cry I hold out the vision of God as with me in my grief, of God as grieving with me; God is with me on the mourning bench. I know that one of the attributes traditionally ascribed to God is impassibility—the inability to suffer. I think the traditional theologians were mistaken on this point. I find the scriptures saying that God is disturbed by what transpires in this world and is working to redeem us from evil and suffering. I do not see how a redeeming God can be impassible. . . . Why does God allow what God endures in tears?

I do not know the answer. In faith I live the question.

—Nicholas Wolterstorff, "Rights and Wrongs, an Interview with Nicholas Wolterstorff"

THE GRIEF BEAST

THE GRIEF BEAST is enormous—a hybrid of Jabba the Hutt, Sasquatch, and Grendel. His head scratches any twenty-foot ceiling and he doesn't speak; he transudes. He is warted and hairy and lumpy—a shaggy, slate-khaki thing with hair balls and sodden patches of a matted, grimy pelt from sitting for long stretches in pools of tears and mucus.

The Beast emits a sharp-sweet rotting compost odor that can make your eyes burn, which makes you wonder how others—the non-grieving—cannot smell him out; or if they do smell him out, how they can pretend he's not there. He trails you everywhere, tethered to your heart, shedding molting fur and spreading his sickly aroma wherever his deep sloppy footprints leave their trail. His breathing, if you want to call it that, is gravely and loamy—subterranean—with moistness that slithers inside of your collar, suffocating you when you have to go out in public or respond to the flip line, "So! Tell me about your kids!"

When you awaken day or night, he is right there, squat at the side of your bed, skulking, glaring, glowering. Most days, you have to bear not only the presence of The Beast himself, but also the weight of the chain that links you to him as you drag his blubbery, slavering mass along with you everywhere you go. This makes every effort arduous and awkward, like slogging through tepid, thigh-deep tar. "Good" days are the ones where at least he walks behind you, albeit menacingly—your hulking, stinking, unwelcome sidekick.

You recall the exact instant he appeared—just like *that*—and you mistakenly thought he was a passing apparition, a totem linking you to your loss. In those first days and weeks—and this is the dilemma his presence creates—you were struggling to learn how to live with him. Then on top of that you had to learn how to respond when others asked, even if just with their eyes, *what on earth the matter was.*

Well, clearly, *he* is the matter. Grief matters. One's Beast is the matter with the earth and the whole universe, into whose every corner his shadow seems to spread. No wonder bystanders usually prefer to retreat to bright, clean air rather than stay in the choking shadow of another's Beast. Who, when met with someone else's Grief Beast, can bear it, bear it at least for a while, can bear this shadow's dank hollowness for the duration? What's more, who would willingly draw close?

At some point in every mortal life, The Grief Beast arrives. He becomes our own. But when The Beast is not our own, how do we respond to his presence in the lives of others? Some of us, when we meet another's Grief Beast, react like we've come face-to-face with a grizzly bear: we slap our hands over our eyes and run, shrieking. Others of us are initially paralyzed, then tiptoe slowly away, sidling up against a wall, holding our breath. Others of us find the sight of a human being strapped to The Beast so sad, so tragic, that we are struck dumb.

Others of us grab for weapons. We want to do something to beat The Beast back, beat it up. "You need to be strong," we tend to advise. Or, "Don't let anyone see you crying—being weak." We think, "Hold on now here. I've seen beasts maybe somewhat like this one before. I'll do the same thing to this one that I did to that other one to get rid of it. Quickly."

Others of us launch headlong into a feverish jollity jig, reasoning that what this whole scene needs is nothing more than a little pepping up. And so we start handing out tap shoes, and we crank the music, tightening our stage smiles. Others arrive with wheelbarrows full of distractions—shopping, TV, movies, endless catatonic rounds of golf—reasoning that The Beast can be suffocated or at least anesthetized by a big enough pile of amusements.

Others of us size up The Beast, concluding that, *meh*, he's not such a big deal after all. A bit exaggerated, perhaps. A device for getting an audience's attention. A big, Spielbergian Special FX. A ploy for pity. Or we pretend that The Beast is a trumped-up phantasm that, if only ignored long enough, will eventually wobble off into a forest, gone for good and forever.

Fidgeting, denying, ignoring, escaping, avoiding, laughing, minimizing, jigging, juggling, judging, or whistling in the dark—each is a possible reaction to grief, our own or another's. And each points to how challenging bearing the burden of grief actually is. We might naively (and devastatingly) underestimate grief's qualities and proportions. Then again we might, in an act of self-preservation, deliberately deny the realities of grief.

Why do we react so awkwardly and sometimes ineptly to grief? Partially, at least, because pain (whether our own or someone else's) incites fear, and fear intensifies pain. We feel obliterated by the cycle; we recoil, unable to reach out to receive or to give love.

We might have learned some forms of faux courage along the way—toughness, callousness, brazenness, flippancy, stoicism, dare-deviling our way through life. But those are lower forms of courage because they are in their most elemental particulars self-preserving, not self-giving. They ask not about how The Beast affects its owner, but about how The Beast might affect *me*? Is this Grief Beast dangerous? Am *I* going to get hurt? Infected? Shredded? Will I end up being just like *that person* chained to the Beast? Or, if I reach toward him will I get his Beast riled up and it will run amok? And what if someone . . . well, what if . . . what if *I* should lose composure? Cry?

Fearing for everyone's lives, we start to slink away graciously, deftly, eyes darting, chins dipped, heads turned slightly to the side, hands steadied. Surely we don't want anyone around here to get their heads grizzled off. Under our breath, the grieving can almost hear our whispers, "Easy boy, *eeeeasy.*"

Fake courage tells us to ignore the distress, no matter how unwieldy and pernicious it might be. We never bring up the horrible, sad thing. We don't say a single word. Not even the name of the thing that summoned The Beast in the first place: the name of the deceased or the diseased. We think, with our own Beast, that not mentioning him will make him go away. And when it is someone else's Beast, we mistakenly assume that someone chained to The Beast wants to forget about it, too, wants to talk about anything—snow tires, the best antacid medication, Snooki's lipgloss—anything but The Beast.

It takes a certain breed of courage—a courage-in-vulnerability—to address and enter pain, to look right into the eyes of our own or another's Grief Beast. It takes courage both to live with one's own grief and to face grief in another. It takes great courage to give or to receive love when paralyzed by fear and when pinned stiff with pain.

This courage is not casual or flippant; it's not the kind of pretended courage that tosses its head back cavalierly, or dismisses with lots of proverbs and greeting card couplets the threatening dimensions of The Beast.

In fact, I'm not entirely sure that someone possessing real courage needs to *talk* that much. Courage can also be resoundingly silent, as long as it is resonantly present.

This kind of courage walks up to you. He looks at you, your chain, your Beast. He reaches for the chain, asking to hold it, weigh it. (He had no idea, until he held it in his own hands, just how impossibly *heavy* that thing was.)

And then courage takes a seat next to you, your Beast. There, courage can feel the struggling unevenness of your heartbeat, the coldness of your skin. Courage will certainly sense The Beast's muggy breath, its putrid stench, its murky far-reaching shadow. Courage might ask, after a spell, and if only with a turn of the shoulders and eyes focused to eyes, "Please . . . can you *tell* me?"

Or . . . it might not ask.

Because courage is able to sit. It is able to wait right next to you, right beneath The Beast. It will sit, in fact, as long as both you and The Beast allow, and in that silent sitting, courage will discover that your most pressing needs are somehow wordlessly met. True courage won't need to say a thing.

SUCCOR AND MOURN, CONSOLE AND COMFORT

THE ORIGINAL MEANING of *succor* is to run or dash to someone's aid. How soon we go, how easily we drop everything to help, says something about our esteem for the person in need. Zeal sends one message; hesitation another. The best time and most eloquent way to succor is to do so when need arises. After all, service is seldom convenient.

—Wayne E. Brickey, *Making Sense of Suffering*

TO SHOW COMPASSION means to share in the suffering "passion" of another. Compassion understood in this way asks more from us than a mere stirring of pity or a sympathetic word.

To live with compassion means to enter others' dark moments. It is to walk into places of pain, not to flinch or look away when another agonizes. It means to stay where people suffer. Compassion holds us back from quick, eager explanations when tragedy meets someone we know or love.

— Henri Nouwen, *Turn My Mourning Into Dancing*

ONE WORD FREES us of all the weight and pain of life: That word is love.

—Sophocles, quoted in *To My Soul Mate*

———————————

CAN I SEE another's woe,
And not be in sorrow too?
Can I see another's grief,
And not seek for kind relief?

Can I see a falling tear,
And not feel my sorrow's share?
Can a father see his child
Weep, nor be with sorrow filled?

Can a mother sit and hear
An infant groan, an infant fear?
No, no! never can it be!
Never, never can it be!

And can He who smiles on all
Hear the wren with sorrows small,
Hear the small bird's grief and care,
Hear the woes that infants bear—

And not sit beside the nest,
Pouring pity in their breast,
And not sit the cradle near,
Weeping tear on infant's tear?

And not sit both night and day,
Wiping all our tears away?
Oh no! never can it be!
Never, never can it be!

He doth give His joy to all:
He becomes an infant small,

He becomes a man of woe,
He doth feel the sorrow too.

Think not thou canst sigh a sigh,
And thy Maker is not by:
Think not thou canst weep a tear,
And thy Maker is not near.

Oh, He gives to us His joy,
That our grief He may destroy:
Till our grief is fled and gone
He doth sit by us and moan.

—William Blake, "On Another's Sorrow," *The Poetical Works of William Blake*

A PHYSICIAN WHO lost one of his own children says that before his loss, when he would hear of a child's death, he would send a card; now he sends himself.

—Joyce and Dennis Ashton, *Jesus Wept*

ONE COMPASSIONATE GAZE or one affectionate handshake can substitute for years of friendship when a person is in agony. Not only does love last forever, it need only a second to be born.

—Henri Nouwen, *The Wounded Healer*

NO MAN IS an island, entire of itself; Every man is a piece of the continent, a part of the main . . . any man's death diminishes me because I am involved in mankind, and therefore never send to know for whom the bell tolls; it tolls for thee.

—John Donne, "Meditation XVII"

HEALING IS IMPOSSIBLE in loneliness; it is the opposite of loneliness. Conviviality is healing. To be healed we must come with all the other creatures to the feast of Creation.

—Wendell Berry, *The Art of the Commonplace: The Agrarian Essays*

IT IS NATURAL, in sorrow, to be consoled if a friend shares our grief. . . .

First, sorrow weighs one down; it is a load which, of course, one tries to lighten. When therefore a person sees others joining him in sorrow, it feels as if they are helping him carry the load, trying to lessen its weight on him; so the burden weighs on him less heavily, just as in the case of carrying physical weights.

—St. Thomas Aquinas, quoted in *Consoling Grace*

WHAT IS THE difference between grieving and mourning? Mourning has company.

—Roger Rosenblatt, *Kayak Morning*

THE SUFFERING OF the world has worked its way deeper inside me. I never knew that sorrow could be like this. Six months before, I had gone to the funeral of the twenty-three-year-old son of friends. I tried to imagine the quality of their grief. I know now that I failed miserably.

—Nicholas Wolterstorff, *Lament for a Son*

IF YOU WANT others to be happy, practice compassion. If you want to be happy, practice compassion.

—Dalai Lama and Howard C. Cutler, *The Art of Happiness in a Troubled World*

DO NOT ASSUME that she who seeks to comfort you now, lives untroubled among the simple and quiet words that sometimes do you good. Her life may also have much sadness and difficulty, that remains far beyond yours. Were it otherwise, she would never have been able to find these words.

—Rainer Maria Rilke, *Say Hello*

A SIMPLISTIC SOUNDING answer to the question of how to help families face tragedy is that, paradoxically, there are no "right things to say," nor is there even a need to say anything that speaks of the intellect at a time like this. The need is for sincere human love, reaching in its own unique, spontaneous, fumbling way with a "built-in" message: "Though I don't fully understand how you feel, I care enough to come to you and to try to share your hurt with you as much as I can, and as much as you will allow me to at this time. I'll leave you alone if I get any vibrations from you that you prefer to be alone, yet I'll leave with a readiness to come back when you give the signal you want me to come back."

—Vern Albrecht, quoted in *Grieving: The Pain and the Promise*

THE REALITY OF grief is the absence of God—"My God, my God, why hast thou forsaken me?" The reality of grief is the solitude of pain, the feeling that your heart's in pieces, your mind's a blank, that "there is no joy the world can give like that it takes away" [Lord Byron]. . . .

That's why immediately after such tragedy people must come to your rescue, people who only want to hold your hand, not to quote anybody or even say anything, people who simply bring food and flowers—the basics of beauty and life—people who sign letters simply, "Your brokenhearted sister." In other words, in my intense grief I felt some of my fellow reverends—not many, and none of you, thank God—were using comforting words of Scripture for self-protection, to pretty up a situation whose bleakness they simply couldn't face. But like God . . . Scripture is not around for anyone's protection, just for everyone's unending support.

And that's what [you] understood so beautifully. You gave me what God gives all of us—minimum protection, maximum support. I swear to you, I wouldn't be standing here were I not upheld.

—William Sloane Coffin Jr., quoted in *This Incomplete One*

MAY I TRY to tell you again where your only comfort lies? It is not in forgetting the happy past. People bring us well-meant but miserable consolations when they tell us what time will do to help our grief. We do not want to lose our grief, because our grief is bound up with our love and we could not cease to mourn without being robbed of our affections.

—Phillips Brooks, quoted in *A Broken Heart Still Beats*

TIME DOES NOT bring relief; you all have lied
Who told me time would ease me of my pain!
I miss him in the weeping of the rain;
I want him at the shrinking of the tide;
The old snows melt from every mountain-side,
And last year's leaves are smoke in every lane;
But last year's bitter loving must remain
Heaped on my heart, and my old thoughts abide!

There are a hundred places where I fear
To go,—so with his memory they brim!
And entering with relief some quiet place
Where never fell his foot or shone his face
I say, "There is no memory of him here!"
And so stand stricken, so remembering him!

—Edna St. Vincent Millay, *The Selected Poetry of Edna St. Vincent Millay*

ONE DOES NOTHING who tries to console a despondent person with word. A friend is one who aids with deeds at a critical time when deeds are called for.

—Titus Maccius Plautus

WHAT DO YOU say to someone who is suffering?

Some people are gifted with words of wisdom. For such, one is profoundly grateful. There were many such for us. But not all are gifted that way. Some blurted out strange, inept things. That's OK too. Your words don't have to be wise. The heart that speaks is heard more than the words spoken. And if you can't think of anything at all to say, just say, "I can't think of anything to say. But I want you to know what we are with you in your grief." Or even, just embrace. Not even the best of words can take away the pain. What words can do is testify that there is more than pain in our journey on earth to a new day. Of those things that are more, the greatest is love. Express your love. How appallingly grim must be death of a child in the absence of love.

But please: Don't say it's not really so bad. Because it is. Death is awful, demonic. If you think your task as comforter is to tell me that really, all things considered, it's not so bad, you do not sit with me in my grief but place yourself off in the distance from me. Over there, you are of no help. What I need to hear from you is that you recognize how painful it is. I need to hear from you that you are with me in my desperation. To comfort me, you have to come close. Come sit beside me on my mourning bench.

—Nicholas Wolterstorff, *Lament for a Son*

ATTEMPTING TO CONSOLE those who have lost loved ones . . . by saying it will be better in the next life tends to minimize their immediate pain: "It's like you're on a desert island and you are dying of thirst, and someone says, 'Yes, you can have a drink, but not for thirty years!'"

—Joyce and Dennis Ashton, *Jesus Wept*

WE NEED PEOPLE who most sensitively mediate God's love for us.

—Wayne Simsic, *Cries of the Heart*

[Y]OU ARE PASSING through a darkness in which I myself in my ignorance see nothing but that you have been made wretchedly ill by it; but it is only a darkness, it is not an end, or the end. Don't think, don't feel, any more than you can help, don't conclude or decide—don't do anything but wait. Everything will pass, and serenity and accepted mysteries and disillusionments, and the tenderness of a few good people, and new opportunities and ever so much of life, in a word, will remain. You will do all sorts of things yet, and I will help you. The only thing is not to melt in the meanwhile . . . Try not to be ill—that is all; for in that there is a future. You are marked out for success, and you must not fail. You have my tenderest affection and all my confidence.

Henry James, "Letter to Grace Norton," *Henry James: Selected Letters*

WHEN OUR PAIN is so deep and real that we can't see or feel anything else, we need the witness of the saints about us; saints who, on the basis of their own experience of life's pain, can assure us that though our pain is true, it is not the ultimate truth. In all our pain, and beyond all our pain, always is the beauty, truth, and love of God in Jesus Christ, which never dies, and which will never allow us to die.

—Jeffery J. Newlin, "Standing at the Grave," quoted in *This Incomplete One*

STANDING ON THE HINGE

IT DOESN'T MATTER how educated, moneyed, or smart you are: when your child's footprints end at the river's edge, when the one you love has gone into the woods with a bleak outlook and a loaded gun, when the chaplain is walking toward you with bad news in her mouth . . . [y]our life will swing suddenly and cruelly in a new direction, and if you are wise . . . you will know enough to look around for love. It will be there, standing right on the hinge, holding out its arms. And if you are really wise, you will fall against it and be held.

—Kate Braestrup, *Here If You Need Me*

STANDING AGAINST THE plaster wall in the old apartment in Widen-mayerstrasse, a dark sweater drawn up to my jawline in spite of the August sun that reflected off the Isar river outside our window, and surrounded by stacks of moving boxes marked "Paris → Munich," I stared at Randall. He was leaning heavily into the corner next to me, telephone receiver in hand. The conversation was with Mr. H., the assistant headmaster from our children's school in Paris, the school from which Parker had graduated just two months earlier. One month before his accident.

"You still there? Randall? Uh . . . Melissa?"

Listening to what I could make out from Randall's receiver, my head tipped toward his, my arms wrapped firmly around my ribs, eyes closed for comfort and concentration, I could just make out what Mr. H. was saying.

Randall cleared his throat. "Here, yeah, yes. We're both here."

There was an unfamiliar vacancy to my husband's voice, a hollow quality that, had you not known better, might have pointed to grave illness, a stroke, even Alzheimer's. His trademark tip-of-toes vitality had vanished in one yank, and like a Christmas tree that has lost not only its sparkle but its very purpose the instant its string of lights is unplugged, so had Randall lost the high voltage that had always been his essence. I opened my eyes and looked at his face, aged two decades in less than one month. *Have I lost him, too?*

"Okay, well . . . are you and the kids . . . " Mr. H.'s voice was a warm murmur, "are you going to make it?"

"We're making it," Randall offered, pacing around the quicksand of emotion. It was hard for him to open his mouth and make sounds without being swallowed up in the suction of despair. "But we're not sure . . . we might need to move back to Paris. To our school. We need community. We need *our people*."

"And we're not finding it, *them* . . . yet," I said, speaking in the direction of the phone, and just loudly enough for Mr. H. to hear.

Each passing day made our son's absence more impossible to live with. I tried, unsuccessfully, to unpack boxes in this new place. I couldn't look at pictures of him. His features—an unsuspecting smile, those blue-gray eyes alert and glinting, especially the toothless little boy, all heart-splitting— made me noiselessly wild, dizzy with pain.

Every day I vowed inwardly I would try to finish the unpacking. My limbs were full of cement, and the thought of even picking up a box cutter made me ache with fatigue. Only five weeks ago—before I'd flown to the States to visit our firstborn at his initiatory week at college; before I'd received the policeman's late-night phone call at my parents' house; before that call that slashed open the skin of the universe, gushing reality in all directions; before in the Land of Before—I had been singing and dancing along with "September" from Earth, Wind & Fire while bulldozing through the chaos of over three hundred just-delivered moving boxes. Rhythmically, confidently, I'd been ripping into this new life, into these boxes, the same way I'd torn into every one of our many international moves.

Now, as I propped my body against the chilly plaster, dense and inert as a big burlap bag of wet flour, Randall must have also wondered, *Have I lost her, too?*

"Hey, um, I've been working on an idea," Mr. H. continued, with the faintest hint of fragility underneath his voice. Though he'd never struck me as a man who could crack, now I heard undeniable fissures creeping up the contours of his voice.

"See . . . this week alone I've had student after student in my office. Faculty, too. Every day, all day long, it seems. They've all needed to talk about . . . Parker."

Speaking that name was like hitting a speed bump, and his voice stalled, before heaving itself over the hurdle.

"This is the idea," Mr. H. went on. "I've been discussing doing a Parker Fairbourne Bradford Memorial at the school as soon as possible. End of this month, even. The more I talk with the administration about it, the more I see it might be a healthy thing, even a powerful thing. Good for us, for you, for Parker's memory."

"A memorial?" I mouthed the words to Randall, wondering if I'd heard correctly, and I started to feel heat kindle behind my ribs and through to my spine. Now I straightened, moved closer, and put my cheek against Randall's so I could hear every word.

"People need to make sense of what's happened, you know?" Mr. H's voice was clearer. "Most found out through email and Facebook and texts over the summer. That went like wildfire. Lots of people have had to process it alone. Some were out of the loop and have just found out this week. Seems to me everyone needs a place to express their feelings and their love, to make sense. They really need to see you. They need to come together."

———

Come together.

Those were the very words I had heard in my mind throughout the week preceding Parker's funeral services. *Come together right now,* I had heard echoing inside my body as I sat with Randall and our three children looking out over the guests, an assemblage of the world sitting shoulder to shoulder. School friends, work colleagues, church friends, lifelong friends. Those who'd walked down the street. Those who'd flown across the ocean.

Come together. Right now. Over me.

Coming together had made for a funeral that wasn't mere anodyne for our pain, or a distraction from bitter reality, but a fiery outpouring of purest, purifying love. For just a few hours, the rawest edges of our sorrow had felt blowtorched away, darkness had been blasted through with brilliant white, and our leaden hearts had been lifted on the surge of spirit.

Coming together over our boy happened again on an evening in September as our family sat on the front row of a packed school auditorium in Paris. Behind us sat youth and their parents as well as several of Randall's work colleagues from all over Europe. To each side we saw many church and neighborhood friends. Faculty members and students closest to Parker spoke (tenderly, frankly, humorously, musically, poetically, mailed in from abroad, recited across the silence), and above the stage there hung a large screen with projections of pictures and video footage. Randall looked alive, radiant, and for two hours, at least, he was back on his toes. I got a blood transfusion with fire. My body shook like a furnace overstocked with coal, on the verge of exploding.

Coming together happened again when Parisian church friends John and Renée arranged a gathering in their apartment. I recall the moment the door opened and we crossed over their threshold into their care. It was like passing from gunmetal cold into goldenrod heat, and we sunk wordlessly into a circle of reaching arms and knowing eyes. Without hurry or agenda, we all whispered and wept until the sun set and then rose again on the city streets outside.

Coming together happened when a church leader in Paris called to ask if we could come "back home" and speak to those in our congregation who'd been shocked by the news of our tragedy. "Of course," we answered, and did it enthusiastically, even though at the same moment in Munich we were hardly able to form the words to greet the local postman.

Were we really the same people? Hadn't we been shivering and stiff in that dank prison cell in Widenmayerstrasse? Yet when we came together with those who loved us and our boy, we were flushed, fresh, and on our toes? Who can account for it? Where does that kind of transformation come from?

Love, if we risk turning in its direction and moving toward it, holds the power to pull our pain into its embrace, absorbing it, coaxing us toward healing. If we can lean out of our corners of isolation and our frosty walls of self-protection and "look around for love" as Braestrup suggests, we find that regular-body-temperature folks—nice, decent people, neighbors, professional colleagues, church brothers and sisters, teachers who pass in the hallways, friends of the friends of parents of students who sat next to someone's child in a history class or in a jazz band or on the bench during basketball season—can stoke a saving fire in the ice-cold bones of the suffering.

And when that heat spreads through a whole community, it becomes a living firewall against the encroaching winter in everyone's souls.

When sorrow pushes us to where a blue glacial wind threatens to plunge us off a cliff and into a crevasse of despair, part of our nature might stare blankly—drained, as it feels, of will—into that icy bottomlessness. Maybe for the length of one breath we stare. Maybe longer.

But there is another part of us, a wiser part, as Braestrup calls it, that will look around for love. It might only glance at first, eyelids low, fearing what it will or will not find. But in time, it will scavenge like a beast dying of hunger. It will yowl to the empty clouds and bray across the flat horizon for love. It will howl from the bottom of its lungs rendered rigid and brittle from cold. It will limp and then collapse and then belly-crawl for love.

And there, right there, love will be.

Right there, next to us, will be love holding out its everyday arms. Its stranger or next-door-neighbor or school administrator-made-brother arms.

Right there on the hinge we find it so that, instead of closing our eyes and waiting to die of the cold, we fall into the radiant reach of love. And we are held.

KINDNESS AND LONG-SUFFERING

BEFORE YOU KNOW what kindness really is,
you must lose things,
feel the future dissolve in a moment
like salt in a weakened broth.
What you held in your hand,
what you counted and carefully saved,
all this must go so you know
how desolate the landscape can be
between the regions of kindness.

Before you know kindness as the deepest thing inside,
you must know sorrow as the other deepest thing
You must wake up with sorrow.
You must speak to it till your voice
catches the thread of all sorrows
and you see the size of the cloth.

Then it is only kindness that makes sense anymore,
only kindness that ties your shoes
and sends you out into the day to mail letters and purchase bread,
only kindness that raises its head
from the crowd of the world to say

it is I you have been looking for,
and then goes with you everywhere
like a shadow or a friend.

—Naomi Shihab Nye, "Kindness"

IN SO MANY encounters we try to look away from the pain. We try to help our friends quickly process grief. We hastily look for ways to bring cheer to a child or ailing aunt. All the while, however, we act less out of genuine "suffering with" and more out of our need to stand back from the discomfort we fear we might feel. We secretly, restlessly want to move from the place where it hurts. Our evasions do not help others, of course, but rather cause them to put up defenses and drive away those who need someone to care.

—Henri Nouwen, *Turn My Mourning Into Dancing*

DYING WAS ONCE a public process in the life of the individual and a most exemplary one; think of the medieval pictures in which the deathbed has turned into a throne toward which the people press through wide-open doors of the death house. In the course of modern times dying has been pushed further and further out of the perceptual world of the living. There used to be no house, hardly a room, in which someone has not once died. . . . Today people live in rooms that have never been touched by death, dry dwellers of eternity, and when their end approaches they are stowed away in sanatoria or hospitals by their heirs.

—Walter Benjamin, quoted in *The Novel*

EVEN THE MOST devastating loss—that of a child by a parent—seems to carry an unwritten statute of limitations on grief.

—Stephanie Salter, "The Myth of Managing Grief," *San Francisco Chronicle* online

THERE IS A cold chill that goes through your body each time some unthinking acquaintance tells you "it's time to get over it." There is no "getting over it." You will carry every detail of what happened throughout every day of your life, and you will forevermore categorize all events as occurring either "before" or "after" your child's death.

—Ellen Mitchell, *Beyond Tears*

FIVE YEARS AGO, I found my 17-year-old son dead in his bed, and apparently five years is too long to be manifesting symptoms of sadness: sleeplessness, the sudden and inexplicable onset of overwhelming memories and tears, the occasional entire day spent lying in bed. My time was up two weeks after we found him, according to the proposed fifth edition of the Diagnostic and Statistical Manual of Mental Disorders. If the new edition is approved, my symptoms will be diagnosed as a major depressive disorder.

—Marianne Leone, "A Mother's Grief—Without Time Limits," *The Boston Globe*

OUR CULTURE HAS not been educated to acknowledge the length of time necessary to overcome a major loss. This lag of information adds to the burden on the bereaved because they themselves feel that they should have been "back to normal" long before this.

—Catherine M. Sanders, quoted in *When the Bough Breaks*

IN AN AMERICAN society that is so defiant about death; which reveres youth so highly; which conceals the aged and the ill in institutions; which portrays death in the media as tragic, horrible, unlawful, unwanted, seldom as peaceful or wanted; which wants everything so comfortable and so convenient; which attempts to manipulate and control its total environment; in that kind of society death is frequently interpreted as an insult, an intruder, as unnecessary, as superimposed on life. The acceptance of death and the resulting ability to move through grief work is severely inhibited by the notion that death cannot possibly be part of the American Dream and the Good Life.

—Elisabeth Kübler-Ross, *The Final Stage*

RESEARCH HAS INDICATED that the death of a child may take years to resolve, if it can be resolved at all. One thing is clear: Grief can't be rushed and it can't be avoided. . . .

I eventually learned that the pain cannot be circumvented. It must be borne in its full vengeance, with awareness. . . .

When a child dies, the parents grieve not only for the deprivation of being without their child, but also for the lost aspects of themselves. Identification is experienced so personally that parents often report actually feeling the impact that killed their child or suffering the pain that accompanied the fatal illness.

—Catherine Sanders, *How to Survive the Loss of a Child*

THE BEREAVED PARENT after a time, will cease showing the medical symptoms of grief, but the parent does not "get over" the death of the child. Parenting is a permanent change in the individual. A person never gets over being a parent. Parental bereavement is also a permanent condition.

—Dennis Klass, quoted in *After the Death of a Child*

THE ONE THING that should never be said when someone dies is, "It was the will of God." Never do we know enough to say that. My only consolation lies in knowing that it was not the will of God that Alex die; that when the waves closed in over the sinking car, God's heart was the first of all our hearts to break.

—William Sloane Coffin, "Alex's Death," in *This Incomplete One*

"YOU HAVE TO understand," she said. "Grief lasts forever."

"Like death," I said.

"Like death. Except death is someone else's condition, and grief is yours."

"I feel worse now that I did shortly after she dies."

"And you'll feel even worse next year. And worse the year after that, unless you find a way to transform your grief."

"We're back to that."

"We've never left it," she said. "Grief comes to you all at once, so you think it will be over all at once. But it is your guest for a lifetime."

"How should I treat this guest? This unwelcome, uninvited guest."

"Think of the one who sent it to you," she said.

—Roger Rosenblatt, *Kayak Morning*

BEREAVED PARENTS NEED to know that others may minimize or misunderstand their grief. Many don't understand the power, depth, intensity, or duration of parental grief, especially after the death of a very young child. In some instances, bereaved parents are even ignored because some individuals are not able to deal with the tragedy. They find the thought of a child's death too hard, too inexplicable, or too threatening. Many simply don't know what to say or do and so don't say or do anything.

—Joani N. Horchler and Robin R. Morris, "The Death of a Child—The Grief of Parents"

IT SEEMS IMPOSSIBLE to me to understand the cruelty of friends and family who desert parents at such a time. But in my research I found countless couples who had horror stories to relate, such as a brother, once close, who stopped calling his sister shortly after her child died, or friends who were never heard from again after the funeral.

—Harriet Sarnoff Schiff, *The Bereaved Parent*

THE WAY WE resolve our grief is a process. Timing is everything. What is inappropriate at one time is a lifeline at another. At the beginning, it is necessary for the one who has suffered loss to admit the pain and feel it deeply. No one can ever resolve grief without doing this. To deny that the experience of death is the experience of the absence of God is a pious lie that disqualifies anything else one might say. But once one admits the reality of the emptiness and despair and meaninglessness of death, one is also ready to admit that there is something else present in the darkness as well. Something that at first seems only a hint of light on the horizon, but in time becomes a warm glow bathing everything: There is also love; there are also happy memories and gratitude; there is also God. A simplistic life based on despair is no more adequate to the human condition than a simplistic life based on rose-colored theology. In the end, only contact with the living God satisfies.

—Jefferey J. Newlin, "Standing at the Grave," in *This Incomplete One*

WHILE GRIEF IS fresh, every attempt to divert only irritates.

—Samuel Johnson, quoted *The Life of Samuel Johnson*

MY MOTHER GREW up in the Abruzzo region of Italy, where the inhabitants of that old culture have experienced war, earthquakes, famine. They are not afraid to acknowledge death and the sadness that follows; a folk song about death is called "scura mai"—you have left me dark. They are not afraid to represent the archetypal mother, Mary, with seven swords in her heart after the death of her Son. What are we afraid of here in the United States?

—Marianne Leone, "A Mother's Grief—Without Time Limits," *The Boston Globe* online

ACROSS THE YEARS I have met countless men and women who have used drugs, alcohol, sex, food, gambling, work, hobbies, or shopping to drown out the painful scenes [of the death of a loved one] in their minds. My drug of choice was work. My hectic schedule was a convenient distraction, and it was something I used in my attempt to outrun the pain. . . .

Along my grief journey I have met countless men who, like me, have tried to outrun their pain by replacing it with something else. . . . For grievers, the message is clear: if we try to stifle, ignore, outrun our sadness, and not talk about the pain we feel inside, there will be serious consequences down the road.

—Dennis L. Apple, *Life After the Death of My Son*

I HAVE HEARD many such things: miserable comforters are ye all. Shall vain words have an end? or what emboldeneth thee that thou answerest? I also could speak as ye do: if your soul were in my soul's stead, I could heap up words against you, and shake mine head at you.

—Job 16:2–4

GRIEF TAKES TIME, and nothing speeds up the process, not even hope. Why? Because they are two different realities. I cannot press on the horn to make the car go faster: The horn and the accelerator involve two essentially different realities, however united they are in the body of the car. The same is true of grief and hope.

—Gregory Floyd, *A Grief Unveiled*

A WAITING PERSON is a patient person. The word patience means the willingness to stay where we are and live the situation out to the full in the belief that something hidden there will manifest itself to us.

—Henri Nouwen, *Eternal Seasons*

SPIRITUAL GROWTH WILL be enhanced as individuals come to understand and accept the grief process, its duration, and, most importantly, its compatibility with faith and spirituality.

—Joyce and Dennis Ashton, *Jesus Wept*

PART III

LIVING AFTER DEATH

GIVING HYMN THANKS

GIVE THANKS? I wasn't so sure about that one.

I didn't know how our family could face any holiday without Parker, and Thanksgiving posed its own set of problems. That particular holiday of 2009 was especially hard for me, since it was the first Thanksgiving I had acknowledged in three years. I'd managed to sidestep the date the previous two years, reasoning with myself and my family that if Europe didn't celebrate the holiday, we didn't need to either.

But something was brewing in my soul already at the beginning of that November. And so I braced myself against that gentle internal imperative that this year needed to be the year we returned to giving thanks.

I had reason to fear this holiday. Giving thanks as we'd done every Thanksgiving for the last twenty years was fraught with the potential for a nasty emotional crash and burn. For as long as our children could recall, Thanksgiving had been synonymous with gathering to our home those who were far from their homes. These were students, refugees, young professionals with families several time zones away, and most often, volunteer missionaries for our church. They were famished—especially the missionaries—for more than just food.

So we brought them under our roof and to our table. This was one of the main reasons we'd invested in our long, massive pine slab of a Norwegian dining table in the first place. We knew that on this important American holiday, more than any other, we would need room for many extra bodies.

Sometimes we would get a real throng packed into our home; one year we had eight young men and women and a few random friends who filled not only the massive Norwegian table but the extra tables we'd crammed into every corner. Music played through the house or floated from the piano where all those radiant kids gathered, pulling our children between them, to sing harmony. Scented candles mingled with the smells of a holiday kitchen. I wore a rarely-used apron. Randall, oven mitts. Luc, his French chef's hat. Dalton, a construction-paper pilgrim's collar. Claire, an Indian headdress. And Parker wore a look of such head-to-toe hunger you'd have thought he had been stowed away on the *Mayflower* itself.

Parker was always especially preoccupied with the details of the feast. Like the other children, he knew full well that this kind of cornucopial spread was nothing like Mom and Dad's normal culinary offerings. They knew they had better enjoy it, and plan on leftovers until well past Christmas. Consequently, Parker really threw himself into making it all happen. He would baste the turkey, mash the potatoes, crimp the piecrust edge. With Claire, he would set out silver and china, fine stemware, and the harvest centerpiece, his anticipation and appetite mounting as he awaited the missionaries' and our other guests' arrival.

As much as he had an appetite for food, he was an even more voracious social creature. More than turkey and stuffing, it was the gathering of young men and women—all those temporary church representatives who as the years advanced were not much older than he—that gave him his biggest charge.

Another part of that charge came from learning over the years how to fill in the blanks in Randall's pre-dinner presentation on the saga of the pilgrims and the history of Thanksgiving. Dad and son would swap lines telling how Governor William Bradford, mayor of Plymouth Colony and founder of the Thanksgiving feast was in fact our grandfather ten generations back. The holiday belonged to us, Parker claimed, proud of the pilgrim blood running in his veins.

After that lecture on the origins of the feast, we'd dig in. Then we'd sing, tell stories, list our rounds of Thankful-Fors, laugh and thank and sing and thank again, and feast all over again until the three turkeys, two hams, eight pies, bread pudding, six dozen rolls, stuffing, cornbread, cranberry sauce, and the ten side dishes (as well as the hidden coffers of chaser chocolates) were gone. Or at least thoroughly decimated.

Maybe the children would not notice if we skipped that whole production again this year, I kept telling myself as November of 2009 crept along. If they did, I hoped they would also understand that, well, Mom and Dad just couldn't do that song and dance routine anymore. Maybe intuitively they would know that it was not the singing, dancing, or feast-spreading that was painful, but the presence around our table of those young male missionaries.

For eighteen years, our family had discussed and looked forward to the year 2009. With the missionaries themselves, we'd talked—over third and fourth servings of stuffing with turkey gravy—about when little Parker (then bigger Parker, then taller-than-most-missionaries Parker) would one day do what they were doing. The dates when he would be serving his two-year mission had been on my mental calendar his whole life. I'd—we'd all—been counting down essentially since his childhood. At long last, *this* was the year when he was supposed to have been one of *them*.

I could not get past this. Even in mentally projecting forward to the feast day, the pain of my son's absence felt too big, too heavy, too loud and obvious for any feast-covered Norwegian table to hide.

I knew rationally that I had much for which to be grateful, endless much for which to thank my loving Father in Heaven. But I still felt sad and pensive and inescapably lonely. Lonely in the world. Lonely for my boy. Loneliest in a crowd that did not know and therefore did not acknowledge the existence of my son. The possibility of being surrounded by but estranged from a crowd triggered a number of concerns: What if I stared for too long at the back of the head of that one young guy who looked just like Parker from behind? Or almost as bad, what if I turned so stony that everyone would feel the glacial winds whipping from my direction, and they'd have to edge, head down and sideways, around my flintiness? What if, somewhere between cranberry sauce and pumpkin pies, I actually spoke my son's name? And choked? And turned our happy little feast into a brittle bust?

I feared that trying to celebrate was going to require that I be stagey to the point where my voice, if not my actual face, might crack. For a while, I held those feelings in check by strapping them down with several spools of psychological duct tape. This, to protect myself, others, my family, and not least, the memory of my son.

Then, one Sunday at church meetings while casually eyeing from behind the four young missionary men, two young missionary women, two lovely retired couples also volunteering as missionaries, and the fine gentleman and his wife who led this regional mission, my duct tape stretched, strained, and snapped. From nowhere, I felt ambushed by a crowding sense of—where on earth did this come from?—*affection and compassion* for them. The *pop!* of that duct tape catapulted me up out of my pew and straight in their direction. I strode up as if it had always been my plan—it had *not* been my plan, indeed it was strictly *against* my plan—and I (*what?!*) invited them all to our home for what I proclaimed was going to be a "fabulous Thanksgiving feast!"

———

The night before said "fabulous Thanksgiving feast!" I found myself on edge and on my knees. I was praying to God to guide me, to show me what to do with this permanent cargo load of sorrow. It held me down, wrapped my better inclinations tightly, made me fearful of things *as harmless as missionaries*, for Pete's sake. And it made me sometimes feel resentful of others' basic aliveness, judgmental of why *they* were here and *not* my son. All those internal churnings that made me extremely, existentially lonely.

How, I asked in prayer, could I go on? And as God wanted and needed me to go on? How could I bring anything good to others when they, through no fault of their own, embodied the very thing I had lost? I needed a paradigm (I instructed God about this) or a model or something—anything—to show me how to live with the ever-presence of Parker's absence. I was waiting, hoping. I would follow instructions, whatever they were.

As I kneeled, prayed, and then waited, I knew that to feel God guiding me I had to do one thing first. I had to peel off any duct tape that might be corseting the whole thoracic cavity of my soul. With my nails, I had to pick at the duct tape's gluey corners, and just peel it back, open up. Raw pinkish swaths of stinging skin and all—I needed to lose the encasing. Ribs almost crackling as I expanded my lungs fully for the first time in ages, I settled in to receive direction.

Read in the Old Testament.

"Old Testament?" I thought. "But I'm studying the New Testament right now." (I think I even motioned with a finger to the scriptures lying open on my nightstand, in case the impression thought I was just making excuses.)

Old Testament. Go to Samuel. First Samuel.

"All right. But the chap—?"

First Samuel, chapter one . . . and focus on verse eighteen onward.

I got up from my knees, retrieved my scriptures from my nightstand, closed the Gospel of John and opened to First Samuel.

In one glance at the chapter heading I felt gentle heat expanding across my shoulders and chest. Only then did I remember what First Samuel was all about. I sat there in bed while an electrical storm shizzed through my room and through me.

There she was, my paradigm: magnificent Hannah.

Hannah, who leaned against the temple pillar, weeping in bitterness of soul because she longed for a child but was barren. Whose sad countenance disappeared when she was promised by Eli that she would have a child, and promised in return to give her child to the Lord to serve in His house. Who bore Samuel and brought him up to the point where he was weaned. And then, who handed her boy back to God, where he would be part of the temple and "appear before the Lord, and there abide forever."

That was not all.

Something nudged me to read on into chapter two. Hannah did not then curl up and retreat forever in her mother sorrow. Was she not heartsick? Empty-armed? Desolate? Duct-taped, constricted, self-bound against the threat of exploding into a million shards of sorrow? Like me? Certainly she was.

But Hannah did something that I had not been able to do, something I still can scarcely fathom. She took a deep breath, threw back her head, and *sang.* For ten whole verses straight, Hannah sang prophetic praises to the Lord.

I am a singer, and singing was a principle part of the mother my son Parker knew. Throughout his life, Parker had accompanied me to my many rehearsals, recitals, shows, and concerts; he had become friends with my accompanists; he had even learned many scores with me. In fact, we had performed together—Mom at the microphone, son on the drums. We used to joke that with his dad, he spoke fluent basketball. With his mom, fluent music.

His death threatened to shut down my vocal cords completely, permanently.

Sing.

The thought stuck in my throat like the wishbone of a forty-pound Butterball turkey. I held my eyes on those words at the bottom right-hand corner of my page: "Hannah sings praises to the Lord."

I stared at those words, hoping, I suppose, that they'd change. Instead I felt Parker prompting: "Keep singing, Mom. Don't stop singing." Whatever "singing" would mean—at that time I couldn't get beyond a hazy notion of just squeezing air through my throat—I was supposed to keep doing it.

I turned the page and there again was Hannah, the same woman who in chapter one had been drooping in despair like a drunk leaning against the temple pillar. But here, one page later, I saw instead Hannah standing as firmly *as* a temple pillar, raising her eyes, head, and voice in song: "For the pillars of the earth are the Lord's, and he hath set the world upon them."

Hannah, *in spite of* what unquestionably was great hurt and deep grief, trusted God and entrusted her child to God's care. And so trusting, she was able to be rebuilt straight up from rubble. She was not denying grief or suppressing it. She was not trying to *look* strong for others or put on a cheery social face or have a positive mental attitude.

It wasn't stoicism. Not escapism. Not put-it-behind-you-ism, move-on-ism, get-a-life-ism. And in spite of what modern psychology might call it, it was not resilience.

It was reliance. It was trusting God, who helps to un-duct-tape our spirits so that we can expand and receive strength and flourish. So that we can become pillars against which others in distress can lean. So that we can celebrate with family, friends, and missionaries—even those who bear an uncanny resemblance to our beloved, departed son.

That year, I let the young men in missionary suits take over kitchen cleanup. While they packed all the leftovers into plastic bags to take home, while they scrubbed and dried serving platters with their white shirtsleeves rolled up to their elbows, dark ties flipped over shoulders to keep them out of the sink full of soap suds, I sat in the next room at our piano.

Encircled in a comforting radiance, I was surrounded by good people, whose elbows rested right where my son's once had, folks who, had the thread of life been a bit sturdier and my son had not died, would have been Parker's best friends. Yes, they would have been. I told them as much.

With these friends, I sang hymns of Thanksgiving. Head thrown back. Eyes glistening. Heart and soul loosed with love, expanded with thanks, filled, as they would be every year to follow, with the true feast.

SHADOWS OF THE VALLEY OF DEATH

AFTER GREAT PAIN a formal feeling comes—
The Nerves sit ceremonious, like Tombs—
The stiff Heart questions—was it He, that bore?
And Yesterday—or Centuries before?

The Feet mechanical, go round—
Of ground or Air, or Ought,

A Wooden way

Regardless grown,
A Quartz contentment, like a stone—

This is the Hour of Lead—
Remembered, if outlived,
As Freezing persons, recollect the Snow—
First—Chill—then Stupor—then the letting go—

—Emily Dickinson, "The Hour of Lead," *The Poems of Emily Dickinson*

CONTRARY TO THE general assumption, the first days of grief are not the worst. The immediate reaction is usually shock and numbing disbelief. One has undergone an amputation. After shock comes acute early grief which is a kind of "condensed presence"—almost a form of possession. One still feels the lost limb down to the nerve endings. It is as if the intensity of grief fused the distance between you and the dead. Or perhaps, in reality, part of one dies. . . . If one is lucky, one is reborn. Some people die and are reborn many times in their lives. For others the ground is too barren and the time too short for rebirth.

—Anne Morrow Lindbergh, *Hour of Gold, Hour of Lead*

IN A FEW weeks she will have been dead five years.

Five years since the doctor said that the patient has been unable to get enough oxygen through the vent for at least an hour now.

Five years since Gerry and I left her in the ICU overlooking the river at New York Cornell.

I can now afford to think about her.

I no longer cry when I hear her name.

I no longer imagine the transporter being called to take her to the morgue after we left the ICU.

Yet I still need her with me.

—Joan Didion, *Blue Nights*

IN THE LONG, sleepless watches of the night,
    A gentle face—the face of one long dead—
    Looks at me from the wall, where round its head
    The night-lamp casts a halo of pale light.
Here in this room she died; and soul more white
    Never through martyrdom of fire was led
    To its repose; nor can in books be read
    The legend of a life more benedight.
There is a mountain in the distant West
    That, sun-defying, in its deep ravines

Displays a cross of snow upon its side.
Such is the cross I wear upon my breast
   These eighteen years, through all the changing scenes
   And seasons, changeless since the day she died.

              —Henry Wadsworth Longfellow, "The Cross of Snow,"
              The Poetical Works of Henry Wadsworth Longfellow

THE DEATH OF any familiar person . . . whether loved or not leaves an emptiness. The great tree goes down and leaves an empty place against the sky. If the person is deeply loved and deeply familiar the void seems greater than all the world remaining. Under the surface of the visible world, there is an echoing hollowness, an aching void—and it cuts one off from the beloved. She is as remote as the stars. But grief is a form of love—the longing for the dear face, the warm hand. It is the remembered reality of the beloved that calls it forth. For an instant she is there, and the void denied. It is not the grief, involving that momentary reality, that cuts one off from the beloved, but the void that is loss. In the end one can no longer summon forth that reality, and then one's tears dry up. But while it lasts, it is a shield against the void; and by the time the grief wanes, the terrible emptiness of loss has given way to a new world that does not contain the shape of the beloved figure.

              —Sheldon VanAuken, *A Severe Mercy*

WHEN YOU FACE disappearance and death head-on, vanity falls right off the radar. Fear illuminates what matters, and leaves the rest in shadow, perhaps forever.

              —Kate Muir, *Left Bank*

THY DAY WITHOUT a cloud hath pass'd,
And thou wert lovely to the last;

Extinguish'd, not decay'd;
As stars that shoot along the sky
Shine brightest as they fall from high.

Yet how much less it were to gain,
 Though thou hast left me free,
The loveliest things that still remain,
 Than thus remember thee!
The all of thine that cannot die
Through dark and dread Eternity
 Returns again to me,
And more thy buried love endears
Than aught except its living years.

—Lord Byron, "And Thou Art Dead, As Young As Fair," *The Poetical Works of Lord Byron*

I PROMISED MYSELF that I would maintain momentum.

"Maintain momentum" was the imperative that echoed all the way downtown.

In fact, I had no idea what would happen if I lost it.

In fact I had no idea what it was.

—Joan Didion, *Blue Nights*

WHEN I ASK [author Joan Didion] if this grief [at her daughter' death] is different from what she has so carefully described in her book [about her husband's death], she says, "It is and it isn't. I recognize a lot of the things I'm going through. Like, I lose my temper a lot and I become unhinged and kind of hysterical. Like if someone calls to update their Rolodex." She laughs. "I recognize little things like that as being part of the process, so they're not quite as frightening. But on the other hand, it's a whole different level of loss." She stops and stares at the table again. "This is the part I don't want to talk about." She takes off her glasses, sets them down, and her eyes are flooded with tears. When she finally looks up, she says, "What I want to do as soon as I get through this . . . all of this . . . is basically be too busy. Take too much work. I figure that will get me through."

—Jonathan Van Meter, "When Everything Changes," *New York Magazine*

IN THIS SAD world of ours sorrow comes to all and it often comes with bitter agony. Perfect relief is not possible except with time. You cannot now believe that you will ever feel better. But this is not true. You are sure to be happy again. Knowing this, truly believing it will make you less miserable now. I have had enough experience to make this statement.

—Abraham Lincoln, "Letter to Fanny McCullough," *Collected Works of Abraham Lincoln*

I BEG FOR your pity, You, the only one I love,
from the bottom of the dark gulf where my heart has fallen.
It is a drab universe with a leaden horizon,
where horror and blasphemy swim in the night.

A sun without heat floats over six months,
and the six other months night covers the earth;
it is a country more naked than the polar land;
—no animals, nor streams, nor green, nor woods.

Now there is no horror in the world that's worse
than the cold cruelty of this icy sun
and this immense night resembling the Chaos of old,

I envy the lot of the lowest beasts
who can dive into a stupid sleep,
while the skein of time slowly unwinds!

—Charles Baudelaire, "The dark gulf where my heart has fallen,"

GETTING OVER IT so soon? But the words are ambiguous. To say the patient is getting over it after an operation for appendicitis is one thing; after he's had his leg off it is quite another. After that operation either the wounded stump heals or the man dies. If it heals, the fierce, continuous pain will stop. Presently he'll get back his strength and be able to stump about on his wooden leg. He has "got over it." But he will probably have recurrent pains in the stump all his life, and perhaps pretty bad ones; and he will always be a one-legged man. There will be hardly any moment when he forgets it. Bathing, dressing, sitting down and getting up again, even lying in bed, will all be different. His whole way of life will be changed. All sorts of pleasures and activities that he once took for granted will have to be simply written off. Duties too. At present I am learning to get about on crutches. Perhaps I shall presently be given a wooden leg. But I shall never be a biped again. . . .

How often will the vast emptiness astonish me like a complete novelty and make me say, "I never realized my loss until this moment?" the same leg cut off time after time. The first plunge of the knife into the flesh is felt again and again.

They say "The coward dies many times"; so does the beloved.

—C. S. Lewis, *A Grief Observed*

WHEN I TRY to take myself back to that time, to recall the terrible numbness that I lived in, I recoil in fear. I never want to go through anything like that again. Originally, these songs were never meant for publication or public consumption; they were just what I did to stop from going mad. . . .

When ["Tears in Heaven"] came out, it was the biggest-selling album of my entire career. . . . But if you want to know what it actually cost me, go to Ripley, and visit the grave of my son.

—Eric Clapton, *Clapton: The Autobiography*

I AM A man without a country. Wherever Livy was, that was my country.

—Mark Twain, "I am a man without a country"

THE MOST PAINFUL state of being is remembering the future, particularly one you can never have.

—Søren Kierkegaard, quoted *Geary's Guide to the World's Great Aphorists*

FIRST DEATH DEPRIVES us, then bereavement turns the screws. We may suspect that the intensity of early pain and anguish will wane. But we dread that our loss will permanently drain our lives of all vitality. We anticipate an empty future. Our hurt transfixes us. It is as if we lie immobile and exposed waiting for more dreadful things to happen. We must choose not to linger in the lethargy of bereavement. If we do, our fears will be realized and our helplessness perpetuated. Coming to terms with pain and anguish requires that we move, however small and halting our first steps may be.

—Thomas Attig, *How We Grieve*

THERE IS SOMETHING sustaining in the very agitation that accompanies the first shocks of trouble, just as an acute pain is often a stimulus, and produces an excitement which is transient strength. It is in the slow, changed life that follows—in the time when sorrow has become stale, and has no longer an emotive intensity that counteracts its pain—in the time when day follows day in dull unexpectant sameness, and trial is a dreary routine—it is then that despair threatens; it is then that the peremptory hunger of the soul is felt, and eye and ear are strained after some unlearned secret of our existence, which shall give to endurance the nature of satisfaction.

—George Eliot, *The Mill on the Floss*

SURPRISED BY JOY—IMPATIENT as the Wind
I turned to share the transport—Oh! with whom
But Thee, long buried in the silent Tomb,

That spot which no vicissitude can find?

Love, faithful love, recalled thee to my mind—

But how could I forget thee?—Through what power,

Even for the least division of an hour,

Have I been so beguiled as to be blind

To my most grievous loss!—That thought's return

Was the worst pang that sorrow ever bore,

Save one, one only, when I stood forlorn,

Knowing my heart's best treasure was no more;

That neither present time, nor years unborn

Could to my sight that heavenly face restore.

—William Wordsworth, "Surprised By Joy"

ALAS, BELOVED, IS it not a great pity
  how the water rocked you,
your pulses powerless and no one near you
  to bring relief?
No news was brought to me of my child in peril
  or his cruel hardship
—O, I'd go, and eager, to Hell's deep flag-stones
  if I could save you.
The moon is dark and I cannot sleep.
  All ease has left me.
The candid Gaelic seems harsh and gloomy
—an evil omen.
I hate the time that I pass with friends,
  their wit torments me.
Since the day I saw you on the sands so lifeless
  no sun has shone.
Alas my sorrow, what can I do now?
  The world grinds me

—your slight white hand, like a tree-breeze, gone from
   my frowning brows,
and your little honeymouth, like angels' music
   sweet in my ears
saying to me softly: "Dear heart, poor father,
   do not be troubled."

—Pádraig Ó hÉigeartaigh, "My sorrow, Donncha"

GRIEF IS NOT a hurdle that we jump over at will or a barrier that we can avoid if
we are careful. After his wife's death from cancer, C. S. Lewis recognized the all-en-
compassing reality of grief: "Her absence is like the sky, spread over everything" (A
Grief Observed, 11).

—Wayne Simsic, Cries of the Heart

I TAKE JESSE'S pillow for my new bed downstairs, the pillow I carefully hid from
Chris all these months because I didn't want him to wash it. It's the last place Jesse's
head touched. It has his dried saliva on the pillowcase. This is how deranged I am
now. I quickly rip off the pillowcase like a Band-Aid on a sore and put it in the
wash. I put the freshly covered pillow on my new bed. Maybe Jesse will give me a
dream, too, where he's laughing about my fear of taking down his dolphins and my
madness in preserving his saliva and petting his socks.

—Marianne Leone, Knowing Jesse

IT'S THE NEVERNESS that is so painful. Never again to be here with us—never to
sit with us at the table, never to travel with us, never to laugh with us, never to cry
with us, never to embrace us as he leaves for school, never to see his brothers and

sisters marry. All the rest of our lives we must live without him. Only our death can stop the pain of his death.

A month, a year, five years—with that I could live. But not this forever.

I step out into the moist, moldy fragrance of a summer morning and arm in arm with my enjoyment comes the realization that never again will he smell this. . . .

One small misstep and now this neverness.

—Nicholas Wolterstorff, *Lament for a Son*

MORSDAG

MORSDAG: **MOTHERS' DAY** in Norwegian. I braced myself for Mother's Day 2010. I would try to be gracious and pleasant, although I knew I'd be traversing a potential emotional minefield. Markers like holidays underscored the droning reality: another year without him. Every Mother's Day of every year for the rest of my life would be without him. And what did it mean to be the mother of a dead child?

Then Randall arranged a trip to Norway in May that would span the weekend of Morsdag. As it turned out, that put us exactly where we needed to be to receive a rather special gift from an attentive oldest son, who had never missed a Mother's Day while he'd been alive.

To explain the gift, I have to go back to another weekend, this one in July of 2007. And I have to begin not in Norway, but Idaho.

Eighteen-year-old Parker had flown ahead from Paris to Utah with our younger children, Claire, Dalton, and Luc, while Randall and I negotiated a big, complicated move from Paris to Munich. Parker left his siblings with family and traveled to Idaho, where he would enroll for the summer at a small liberal arts college. After his first semester, he would take a leave of absence to serve for two years as a volunteer representative of our church.

On the weekend before Parker entered his summer course, he stayed in the Idaho home of Melanie, a friend of mine from college days. There, Parker met and quickly befriended Melanie's nephew Nathan. Nathan was visiting from Chile, where his family lived as military expatriates. Parker and Nathan stayed up over twenty-four hours straight, just talking about their upbringings as two frequently displaced global kids. Parker shared tales of his French years, but also of his childhood on an island in Norway. The young men hit it off immediately and at the end of thirty-six hours together, Nathan and Parker decided to room together at college that fall.

Parker told me all about this talk-a-thon when I arrived in Idaho to see him safely settled at the university. After some hours together, we parted with a big, firm hug, sure to see each other in "just a couple of days!"

It was the last day I would see him alive.

More than a year after Parker's funeral, I received word from Melanie that Nathan had applied to serve a mission, and he had been assigned to Norway. Nathan had as good a chance of being assigned to Montana or Mongolia, Madagascar or Melbourne, Moscow or Mississippi. Of all places, Norway. *Norway*, the place where one of his "best friends" (as Nathan called Parker) had hoped to be assigned as a missionary.

The Norwegian coincidence didn't feel coincidental to Nathan. As the newly minted "Elder Smith" ("Elder" is an office of responsibility within our church) he launched into his service "way in the heck up there," as he said. Over the months, Melanie forwarded me short excerpts of Elder Smith's emails to his family—all bright and vibrating with enthusiasm, and speckled with tokens of the Norwegianness our family knows so well. One email referred to Parker by name, and the impact Parker's friendship and passing from this life had made on Elder Smith's life and, in turn, on other missionaries serving in Norway.

Sometimes these letters were heavy reading for me. I would pace through the effervescent descriptions of the places Parker so loved and where he had always hoped he would serve, and I would find myself holding my arms around my torso so I wouldn't disintegrate or detonate.

=====

Now, throughout the spring of 2010, Randall had been trying to find a three-day break so our family could make this last trip up north before our July move, this time from Munich to Singapore. But with the move itself gathering momentum and devouring time, and with Randall's weekly travels crowding his calendar, it didn't look likely. Then a certain video conference got canceled, a business trip got bumped, and he managed to snap up frequent-flyer tickets for a Mother's Day weekend in Oslo. We squeezed in seventy-two hours of Norway's awesome early-summer splendor. And then we let serendipity spin its shimmer, the magic of which settled upon us somewhere in the middle of our church meetings.

Before those meetings, as we'd knelt in our hotel room in family prayer, I prayed inwardly for something notable—something quiet and personally significant—to happen at church that day, something that would boldface this day, something that would bless us with Parker's recognizable touch. On the road to the Sandvika chapel I remembered an Elder Nathan Smith, and fished in my handbag for a pen so I could write a little message to any missionaries I might see there, which they could in turn somehow get to Elder Smith. Norway is a huge country; this Elder Smith could easily have been serving a long plane ride northward, somewhere near the Arctic Circle, or anywhere in between.

As the church meeting started, I scanned the congregation, seeing many familiar faces that took my heart back to some of the sweetest friendships and years of our lives. It was delicious to hear and speak Norwegian again. It was striking to be surrounded by such reverence, even with many children in the congregation. It was healing to be with people who knew our family as a whole—and therefore acknowledge the *hole*—who with moist eyes looked into our eyes and wanted to know how we were *really* doing. This, as I felt it happening, was the gift of the day, I thought. It was so much. My soul was brimming.

I tapped the arm of a young man in front of me, asking if he'd ever heard of a missionary named Smith. He hadn't, but there was a new missionary who had just arrived in this small congregation. Maybe I could ask him if he knew someone named Smith. The young man gestured to the dark-haired, dark-suited young man sitting on the other side of the chapel elbow-to-elbow with Dalton in the row of young men who would administer the Sacrament (Holy Communion) that day.

My eyes settled on Dalton, born in this congregation but now fourteen and almost as tall as his mom. That little white-blonde Viking child had taken his first wobbly steps on the light rose carpet in this very chapel, and here he was, lanky and at ease in his skin, those dimples in his cheeks marking him as, yes, that same little boy. He looked a lot like Parker at that moment: his darkening blonde hair cropped very short, gelled up in the front; his shoulders the same shape as his older brother's had been at that same age; the ready smile; the bright eyes; the adoring but comfy glance to the new missionary sitting tight against him on his right.

The two whispered something to each other and laughed a bit, my Dalton and the big-shouldered kid with bright eyes, dimples like Dalton's, and a broad smile. In that instant I saw all the long chain of so many missionaries our Parker had known and called his best friends, the ones he wanted to be just like. That same look was in Dalton's eyes.

And then I felt it: *Elder Smith*.

After the Sacrament, that missionary came and sat two rows ahead of us, just close enough that, if I strained, I could make out the name on the nametag. I nudged Randall, and whispered "Smith. *Smith*. Got a notepad? He's the one." Handing him my pen, I added, "*Chile*. Find out if he grew up in *Chile*."

(Randall had not been in on every detail of Melanie's forwarded emails from her nephew. He wasn't even looking for an Elder Smith as I was, but was quickly getting the message—I was serious about cornering this kid.)

What follows are the little pink Post-It notes that then went back and forth between the Elder and Randall.

Randall writes in Norwegian:

> *Elder Smith,*
>   *Would you be so kind and tell me where you come from original-ly/where you grew up? We happen to know an Elder Smith who's supposed to be in Norway on a mission.*
>   *Thanks,*
> *Randall Bradford*

Elder Smith, the back of whose head I am studying intently, responds in Norwegian (I'm practically prostrate across Randall's lap trying to read the little message):

> *I grew up around the world and lived in Chile and Germany most recently because of my Dad's job as a diplomat in the American Air Force. So what I usually say is that I grew up outside the USA, since I don't remember much of my childhood in the USA.*

I'm jab-jab-jabbing with my fingertip on the written word *Chile*, trying to stay calm and inconspicuous, hoping I'm not distracting the speaker who has risen to the pulpit. Randall now writes in English:

> Elder Smith,
>
> I think you are the Elder Smith I'm talking about. Do you remember meeting a young man named Parker Bradford who was planning to attend college in Idaho before serving his mission? If you do, you must be the nephew of Melanie Smith. Parker is our son, our oldest. He lived in this congregation for five years of his childhood.
>
> Are you Melanie Smith's nephew?

We pass the note forward two rows. I watch the nape of the missionary's neck and the back of his ears. Maybe he will turn around and meet our eyes. Or grin. Or wink while giving us a low "thumbs up."

Instead I see this: Those big shoulders draw up in sharp jerks and then begin shaking as the young man lowers his head, his right hand wiping both his eyes, then down his cheek and across his jaw. It takes a few minutes for him to write a response.

His words:

> Yes, that's me. Parker is one of my heroes and I think about him every day since I have known him. Melanie is my aunt through marriage.

I have to pull myself together quickly, because I'd been asked to sing, and right then it is my turn. As I stand to walk to the front of the congregation, I stoop to whisper to *the* Elder Smith, "I sing this for you and for Parker." Then, as clearly and as full of strength as I have managed since burying my son, I offer a Norwegian anthem. I sing to this miraculous kid hunched over in his white shirt and tie, the one whose rugby player's hands smudge away tears that flow streaming down his face.

Grief is often isometric. There is so much holding in and bracing that one must master. I eventually learned that, eyes closed, I could extend my eye of faith and envision Parker watching over his friend Nathan's service. Pleased for his joy. Grateful for his service. Proud of his goodness. And in that act of imagining and stretching my vision, I saw in small moments like this, how there was a sort of synergistic interaction between my mortal reaching, and heaven's whispered rush right back at me.

LET US, THEN, learn that we can never be lonely or forsaken in this life. Shall they forget us because they are "made perfect"? Shall they love us the less because they now have power to love us more? If we forget them not, shall they not remember us with God? No trial, then, can isolate us, no sorrow can cut us off from the Communion of Saints. Kneel down, and you are with them; lift up your eyes, and the heavenly world, high above all perturbation, hangs serenely overhead; only a thin veil, it may be, floats between. All whom we loved, and all who loved us, whom we still love no less, while they love us yet more, are ever near, because they are ever in His presence in whom we live and dwell.

—H. E. Manning (1808–1892), Archbishop of Westminster

MAN, WOMAN, CHILD

HOW DO YOU survive as a couple? How did we work out our differences? We talked, we love each other, and we held each other and we began to appreciate that we were different. . . . Each of us was grieving on different levels. I was very sad at the beginning, and he was very rational. . . . When we went to bed, I would talk about my feelings so I could go to sleep—and then he would have it all and he couldn't sleep. He got to the point where he said, "Don't talk," and then that would breed resentment in me. It was a while after Ellen died, but we got to a place where we could hear each other.

—Interview in *A Parent's Guide to Raising Grieving Children*

I KNEW, SEEING the radiant happiness of the parents, the secret that they had shut away from public view; that this day of joy was also tinged with grief.

The parents rejoiced for the bride's good choices, her well-founded hope of happiness in marriage. But the parents also remembered, and in private perhaps shed tears for the children who would not marry, would not bring them grandchildren, would not grow old in the joy of seeing their own children marry. . . .

No one spoke of the missing children, just as no one at our son's wedding not many years ago spoke of our other son, his younger brother, who, even had he lived past the age of seventeen, could never have married; or of our little girl who died the day she was born.

The funeral does not intrude on the wedding day.

But still it is there, in the parents' hearts. The memory of the missing children whispers to us.

—Orson Scott Card, "When joy, grief share the same day," *Deseret News* online

---

THE CHILDREN WERE very blunt. They said: "We want our mother and father back." It wasn't easy, but we listened. They were really surprised when we told them, "Those people are gone forever; you have to live with the mother and father you have now. Everything has changed. Your sister's death has turned everything around, and we all need to learn new ways. We are all hurting and we are in this together." It made a big difference in the way the children, even the six-year-old, reacted. They seemed to relax. We think it was because they felt included and began to understand what was happening.

—Parents interviewed in Silverman, *Never Too Young to Know*

WE WERE . . . raising grieving, horribly sad, mind-bogglingly destroyed children. . . . They looked at us, and they were scared. . . . They were looking at mothers who were flattened, totally smeared into the earth. I wanted to be able to say to them: you don't have to be victims—you could be survivors.

—Kristen Breitweiser, interviewed in "Hell's Angels," in *Live Your Best Life*

ALLIE WAS IN his senior year of high school, we had smoothed the rough edges of our marriage and the future looked bright.

Then tragedy struck . . . and I wanted Peter to hang on with me. I was terrified that he would succumb to despair. We knew immediately that it was impossible to console each other. Allie is an inconsolable loss. The best we could do was stick together and try not to cause each other more pain.

Seven years later we felt grounded again, but life is very different. The future is a thing of the past, as writer Peter De Vries puts it. We live from day to day, bearing our burden of grief, finding solace when and where we can. . . . It's impossible to live wholeheartedly with a heart that is broken.

—Anne McCracken and Mary Semel, *A Broken Heart Still Beats*

WE HAVE LOST the joy of the household, and the solace of our old age: she must have known how much we loved her. Oh, that she could now know how deeply, how tenderly, we do still and shall ever love her dear joyous face! Blessings on her!

—Charles Darwin, *The Life and Letters of Charles Darwin*

MOST BEREAVED CHILDREN like to remember and talk about the deceased with friends and relatives. Unfortunately, there is a phenomenon called "the conspiracy of silence" that makes it difficult for others to talk about the dead person because they are afraid of hurting the bereaved's feelings. The bereaved person, on the other hand, has hurt feelings when people won't talk about the deceased with them.

—Erin Linn, *150 Facts About Grieving Children*

MY BROTHER CAME in and he said, "Ma died" and he just started crying. Then I started punching walls and stuff. I was punching all over the place. I broke one of the pictures in my room. I smashed it all over the place. I was mad. I just went around the house punching everything. Getting mad and freaking out, punching everything and just crying and stuff. I cried the whole night. I didn't even sleep. I guess my father would have liked me not to be mad and stuff and punch things, but I couldn't stop.

—Interview in *Never Too Young To Know*

NO LIFE. I can't believe it. No blood pumping through all those tiny veins of your hand. I am in shock. No life. How can that be? When I looked at you there, it was as if all time had stopped, all time had come to a halt. All those molecules, all those atoms, all those neutrons and electrons that are supposedly in constant motion, were not moving, for there was literally no minute, no second, no split second, no nanosecond. You did not breathe. You did not sit up. You did not open your eyes. I expected you to sit up. I expected you to look at us with your blue eyes and sly smile and shyly say something cute, or softly ask us, "What's wrong?" or flippantly say, "I don't know what the big deal is; I'm just up here with God." But there you lay, in a fine mahogany box. You're wearing a powder blue necktie and a plaid jacket. You hair is parted over too far and swept to the side just a bit too neatly. You face is waxy and your long, fine nose seems more prominent than usual. Your hands are crossed just a bit too politely over your waist. I realize that the only time I would have seen you like this would have been in slumber. I realize that the only time I have seen you asleep was when you were a baby. It is only in dreams and in memories that I meet you now. I cry, but there is only the sound of my own echo.

I read your poetry and remember how I knew you. The thought that crossed my mind first when I first found out was that I would never speak with you again. I thought of this, and the breath was taken out of me. I could not find the breath, and the silence crackled cold and hard, a sheet of ice across what is now an ocean of space. My mouth stands open, gaping, speechless, a silent red gash.

—Meg Edington Sefton, "When the Waters are Deep," quoted in *This Incomplete One*

Life is fragile,
Living is like a twig,
Fragile, thin, and broken with a finger
Greif is like a stone,
Sadness like a boulder,
Weighing down your every move,
Crushing, crushing impenetrable.
Agony is like a blanket
Covering all around,

But alas, there is one difference,
A blanket is warm, comfortable, and forgiving.

—Chet Garlick, "Life"

"SO, WHAT ELSE have you learned by making tear soup, Grandy?"

"I've learned that grief, like a pot of soup, changes the longer it simmers and the more things you put into it. I've learned that sometimes people say unkind things, but they really don't mean to hurt you."

"And mostly importantly, I've learned that there is something down deep inside all of us ready to help us survive the things we think we can't survive."

"Grandy, you know so much. What will I do after you die?"

"Don't worry, I'll leave you my recipe for tear soup."

—Pat Schweibert and Chuck DeKlyen, *Tear Soup*

SCHOOLING GRIEF

IT'S A SPRING afternoon in 2009, nearly two years following Parker's death, and the counselor at our children's school in Munich has invited a short list of students and faculty, whom Dalton has hand selected, to gather in an empty upper floor room during an extended recess and lunch period. The whole building will be empty during that hour, the counselor's assured us, so that we can count on no disturbances whatsoever. We'll need this time. Dalton's been preparing for many months for this moment.

"Now, all of you've been invited here specifically by Dalton," the counselor begins after we're all settled. There are about a dozen girls and boys sitting to my left and my right in a circle, twelve- and thirteen-year-olds all of them. Dalton's favorite teacher, his English professor, is sitting directly across from me, and Randall is to my immediate right. The four chairs to my left separate me from Dalton.

"He's invited you," the counselor continues, "because he has something he wants to share, and he trusts you. What we will discuss today stays here, unless Dalton invites any of you to share this information further. Is that good with you, Dalton?"

He nods.

"Good with everyone else?"

Everyone else nods. I'm focused on the middle of the circle where we've set Parker's djembe, his treasured African drum.

"I wonder," says the counselor, "if you all could just note on this slip of paper I've given you something that you've lost. It can be something intangible or it can be a home or a person, anything. But I want this to be a loss which has really hurt you. Maybe it still hurts you. Just write it down and then you can place your paper on top of here." She points to Parker's drum.

I watch as these kids and their teachers soften, and a spirit of thoughtfulness and sincerity seeps around the circle. I also watch Dalton carefully. He had been sleepless and cramped on the floor of the bathroom all night.

"I'm not sure I can do this, Mom," he said as I wiped his forehead with a cool washcloth around 3:00 a.m. He was on his side in a quasi-fetal position. "What if . . . what if I tell them and . . . "

"And . . . and what?" I asked, running the cloth under cold water again. I squeezed out the excess. I dabbed his face.

"What if I tell them and they just . . . they . . . " He was sweating, holding his stomach.

"They don't do anything? What if they don't care, you mean?" I knew my boy. And I knew this same leaden, justifiable fear. What if I bare my soul to someone and he leans away from, not into, the conversation? What if I expose the enormous hole in my torso and no one sees it, no one feels it?

That's the great fear.

And that is why, for these two full school years, Dalton has made acrobatic contortions at school to avoid any discussion about his family. He's done everything to avoid mentioning his brother. In this new community, everyone asked that thing you always ask when you meet the new student, "So, do you have any brothers or sisters?"

Dalton decided to lie. He had no older brother. But the deception and the denial were making him ill. So on a spring day during a noon hour, we're in a schoolroom where the students are writing down and then talking of their various losses: grandparent, aunt, uncle, pet. They write about lost friendships and missed opportunities and forfeited stability because of moving from country to country their whole lives. Some write down a lost possession—their home in another hemisphere, for instance—some write down "lost time."

Not one, however, writes about losing a big brother.

"Thanks, everyone," says the counselor. "Well, you're here today because Dalton has lost something that is extremely valuable to him, more precious than almost anything else in his life." The counselor is no way maudlin, just serious but warm.

"And because Dalton cares so much about this thing he's lost, and because he cares about you, too," she adds, "he wants to share some of that loss with you. Is that good?" She scans the circle. All eyes are fixed, alert. "Okay, Dalton, would you like to share with us?"

I watch my boy—so blonde, cautious, eyes like chips of aquamarine—I watch him take a breath. I watch the muscles around his mouth, the place you usually catch the first cracks of breaking apart. I also watch his friend, a small Israeli boy named Itamar, who's sitting at Dalton's elbow, his mop of almost-black hair just brushing into his thick dark lashes, those huge soulful eyes watching Dalton, our Nordic prototype, as he begins to speak slowly, deliberately.

"I want to tell you . . . " Dalton begins as he stretches his fingers out on a gold-brown spiral-bound book he's been holding flat on his lap, "I want to *share with you* someone who is important to me. "This," he lifts up the album of Parker to show an enlarged photo of a handsome teenager with a strong chin, a crimson red rugby shirt, and half a grin, "This is my big brother. His name is Parker."

Burning creeps up my face and I look over toward Randall with an impulse to take his hand in mine, but I don't because in the tension of the moment I know the slightest movement could topple things. I wipe my palms discreetly on my pant legs.

The counselor is smiling softly at Dalton, helping him along. His English teacher is quiet, her eyes large and already rimmed in shine. The boys and girls in the circle, as I quietly look around, are motionless, reverent, even.

"Parker is what I have lost," Dalton adds. He lifts his brows, his mouth is pinching and then shaking a bit, "He passed away in a water accident not so long ago when he was trying to save another student from . . ."

And right then, a sound like a rabbit being injured arises from behind Itamar's dark mop of hair that is now hanging toward his lap, and his delicate shoulders sag under a black and rust-speckled sweatshirt. Dalton stops speaking, and turns toward Itamar. The black-haired boy raises his head. There are already tears dripping down the light olive face, and pain transforms those brown eyes. He's crying openly, like this is his own loss.

Dalton's eyes fill with tears, too, but his eyebrows are raised. These are tears of surprise. But more than that, they're tears of relief and joy, the look you'd see on someone who'd slaved day and night for weeks but still never thought he'd deserve to pass the big final exam, but got—*holy cow!*—the highest score in the class. Surprise, relief, joy. Then Dalton touches Itamar's shoulder, as if comforting *him*, while Itamar continues to wipe the flow of tears with his oversized sleeve.

"I want you to know about what happened to Parker," Dalton says, "because he's a great brother and he's so important to me."

While the rest of the world outside our building grows more and more quiet (I wonder what's happened with the afternoon recess and all the children's laughter and screaming from moments earlier), Dalton begins narrating with a stronger voice.

He sits straight and tells about the pages of the album, holding each up and turning the book so everyone in the room can see: Parker holding his arms around his two younger brothers at basketball and volleyball championships,

Parker with arms around his family at high school graduation,

Parker hiking with his family,

Family vacations,

Teaching Dalton and Luc to bike or swim,

Hanging out and watching movies with Claire and his brothers,

Going to church,

Eating his favorite food (ice cream),

Laughing in the sunshine and goofing around beneath starlight.

Pictures of a real live person, a brother, a friend, an actual human being. A reality.

The students are first speechless, and two girls to my right are wiping under their eyes. Everyone—every last person—is leaning into the conversation, reaching their attention toward this story, asking to hold the book themselves if Dalton doesn't mind. Could they just see—*his name's* Parker, *right?*—if they could see *Parker*. If Dalton could just hand them all his pictures of this real person, this brother named Parker.

At this point, the room on that second floor of the school building is rather quiet except for some whispering and the sound of Itamar blowing his nose as Dalton begins turning pages and narrating his photo album. Students start to chat in low tones, two and two, as they pass the Parker book around the circle. I keep my eye on Dalton, whose entire posture has changed from closed and shadowed to open and gleaming.

He's pointing to the page with a shot of Parker playing a drum solo in his senior class talent show at his school in Paris: "Of everything Parker did," Dalton's smiling now, "basketball, volleyball, swimming, hanging out with all his friends, even eating ice cream. . . . I think what he loved the most was drumming. That's why we brought his drum today."

Right then, from directly beneath our feet and as if on cue, someone begins playing a drum set. An explosive, vibrating drum riff that goes and goes and goes. It startles Dalton, the English teacher shoots me a glance, I reach to squeeze Randall's hand, two of the boys look at the floor then all around the walls and then back at each other, perplexed but oblivious. And Itamar holds the tissue at his nose.

I shake my head just once. Randall grins. These kinds of coincidences aren't entirely new to us anymore.

We listen for several more minutes while Dalton tells all he can about his brother, and while some stranger wielding drum sticks tears it up under our feet.

The kids need to return to class, the tin of cookies we've shared is down to crumbs, light is shining through the windows, there are no more tears, and the invisible drummer retreats to whatever mysterious place he'd come from.

But his silent rhythm follows us all the way home and beyond.

A NEW REALITY

THINGS WILL NEVER be "back to normal." Life will be full of peace and joy, love and sorrow, sin and reconciliation, but not "back to normal." We have a new norm for normal. Reality has changed, the psychological and spiritual terrain has changed. We are possessed of a terrible wisdom about life that we did not have before.

—Gregory Floyd, *A Grief Unveiled*

━━━━━━━━━

YOU DO COME out of it, that's true. After a year, after five. But you don't come out of it like a train coming out of a tunnel, bursting through the Downs into sunshine and that swift, rattling descent to the Channel; you come out of it as a gull comes out of an oil-slick. You are tarred and feathered for life.

—Julian Barnes, *Flaubert's Parrot*

━━━━━━━━━

GRIEF IS A strange journey. Each time we embark upon it, it is as though we have never taken its roads before. . . . For we do not only lose another person; we lose the person we were with the one we lost.

—Patricia Monaghan, *The Red-Haired Girl from the Bog*

━━━━━━━━━

I LOST SUSY thirteen years ago; I lost her mother—her incomparable mother!—five and a half years ago; Clara has gone away to live in Europe; and now I have lost Jean. How poor I am, who was once so rich! Seven months ago Mr. Roger died—one of the best friends I ever had, and the nearest perfect, as man and gentleman, I have yet met among my race; within the last six weeks Gilder has passed away, and Laffan—old, old friends of mine. Jean lies yonder, I sit here; we are strangers under our own roof; we kissed hands good-by [sic] at this door last night—and it was forever, we never suspecting it. She lies there, and I sit here—writing, busying myself, to keep my heart from breaking. How dazzlingly the sunshine is flooding the hills around! It is like a mockery.

—Mark Twain, *What is Man and Other Essays*

AND WHAT RIGHT have I to criticize the reactions of others? The memory of my own response to this kind of loss before I became an initiate myself, leaves me burning with shame and embarrassment. The friend I had not seen for years whose seven-year-old was knocked down by a car and killed. The fellow-teacher whose twin daughters died shortly after they were born. The cousin whose child simply dies, inexplicably, in its cot. Did I say anything, send a message of consolation? Did I go to the funerals—as that cousin came to Jonathan and Emma's? I look back at the me of those days—not very long ago at all—with contempt and disgust and bafflement. So busy with my own preoccupations while knowing nothing of these most basic realities. I seem blind and without feeling; hardly human.

—John Tittensor, quoted in *A Broken Heart Still Beats*

AS SOON AS people went back to their routines and you try to go back to your routine, that's when you realize that that routine doesn't exist anymore. We now had to get used to this new reality. Nothing is the same. All of a sudden there was this silence. The expectations of waking up in the morning, of hearing your son stomping up and down stairs going to the bathroom. . . . Suddenly it is too quiet, and that's when it starts to sink in.

—Interview in *A Parent's Guide to Raising Grieving Children*

TIME SEEMS DIFFERENT to me now than it did before you died. At present, it seems to stretch on forever in front of me like an unending road. It has been divided up, forever partitioned by the catastrophic event of your death. The time before your passing will always be "before." It will always seem happy to me now, even though I know that it wasn't always, but I had you in my life. I didn't know then how precious the time was or how blessed we were. The time "before" was filled with so many activities. It was always busy, and it moved so fast. It just flashed by. My only thought regarding time back then was that there was just not enough of it.

Now the time crawls by. It slowly marches on. Everything seems interminable. I wish that I could just close my eyes and be a year older; or better yet, 10 years older.

—Ellen Knell, *Letters to Erica*

I WONDERED THAT other men should live when he was dead, for I had loved him as though he would never die. Still more I wondered that he should die and I remain alive, for I was his second self. How well the poet put it when he called his friend the half of his soul! I felt that our two souls had been as one, living in two bodies, and life to me was fearful because I did not want to live with only half a soul. Perhaps this, too, is why I shrank from death, for fear that one whom I had loved so well might then be wholly dead.

—Saint Augustine, "I wondered that other men should live when he was dead"

WHEN WE TURNED into the road leading to our house, I suddenly felt a deep, inner sadness. Tears came to my eyes and I did not dare to look at my father. We both understood. She would not be home. She would not open the door and embrace us.

She would not ask how the day had been. . . . I felt anxious tension when my father drove into the garage and we walked up to the door. Upon entering the house it was suddenly clear to us: it had become an empty house.

—Henri Nouwen, *A Shared Sorrow*

I DID KNOW that Susy was part of us; I did not know that she could go away; I did not know that she could go away, and take our lives with her, yet leave our dull bodies behind. And I did not know what she was. To me she was but treasure in the bank; the amount known, the need to look at it daily, handle it, weigh it, count it, realize it, not necessary; and now that I would do it, it is too late; they tell me it is not there, has vanished away in a night, the bank is broken, my fortune is gone, I am a pauper. How am I to comprehend this? How am I to have it? Why am I robbed, and who is benefited? . . .

I am working, but it is for the sake of the work— the "surcease of sorrow" that is found there.

—Mark Twain, *The Complete Letters of Mark Twain*

WE KNOW WE have survived the worst life has to offer and in that alone there is strength. Let others who do not know any better speak of "closure." There is no such thing in regard to a dead child. You never close that part of your life. It molds you forevermore.

—Ellen Mitchell, *Beyond Tears*

O! GRIEF HATH chang'd me since you saw me last,
And careful hours, with time's deformed hand
Have written strange defeatures in my face.

—William Shakespeare, *Comedy of Errors, The Riverside Shakespeare*

IN THE CAR accident that killed Jake, I was badly cut by the shattered window shield. Cosmetic surgeons worked hard on my face. They thought they got everything. But nine years later, little slivers of glass, small as grains of sand, occasionally still poke through my skin. Everyone else seems amazed by this. But I like the symbolism in it.

After all, most wounds heal, even deep ones, but not the death of a child. It seems fitting then that glass from that accident keeps emerging as though from the depths of my early pain. . . . When I'm old, if glass still pushes through those scars, I won't be surprised. Or sorry. That glass is my hair turned white.

—Anne McCracken and Mary Semel, *A Broken Heart Still Beats*

GRIEF IS A great leveler. There is no highroad out.

Courage is a first step, but simply to bear the blow bravely is not enough. Stoicism is courageous, but it is only a halfway house on the long road. It is a shield, permissible for a short time only. In the end, one has to discard shields and remain open and vulnerable. Otherwise, scar tissue will seal off the wound and no growth will follow. To grow, to be reborn, one must remain vulnerable— open to love but also hideously open to the possibility of more suffering.

—Anne Morrow Lindbergh, *Hour of Gold, Hour of Lead*

GRIEVING . . . is a life-long process. . . . You have to create a lot of new memories over a long time without that child . . . so that you can rebuild your life. . . . You're never going to have your normal life back, but it doesn't mean it won't be a good life. It will be a different life, a new life.

—Susan Whitmore, "You're never going to have your normal life back"

UNTIL WE MEET AGAIN

WE BURIED OUR son in the narrow groove of time between Paris-as-home and Munich-as-alien. Geographic relocation had never been more inopportune. How, we kept asking ourselves, could we have lost our child at the very moment we also lost everyone who knew and loved him, too?

We initially called our apartment at Widenmayerstrasse 44 "The Monastery." It was a soundproofed cell, a place crowded with emptiness. I couldn't bring myself to unpack boxes and set up house, didn't have the slightest desire for discovery, and didn't even glance at a map of Munich until months into our stay. Given the psychic dislocation, geographic dislocation was a trifle.

When we were finally able to interact with people without stiffening in self-protection or disintegrating into tears, we volunteered for positions within our church community. Randall's responsibility was to make monthly visits to speak to a small congregation in Rosenheim, near the Germany-Austrian border. Something about the long beautiful drive to the little chapel and the simple, subdued authenticity of the people there made Randall look forward to those visits.

Randall was scheduled to speak in Rosenheim over a weekend that happened to coincide with our three monthly memorial markers—the 19th (the date of Parker's accident), the 20th (the day he lay in coma), and the 21st, (the day of his passing). I had also been asked to speak, so we took our youngest two, Dalton and Luc, with us. As we had done every Sunday for a year since Parker's passing, we were fasting for strength and inspiration. I expected something positive—significant, but known only to us—to happen.

As the meeting ended, a woman we had never met approached us. She introduced herself as Ruth Sipus and addressed us in German:

"I have a favor to ask," she said, leaning forward in the church pew and folding her arms across her lap, smiling, eyebrows raised above a smile which, though sunny, readied to offer an apology.

"I am a professional photographer," Ruth went on, "and sometimes do work for our church's monthly magazine. And okay, I'll get right to the point, I wondered if you," she looked at Randall, "and your boys could pose for a photo shoot?" Her pitch swept upward in a question mark. "I'm under deadline to finish for an upcoming edition."

The boys, who could understand a good amount of German by this time, perked up.

"The problem," she said, "is scheduling. I don't have many open days—or hours—left. And we do live an hour apart."

Randall was to fly to London on Tuesday, and then off again for a month, circling the globe. Monday—the next day—was the only time he could do the shoot. "In fact," he explained, "Monday morning would be my only open slot. But it sounds great. We'd love to help out."

Ruth shook her dark hair back from her face, surprised "Well, actually, that's the only time I have available, too." She added that she knew it was asking a lot of us to make ourselves available for an entire morning—taking off work, taking the boys out of school—and on such short notice. Her enthusiasm and certainty in Randall and the boys as the "right subjects" made it easy to say yes.

"Tell me what time you need the boys," I entered the conversation, "and what does this photo shoot entail?"

Ruth said that the photo was supposed to be for a short feature about a father and son biking side by side. "I imagine," said Ruth, "taking this photo from behind, like from here." She moved behind Randall and Luc, who were sitting next to each other, and she crouched a little, holding her hands up as if framing a picture. "And I would have the father place his hand," she reached over to take Randall's hand, "planting his palm—see this?—right *there*." Ruth stepped back while Randall held his hand on Luc's lower back, and Luc looked up at his dad. "Right here, just like that! Yes, on the son's lower back—how does that seem?—as he steadies and pushes his son along."

Over his shoulder, Randall shot a glance at me. Heat streamed into my face, and I bit the inside of my lip to keep my composure. We both smiled.

What Ruth could not have known is that this very image—father and son biking alongside one another, father placing his hand on the son's lower back—existed already in our minds. We had talked about it often in the brutal months since Parker's passing.

It was in Norway that Randall first taught Parker to ride a bike. And it was there that we went on countless family bike rides around the hilly island of Nesøya. When the roads became steep and narrow, I would fall back, trailing Randall and Parker, who were competitive comrades. Soon Claire was biking too, and I stayed next to her. Eventually, little Dalton was seated in the bike trailer attached to Randall's bike.

In those early days on our Nordic island, I saw much about their father-son friendship from where I brought up the back of our family procession. I sensed competition, yes. Parker—determined and athletic—would not get off his bike, even if he could barely turn the pedals on the climb. Randall would not get off his bike, either, although I could hear his puffing and slight grunting with exertion from where I rode. But more than that, I could sense the trust and hope between father and son. We biked so often, and our formation was so consistent that I could anticipate the precise spot on the road where Randall would have to reach over to help Parker. He would stretch his arm and plant his hand on Parker's lower back. From there, the two would ascend the hill together.

After Parker died, we'd wept over that image in our grief. We'd wept with longing. And we'd wept with love. We'd also wept with gratitude over the countless times Randall had figuratively pushed and nudged and encouraged Parker, only an arm's length from him, on the path, uphill, and in the right direction. From Norway to Versailles, where we added Luc to our family and strapped him in the bike trailer while we rode the gardens behind the famous château. To Paris, where Randall rode his Vespa to take Parker to visit members of our center city congregation—young families and widows scattered all around Paris. In every stage of life up until death, father coaxing son along. Father and son riding side by side over the landscape of life.

Ruth Sipus knew none of this. She knew nothing of our family, nothing of Norway or bikes or Paris or Vespas. Nothing of our family's private markers, the 19th, 20th, and 21st. All she knew was that she had this particular assignment and had not yet found the right father and son to photograph. It was only later that she told us she had been inwardly asking for days for some sort of miracle, and then, as we spoke to the congregation that Sunday, something told her, "You must photograph the Bradfords."

Under unusually sparkling early autumn sunshine on the cobblestone roads of the village of Grünwald, Germany, I watched from behind, holding Ruth's photography equipment. Randall reached over to skinny, athletic, determined Luc—a near reincarnation of nine-year-old Parker from Norway—and placed his hand right on the spot where, a decade earlier, he had placed it on Parker.

Some time later, people all over the world opened their copies of a magazine. Toward the very back, they came to an inconspicuous single-page article accompanied by a small photograph. The shot is quiet, simple, and wouldn't grab for attention as much as it might whisper for reflection. The title of the article is "Picturing Fatherhood." And in the border along the top of the page—the thing that made me, when I read it standing alone at the cash register of a bookstore, close my eyes to the flash of surprise that softened to bemusement and then melted to wonder at the heavenly sleight of hand—are the words, "Until We Meet Again."

HOLIDAYS, HARD DAYS

SINCE JESSE DIED, I have felt joy. I have even laughed until tears came to my eyes. I have written a book and essays, I have acted on television and in film, I have hosted huge family parties.

But, full disclosure: I have taken to my bed for the entire day sometimes, on Jesse's birthday, and on the January date I found him dead. Because what makes more sense to me, the actual person who has suffered a loss, are the words C. S. Lewis's character speaks in the film "Shadowlands": "The pain now is part of the happiness then. That's the deal."

—Leone, "A Mother's Grief—Without Time Limits," *The Boston Globe* online

---

I STILL STRUGGLE with depression every August and September.

I think about him every day.

And on those days when my thoughts rest for awhile on some accidental memory of us together, I have a hard time remembering what kind of mother I was to him. I don't see me clearly in those moments, only Michael—laughing, walking through a room in his green plaid pajama bottoms, eating peaches out of the can. Covered under a pile of blankets on his bed, asleep. Playing his guitar. And even though in my mind I seemed to be always laying foundations for what was to come in his life—college and career, mission, marriage, the stuff of his maturity—I don't think of myself as the mom who lived more in my son's future than in his present. I hope I wasn't that mom. I didn't want to be.

But then Michael would never let me get away with that.

Thank Heaven, he wouldn't let me.

—Cheri Pray Earl, "My Grief Observed," *Dance with Them*

A LONGITUDINAL STUDY by Catherine Carnelley, Camile Wortman and their colleagues showed that most bereaved do in fact have strong reactions to important dates related to the loss; the date of the loved one's death, for example, and often major holidays.

—George Bonnano, "Grief and Bereavement During the Holidays"

TOMORROW, STARTING AT dawn, at the hour when the land turns white,
I will leave. You see, I know you are waiting for me.
I will go through the forest, I will go past the mountain,
I cannot stay far from you any longer.

I will walk with my eyes fixed on my thoughts,
seeing nothing else, hearing no sound,
alone, unknown, back bent, hands crossed,
sad, and day for me will be like night.

I will not look at the gold of the falling evening,
nor at the sails in the distance going down to Harfleur.
And when I arrive, I will put on your grave
a sprig of green holly and of heather in bloom.

—Victor Hugo, "Tomorrow, as soon as it is dawn"

I WAS NOT sure whether I should hang my son's stocking or not. I decided to hang it, because after all he is my son. But my husband thought that this was not a good idea. He told me that I was "in denial."

I was taking out the Christmas ornaments and I came across an ornament that Timmy had made in kindergarten last year. It had his handprint on it. I dissolved into tears.

—Interview in "Getting Through the Holidays, Advice from the Bereaved"
This Emotional Life, Grief and Loss Blog

ON NOVEMBER 14, 1970, a plane crashed in the rain in Huntington, West Virginia, killing the entire football team of Marshall University, along with team supporters and crew members. . . .

After nearly 30 years, the pain still is fresh each morning, . . . almost as if it renews itself overnight, culling from the darkness new power to hurt. "You don't forget it. You don't. It's something that happened and you can't do anything about it. I have to accept it.

"I have my bad moments. I do." He paused. "I get in my car and I ride. I ride out to the cemetery and visit his grave. I have a cry." He paused again, longer this time. "Sometimes I can't talk about it."

[Jimi Reese, 72, mother of Scottie Reese] "I think about him all the time," Jimi said. "Sometimes it seems like he's still around somewhere, like he can't be gone. When it gets round close to that day again, I start to think about it harder. Along about that time of (that) month, it gets pretty heavy.

"It ran through my mind the other day, how old he'd be, where he'd be."

Indeed, Scottie—and all of the young men on the Marshall plane—have now been dead longer than they were alive.

—Julia Keller, quoted in "The Marshall plane crash, remembered thirty years later"

EVERYDAY I'M WITH the child
She walks on my dreams

Every place I go she's there
And in the spaces in between

Unfinished business
Keeping us sleepless
Unfinished business
You and me.

— Rachel Perkins, *One Night the Moon*

AS ANYONE WHO has experienced significant grief can attest, waves of sorrow can roll in without a moments notice, brought on by the simplest of stimuli, from the sight of a woman who looks like a beloved spouse now deceased, the sound of a voice like that of a long-dead brother, or a smile like that of a much-missed child. Even the scent of a loved one's favorite meal cooking or a whiff of special perfume or cologne can "set off" intense feelings of longing, the grief of missing a deceased loved one.

—St. Thomas Aquinas, quoted in "The St. Thomas Guide to Surviving Grief"

HOLY DAYS, HARD DAYS

THE EVENTS THAT imploded the lives of twenty-six families in a distant community called Newtown, Connecticut on December 14, 2012 throttled my core in a way I could scarcely share in words. On a morning like any other, a man walked into a public elementary school and, with automatic assault weapons, opened fire on adults and children alike. The gunman killed his mother and ended the carnage by turning a gun on himself.

I know about losing a child. Actually, I only know about losing a particular child—my own—and in a particular way. I cannot claim to know what the Newtown families know. But I do know about losing a child, and by virtue of that horrible truth, such events seize my sympathy. Sometimes they ambush my imagination.

For weeks after the massacre, it was as if everything else that I saw and heard and touched and tasted invoked them, these families who are strangers but who are connected to me by the loss of our children.

Over that subsequent holiday season, I envisioned those families again and again. Each time I saw them, my imagination probed deeper into the scene, and I began filling in the corners with a projection of my own experience with grief. There they were in my mind's eye and in their homes, stumbling upon gifts they'd hidden under the rafters, as I imagined I might have done for my small child. Gifts bought just a week earlier for the now-dead-but-not-yet-buried child.

What happened when they found those hidden gifts for their children? In my sympathetic reaching, I moved alongside these grief-stricken parents—first to my child's clothing, to the school backpack, through papers, into a bedroom, staggering, unable to connect with the new and brutal reality. How does one howl and gasp for breath when huddled under rafters? And without letting the rest of the county—or country—hear?

And knowing how grief stretches far and long, I look ahead for these families and wonder what their experience will be months and even years from impact, how otherwise holy days and other rudimentary holidays—birthdays, anniversaries, the date of a beloved's death itself—might play themselves out in the ongoing lives of the bereaved?

I imagine a home from which just last Thursday the family sent out annual holiday cards, the ones with pictures of smiling children in the laps of smiling parents, cards arriving today in other happy homes of friends and family around the world. Some intended recipients won't receive those cards until much later, because they've flown to Newtown to be close, to attend to the practicals, or to wait in loving silence on their thunderstruck friends.

Some others have remained paralyzed in their corner of the universe, unable to find a way to reach out either in word or in deed. This, because they cannot themselves reach around the vastness of what has happened. Who can? Or because they want to wait until the worst is over, which, they mistakenly think—we all mistakenly think—is the funeral. They'll wait, until after that soul-searing, heavy-lifting moment, until a while later when things will be normalized, they tell themselves, when they find the right words, the right deeds. That's when they'll certainly try to make contact.

So many whose role it is to look on another's grief guess that some months down the road (always months and months too early in the process) things and survivors should be back to normal, back to how they once were. The truth, however, is that this is not the nature of life after major traumatic loss. There is no more "how they once were." That realization disturbs one's expectations, even one's equilibrium. It taxes and wears thin the best in some of us.

Back to that holiday home in my mind. This is the second week of this family's life *After*. There are gifts sitting unopened under a tree whose glinting lights seem to mock the lightlessness this mother and father feel from head to toe. It is a corporeal eclipse whose opaqueness is experienced in measures of weight—ounces, pounds, or tons. It weighs on every emerging thought like an anchor pulling to frozen tautness the movements of a floundering boat.

Strings of Christmas lights—around the fireplace mantle, up the banister, framing the front door—only add to the indecent flashes of the paparazzi lurking everywhere in the streets of town. The town, like everything, feels more foreign to this family than does the moon, whose sallow glow hovers apologetically behind the stiffened tree branches lining Main Street. *How can the world still be turning when our beloved has been ripped away? How will we ever go on? How to survive this hour?*

Limply, the mother pulls out the plug of one of those strings of lights. She has been slumped in an upholstered chair in the corner, her child's favorite, for three hours listening to an endless loop of replayed carols and staring into the blurry, numbing depths. Maybe an hour too long, her husband has dared to suggest.

"Please, don't plug them back in," she says with a voice as wooden and useless as an old picket fence on the beach, hedging back a tidal wave of agony. Fretting in the doorway, her visiting mother-in-law wrings her hands, adding, "I thought maybe we needed . . . the teensiest bit of festive cheer?"

"Please," the mother whispers, gaunt and listless from no food and little drink for eight days. She's growing weak, mostly, after hours of suppressing an unfamiliar, frightening outrage. "I can't take it. I can *not* take the light."

Under the tree, small, fancily wrapped boxes sit. Bows. Glitter. A mockery. On a few of them is a six-year-old's name written in red marker.

"Mommy? See how I write my own name?"

A small voice, birdlike, flies up the length of this mother's spine, perching in her memory. She cannot look at that signature, its broken open letters and jagged strokes, its utter vulnerability. She turns away to stare at a space between these crowding thoughts and the floor. She breathes like a roped bull. And though her back is now to the gift and its sparkly sticker, she only hears the child's name as if the universe were moaning it. She mumbles its familiar syllables, which sends blood engorging the throat, rushing to the cheeks, draining from every limb. The taste of blood.

"And smell the marker! See? See?! Smell it, Mommy. Cherry. Mmmm."

The smell of blood. The sight of blood. It awakens the mother every time she tries to lie down. She retreats down a hallway, pushes open a door, and steps into the heart of impossible. The daughter's bed, untouched since That Last Morning, cold in all its yellowness, the wild pile of pillows, the fuzzy purple slippers under the far end, the crayons of blue, green, and magenta

("*What's magnetta, Mommy?*") clustered precariously on the corner of a nightstand. The jacket with its empty sleeves, hung by its hood on the closet doorknob. The book she'd left under her stuffed tiger on the floor at 8:17 when they drove off to school That Morning. ("*I am hurrying, Mommy. I just can't find my library book!*")

That morning.

The mother kneels, heaves, folds over. She then crawls as if injured up onto her child's bed. She deposits herself on her side.

But there is no rest. Not here. Not anywhere.

There are those other boxes back under the tree. She sees them behind her closed eyes. They'd wrapped them together, this mother with her daughter, the one the media has now appropriated as their own, renaming her, "angel". *But she has a name! Somebody say her name! She was real. She is real. We named her to pin her into this world. Her name binds her to us, the living, the cursed.*

This is the home where human capacity is strained beyond anything most onlookers can fully comprehend. Yet, what has happened—The Event—is already moving quickly into the historical realm for those who produce and consume what's "news." All this, while the true and enduring story, the one of soul-stretching grief and vertiginous absence, is only scarcely taking form. The family itself, uninitiated to tragic loss, doesn't even know this. They cannot begin to envision the contours of what lies ahead. After the funeral. After the holidays. After all the holy days ahead. Life, in its cruel benevolence, will creep and lurch along, continuing as it does, as it must. As we do, as we must.

The real story will last beyond the next news story. And far beyond the next. It will, in fact, outlive all of our collective attention spans placed end to end for years to come. Why? Because grief and longing exponentially outlast ordinary concern and comfort.

This mother, though, might be among those blessed mourners who isn't left to bear the burden of absence and the bruise of loneliness in isolation. For her, there will be exponential, exceptional, even extraordinary love. It will be love—in its many unstudied and imperfect variations—that will hold her up against the bone-crushing weight of loss. The phone call months down the road: "These are the holidays," the voice will say, "and we can't imagine how much you must miss her right now. We miss her, too."

Another person, two years in the future, will follow some faint but persistent impulse: "I saw purple slippers this morning, and I immediately thought of her." With that message is included a picture of the child. "I love her. I love you."

A relative, triggered by a memory, spends five minutes to send a text message: "Tomorrow would be her eighth birthday. I've been bracing myself against this day without her to celebrate with us. What a beautiful daughter she still is. I want you to know again how much we love you all."

And much later, a teacher, the one who'd been her favorite, will buy a simple card, and while waiting at the doctor's office, write: "As school began this week, I saw the middle schoolers line up for the bus and thought, it's been seven years. How you have survived, I just can't imagine. I am so glad you have, because our world needs parents like you. We need her, too, and so do you, and I ache that she is not here with you—with all of us—in middle school today."

The mother will read that card while leaning against a wall in her entryway. It happens to be the same wall against which, seven years ago, she'd collapsed as if hit between the shoulder blades by a meteor out of nowhere, the moment that a policeman's pronouncement—those cruelly blunt syllables—sent the phone tumbling out of her hand and skidding across hardwood.

After such impact—impact as explosive as those that create new planets in the far galaxies—and after seven years of slicing then searing then bruising then aching separation, what has sustained this mother? Has it been lathe and plaster, some timber support beams that have held her up? Has it really been some unyielding wall?

Or has it been the wall's antithesis? A human being that can bend, contour, even conform to that collapsing body. That first blow still hurts, of course. You will bear the scars from it, yes. But you will avoid additional injuries if, instead of hitting that hard wall, there is someone there to fall into.

I imagine that for these families, as for myself, this act of falling and being fallen into is the meeting not of mere surfaces, but of souls, as people bend and shape themselves to support one another in spontaneous saving embraces.

Instead of separation, communion. Instead of detachment, reaching. Instead of hard, repelling surfaces, the softness of words, the absorption of silent presence. A simple, vulnerable authenticity that catches and bends gently with the lean.

PART IV

LEARNING
FROM
DEATH

CASTING HANDS

ON MY WRITING desk stand two statuettes made of white plaster. They are nearly identical in size and shape. Each statuette consists of two hands clasping each other. If you knew the rings my husband Randall and I wear, you would know that in each piece one of the two hands belongs either to him or me. In the first statuette, one of the hands—bony, veined, and with long fingers just right for playing the piano—wears my distinctive triple-linked wedding bands. In the second statuette, one of the two hands is thick, with Randall's substantial fingers, broad oval nails, and custom-made ring with its small stones and the engraving "ASP 2007."

Each of our hands (Randall's hand in one statuette, mine in the other) is wrapped snugly around yet another hand. It is a fleshy mitt of a hand, a hand with slightly swollen fingers that do not bend quite like ours appear to be bending. The nails are gnawed a bit at their tips. The knuckles have wrinkles I could recognize in a line-up of a hundred other hands. These are, after all, the hands of our son Parker.

In one statuette, my left hand grasps Parker's right. In the other statuette, Randall's right hand, which wears Parker's American School of Paris class ring, wraps firmly around Parker's left. A college student who had been at the site of the accident that ultimately took Parker's life had removed Parker's class ring when he was dragged, unconscious and blue-lipped, out of the water. His hands were already swelling while students tried frantically to administer CPR and offer prayer blessings to their friend who was not breathing, and this student knew that Parker would want his family to have his ring. Sobbing and yelling, "Don't leave us, Frenchie! Wake up, Frenchie!" the boy tucked the ring into his swim trunk pocket. He handed it to Randall after we'd turned off the life support and released Parker from two days of coma and from eighteen years and five months of mortality.

Sometimes, that scene of horror is all I can think of when I look at these statuettes. Life cut off too soon, like the two plaster pieces themselves, which stand on their wrists, rising, as it seems, upward from out of this desktop, almost giving the impression that the forearms, elbows, shoulders—the rest of the human forms to which these hands belong, the whole person—might be somewhere below my desk, in an unseen, underground, under-desk world.

Other times, when strangers happen to see them—for instance, the man repairing our Internet line—I let them imagine that these statuettes are nothing more than a lovely, balanced set of clasped hands set in plaster. Like bookends, perhaps. Or artsy paperweights.

But balanced bookends and weights were notions far from our minds in that impossible hour when those hand casts were made. That hour was 11:00 a.m. on Thursday, July 26, a week to the day from the incident that had cost our Parker his life. It was the first day we had seen his body since we had been ushered away from its still-warm flesh lying so leaden in an ICU. There our son lay before us again, but this time a waxy surrogate, a cheap wax museum replica.

Evacuated, I thought as I entered a utilitarian room crammed next to a corner office in the mortuary. *An empty garage*, was the impression that came when I approached our son's form draped with a grayish-green blanket on what must have been an examiner's table. We'd come that late morning with Kristiina, our dear friend, and her sister.

"You might want something solid and lifelike to remember him by," Kristiina had offered when she had visited my parents' home the Sunday night before. She had spoken as she had stood: uncertain, frozen, as if inching out on a tightrope, her half-whisper holding back the panic I knew her spacious heart was trying to clamp down to size.

"Lifelike? Uh . . . uh-huh. Maybe that would . . . be . . . a good idea." Randall had been steady, respectful. I had held my hands beneath the kitchen table, where they were shaking as if with the beginnings of palsy. My legs, as I had stared down at them, felt as if I had just emerged from hibernating in an ice cave.

"My sister has helped make these for the parents of stillborn infants a few times," Kristiina had added, her eyebrows raised in apology, her tone steeped in mourning. "She's never done someone as . . . large . . . and who had been so alive . . . as . . . " Her mouth knitted itself into a curved and twitching pucker, her blue eyes flashed in desperation, and we all hung there for a moment on that incredibly taut but delicate line between knowing an alive Parker and comprehending a dead one.

I had stared at them both, Kristiina and her sister, trying to find words. An impulse hinted that I should respond like the old Melissa would have responded. *How did she used to talk? How did she form words? How did she speak without sobbing?* That person was gone, I knew it. Syllables, like rough wooden blocks, dropped out of my mouth, I think. Clumsy, polite words of habit. But they conveyed nothing of the typhoon that was battering and boiling throughout my mind.

At the mortuary on that Thursday morning, Kristiina and her sister silently mixed buckets of quick-dry plaster, solicitous and servant-like at Parker's feet. Randall and I stood in a dizzy stupor at our stations on either side of our son-replica, tracing his stiff shoulders with our fingertips. In one movement, father and mother took the hands of their firstborn, wrapping their fingers around his, and buried the blended parts wrist-deep into buckets of a mixture the color and consistency of gelatinous oatmeal. I noted how my boy's flesh held less life than did the wet plaster itself. I shook off the plaster, shook off the experience, feeling in the moment as if I'd defiled the sacred, hoping that this would one day end up being worth the desecration.

And Kristiina was right. It has been good to have something solid to remember Parker by. But these hand casts are more than mementos. They are far more than objects reminiscent of the physical closeness we once shared with our son. For us, they are sacred tokens pointing to an expansive spiritual reality that bursts the limits of flesh-and-blood closeness.

To explain the spiritual reality that these plaster casts symbolize, I need to share one of several profound occurrences that marked my early months of grief and has remained with me, vivid and comforting, ever since. It has made these clasped hands into monuments of reverberating, clarifying truth. I don't share this with every visiting Internet repairman, although I sometimes wish I could.

During the weekend of Parker's passing, hours after we left his body to be transferred to a mortuary, days before we would make—or even think of making—plaster hand casts, I was lying on my side in bed, knees tucked up toward my chest, arms wrapped around my middle. My pillow was soaked with tears, and my body was throbbing in acute physical pain, crushed, it seemed, as if by a landslide and torn wide open through the torso. The corporeal sensation of such abrupt and violent loss was like having invasive surgery with no anesthesia, or better, like having a bomb go off in the center of my being. We couldn't escape the feeling of this immense, black, gaping vacancy in that central space—right here, in the fork between our ribs—that our son had just occupied.

Through my silent weeping, I begged God to keep us all—my husband, myself, our three surviving children—from being sucked into the apparent bottomlessness left by this implosion. Although our family was strong and loving, although we were emotionally stable people, although we had profound faith in life being eternal and were certain Parker was in a safe and loving place, we could not imagine, could not physically absorb the impact of life going on without his intertwined with ours. I could not see how we would be able to survive. There had to be help—hoist-you-up-from-under-the-arms-and-keep-you-breathing help—and I knew that kind of help was beyond anything this world could offer.

For several hours, maybe, and probably all night, I whisper-begged continually in prayer, seeking God and Parker, asking that they be close to me and somehow make themselves known to me in a way I could recognize. As nighttime shifted to dawn through the window, another shift began to take place in my mind. Like curtains being quietly drawn open in my spinning and murky mental chamber, I slowly started to see something. I could just make it out—it was initially no more than a foggy, subtle image.

At first I thought it was some sort of textured rope or—no, it was a *chain*. As I focused on it I saw this chain wasn't static, but was gently rhythmic, pulsing. Then I could see that the movement came from the links attaching, separating, and reattaching to each other.

These links, I saw as my inner light grew brighter, were hands. Human hands of many sorts, shades, and shapes, glowing against an opalescent background, gently stretching then clasping firmly, pulling one another. All at once, I understood that these were hands from the past and the present, hands of mortals and immortals, reaching and pulling each other along, binding time and timelessness together.

At the same time as this image grew clearer, a feeling overtook me; it went through my whole body, from the crown of my head to the soles of my feet, expanding in my chest, and that feeling was *joy*—jubilant, singing, surging, soaring *joy*. Part exhilaration, part anticipation, that joy spread through my traumatized body, warming and loosening it, and lifting my spirits with an unmistakable tug.

Something was *pulling. Someone* was pulling *me.* Mighty but tender hands were reaching for my hand. And my task was to reach. Touch. Clasp. Hold on. And then, once linked, to reach to others.

Maybe what I was experiencing in that flash of insight was a glimpse into the way things are, a brief vision of God's cosmic machinery, which is one continuous work going on between us mortals, but also between mortals and spiritual beings, between this realm and the neighboring, immortal one. In only those few seconds, I understood that the living and the dead are joined in a loving, interdependent, interactive chain. There was no difference in that chain between the living and what we call the "dead." They were equally capable beings. Which helped me see that neither I nor my deceased son was alone, forgotten, disconnected, or left without one another.

For the first time, I comprehended in a visceral, palpable way this truth about the interconnectedness of all humans in every stage of existence. As my mind took in this visible chain, my hands felt the unmistakable palms— calloused from basketballs and drums—of my own child's hands. I understood that not only was Parker "*in* good hands," the platitude some had tried to use to comfort me, but that *I* was in good hands, too. Parker himself was among those good hands. *For me.* And I am among the good hands. For him. For anyone. For everyone. There is no one—alive or dead—who does not need the reach and pull of another's hand.

As one person of extraordinary spiritual depth has said:

> We move and have our being in the presence of heavenly messen-
> gers and of heavenly beings. We are not separate from them. . . .
> We are closely related to our kindred, to our ancestors . . . who

*have preceded us into the spirit world. We can not forget them;
we do not cease to love them; we always hold them in our hearts,
in memory, and thus we are associated and united to them by ties
that we can not break. . . . If this is the case with us in our finite
condition, surrounded by our mortal weaknesses, . . . how much
more certain it is . . . to believe that those who have been faithful, who have gone beyond . . . can see us better than we can see
them; that they know us better than we know them. . . . We live
in their presence, they see us, they are solicitous for our welfare,
they love us now more than ever. . . . [T]heir love for us and their
desire for our well being must be greater than that which we feel
for ourselves.*

Eventually I learned that whenever one of my hands reaches to pull along
the hand of another—when I serve in whatever way I can, be that by listening, speaking, laughing, weeping, writing, singing, being silent, acting re-
ceptively to the subtle impressions I attribute to Divinity—I can feel my own
son's hand clasped in mine, pulling me along. Then I do not feel I am only
pressing forward with hope, but that I am being pulled *toward* that hope,
and being pulled toward joy as part of a larger, caring community.

In those moments of clasping onto others, whether by giving strength or
receiving it, I sense the luminous bigger picture. We are all, the living and
the dead, part of an intertwined effort to bring every last one of us to joy.

That image of communal movement redefines much for me. Among other
things, it sets a question mark behind the notions of "alive" and "dead."
There are many of us breathing types who are less alive than those we've
buried. And I've experienced enough to say with total confidence that many
of the "dead" are infinitely more alive than the most "alive" person we have
ever known. My son is one of those, the most living among what convention
insists we call "the dead."

And what about me? Will I, then, while living, remain forever the living
dead because my son is temporarily separated from me in the flesh? What
better mentor than this fully living son who is "dead" to reach back, take my
hand, and guide me to live fully, while alive . . . while living?

In my yearning agony after Parker's death, real comfort and strength
have not come solely from the assurance that life continues after we die, but

from the knowledge that my child is powerfully present in our family here and now. Our relationship with Parker continues. Personal experience has been the sturdiest evidence for me that I don't have to wait until the hereafter to be a co-worker with my son. It can happen here and now. His hand is clasped in mine, and mine in his. In spite of death, a relationship keeps developing. A bond continues to deepen.

Yes, the normal ways of feeling him close are gone—I cannot call him to my room, cannot get a shouted answer from down the hallway or a phone call or a text message or a note under my pillow on my birthday, cannot anticipate his future, cannot delight in sharing him with others, or any of the millions of other things we living people do to knit our hearts to each other. I will never lose my lingering longing for the flesh-and-blood physical presence of my boy. But there are other ways of feeling his presence.

Being able to feel his presence, like feeling any spiritual impressions, requires a mindfulness, imagination, and faithful effort I never needed before. I am on quiet guard against the noisy voices and clattering distractions of our modern world. I have to shelter my spirit at times, the way I would shelter a small seedling from harsh wind and the torch of the sun.

When I focus on those white plaster hand casts as I am doing now, I see them as bookends to a story that has no end, as weights reminding me of the substance of grace my family and I have known. And I have to admit to a little bit of a miracle: When I look at them and let their reality sink in, I am no longer always taken back to that Thursday morning at the mortuary and the son with stone-cold hands. I am, instead, more and more often taken to that internal image I saw and felt of the joyous continuity of God's plan for the whole woven rope of humanity. Hands, like these casts that seem to rise from the hidden realm beneath my desk, are always emerging from an unseen, but nonetheless real, world. And they are always reaching toward us. Parker's hands, the ones whose nails and knuckles I could pick out of a crowd, the same hands that I will in some coming day hold in my own as I stare into his eyes and take in his full-grown spirit self, are firmly cemented—sealed—to mine.

STILLNESS AND REVELATION

THE MOURNERS ARE aching visionaries.

Such people Jesus blesses; he hails them, he praises them, he salutes them. And he gives them the promise that the new day for whose absence they ache will come. They will be comforted.

—Nicholas Wolterstorff, *Lament for a Son*

———

BUT THE COMFORTER, which is the Holy Ghost, whom the Father will send in my name, he shall teach you all things, and bring all things to your remembrance, whatsoever I have said unto you. Peace I leave with you, my peace I give unto you: not as the world giveth, give I unto you. Let not your heart be troubled, neither let it be afraid.

—John 14:26–27

———

IT IS IN [our] helplessness that we come upon the beginning of joy. We discover that as long as we stay still the pain is not so bad and there is even a certain peace, a certain richness, a certain strength, a certain companionship that makes itself present to us when we are beaten down and lie flat with our mouths in the dust, hoping for hope.

—Thomas Merton, *New Seeds of Contemplation*

FOR THE HAPPY man prayer is only a jumble of words, until the day when sorrow comes to explain to him the sublime language by means of which he speaks to God.

—Alexandre Dumas, *The Count of Monte Cristo*

MOURNING MAKES US poor. It powerfully reminds us of our smallness. But it is precisely here, in that pain or poverty or awkwardness, that the Dancer invites us to rise up and take the first steps. For in our suffering, not apart from it, Jesus enters our sadness, and invites us to dance. We find the way to pray as the psalmist did, "You have turned my mourning into dancing" (Ps. 30:11), because at the center of our grief we find the grace of God.

—Henri Nouwen, *Turn My Mourning Into Dancing*

LIFE PROVIDES THE searching child with conflict and pain. The divinity driving the child from the inside and the turmoil of life roiling on the outside make the search for resolution and consolation paramount. It may be, indeed, that pain is among the greatest motivators for spiritual growth. It can be cherished for the revelations and resolutions it ultimately provokes.

—M. Catherine Thomas, *Light in the Wilderness*

BY A DEPARTING light,
We see acuter, quite,
Than by a wick that stays.

There's something in the flight
That clarifies the sight
And decks the rays.

—Emily Dickinson, *The Poems of Emily Dickinson*

EVERYTHING PASSES AND vanishes;
  Everything leaves its trace;
And often you see in a footstep
  What you could not see in a face.

—William Allingham, *The Wadsworth Anthology of Poetry*

SOMETIME DURING SOLITUDE, I hear truth spoken with clarity and freshness; uncolored and untranslated it speaks from within myself in a language original but inarticulate, heard only with the soul and I realize I brought it with me, was never taught it nor can I efficiently teach it to another.

—Hugh B. Brown, quoted in *Eternal Man*

I'VE COME TO know the Lord's death angel here,
His hovering wing and then his sudden flight.
His errand took the one my love holds dear
And hid him now, beyond the veil of sight.
With one swift stroke, my fragile heart is torn,
And as my spirit longs for comfort's balm,
The peace He promised in my soul is born,
And fills my emptiness with God-sent calm.
Beauty for ashes of the mourning heart,
The oil of joy, garment of praise, be mine!
May planting of the Lord within me start

And grow to seek and knit my will to Thine.
I live and love here now the best I can,
With faith to glorify God's perfect plan.

—Moyne Osborn, "The Flight"

OH! I HAVE slipped the surly bonds of Earth
And danced the skies on laughter-silvered wings;
Sunward I've climbed, and joined the tumbling mirth
Of sun split clouds,—and done a hundred things
You have not dreamed of—wheeled and soared and swung
High in the sunlit silence. Hov'ring there,
I've chased the shouting wind along, and flung
My eager craft through footless halls of air . . .

Up, up the long, delirious, burning blue
I've topped the wind-swept heights with easy grace,
Where never lark, or even eagle flew—
And, while with silent, lifting mind I've trod
The high untrespassed sanctity of space
Put out my hand and touched the face of God.

—John Gillespie McGee, "Flying High," quoted in *The American Reader*

LATER IN HIS own experience of grief, C. S. Lewis wrote in a notebook that when he carried his questions about his wife's death and his pain to God, he still received no answer. But now he understood that it was a special kind of silence—not a locked door, as he had once written, but more like his coming under a silent and loving gaze.

As though [God] shook his head not in refusal but in waiving the questions. Like, "Peace, child; you don't understand."

—Greg Garrett, *Stories From the Edge*

THE LAST NOEL

OUR LAST PARISIAN *Christmas*. And because we would be sending Parker, our eldest, off to college in June, we knew it would also be a "Last Christmas"—our last Christmas with all of us together, at least like this.

So I'd run myself ragged with holiday preparations: writing and directing and performing in the church Christmas program; writing and printing out and folding and addressing and sending by snail mail our ninety-five annual Christmas missives; decorating and baking and scurrying and visiting and hosting and "getting into the holiday spirit." At least that was the euphemism.

That Christmas Eve I hit a wall, and the collision landed me in a mental state I am not proud to write about. Instead of making merry with my family, I holed myself up in my bedroom for a couple of hours. In the stillness of that dark room, my body heaped unmoving upon the bed, the universe could have whispered into my heart, warning me that this would truly be *The* Last Christmas, the very last we would ever share with our firstborn son.

Relish this evening, the universe could have stirred in me, as preparation. *Memorize its every detail. Plant yourself in the middle of the scene and draw your family very, very close. Your child's eyes—stare into them right now and learn by heart the patterns of his irises. Do you see their delicate blue-gray, their lively pupils, the way they stretch and contract in darkness and in sunlight? Do you know how much you need those eyes? This boy? His life?*

There were no such messages from beyond. Or if there were, I was too distracted and far too tired to hear heavenly whispers or divine warnings or to feel celestial shoulder-tappings.

Something did, however, tap on my shoulder. And something did whisper. And something did warn me that this would be The Last Christmas with Parker. And that something was Parker himself.

THE LAST NOEL: A TRUE CHRISTMAS STORY

"MOM?"

Her son, whose voice normally had the resonance of a foghorn, was whispering from the doorway.

She was on her side, knees curled up slightly, a dark purple woolen comforter dragged up over her curves and tucked into her hands, which she held against her sternum. Her eyes stayed closed. She faced away from the voice, away from the faint glow of the one night lamp, away from the door, which she'd closed a couple of hours earlier, barricading herself into silence and as far as possible from the everyday holiday noises that emerged from the end of the hall: Kitchen sounds, a swirling, tinkling holiday CD, conversations between teenagers, the low word or two from Dad, the swish-swish-swish up and down the hallway of two younger children in house slippers. A spike of laughter here. A name said with a question mark there. Noises she simply wanted to escape. For as long as it would take.

She was doing it again, that thing she sometimes did. She was retreating into silence. She did this, usually, when she had overdone things. And she did have this tendency to take on too much, to leave herself no room for reverence, for breathing, for reflection, for rest. How many years had she done this? Why did she never learn? Another year-end marker and look, no change. Same old, same old. Old. Old. She felt old.

She tugged the purple comforter up to her eyes, which were leaking a lone, languid line of tears. Like a fine finger tracing with its tip, the saline trail went from the right eye over the bridge of her nose and into the corner of the left, or from the left eye down the left temple, slipping into the ear canal. Her nose grew wet in the same moment, and so she drew in one quiet sniff.

"Mom?" a voice came from the doorway. "Look . . ." the voice was moving closer behind her, "Listen, *Mom*." It was her eldest son, and now he was leaning his weight on the edge of her bed. "Please, don't do this," he said. "Not again. Not tonight." The weight of his hand on the mattress next to her hip was enough to make her flinch and consider shifting away. But she couldn't muster the effort. *Tired. So bone-deep tired. And sad.*

He sighed, her eldest child, and then readjusted himself on the floor with a groan. She could tell from the sound that he was wearing jeans. And wasn't he also in a turtleneck? His maroon one, she remembered.

Should she just turn around and face him, turn around and face the family? Just roll over and brush back the matted hair that's a bit soggy now, with tears drizzling past her ear and down her jawline? Just roll over and swing her legs out and plant her feet on the floor, shake some mirth into her limbs? Just turn it all around like that, switch directions as slickly as a toy train track—switch gears, flip some switch, just head back out? Smiling? Humming Bing Crosby?

She remained silent and still, hoping he'd think she was sleeping deeply.

This is when he tapped her right shoulder. And then he left his hand there. The heat traveled all the way through her, into the mattress (as she envisioned its course) and to the floor. How she wanted to respond. But her jaws were clenched, holding in all the softer feelings her heart held in its pulse.

"Why don't you say something, Mom? What have I done? Okay, so I should have cleaned up the dishes first. But c'mon, they're done now. Just . . . just come out there. Come see."

She had lodged herself too far into the silence to creep out so easily now. *Tired of speaking, giving orders, answering to everyone. Tired and worn out. Another year: gone, wrung out like I feel, squeezed dry to its very last particle. Here we are again. Christmas. I should be keeping everyone's spirit aloft. But I'm flattened.*

Then she heard the lightest tap-tap on the door, and the sound of the door's edge shuuuuushing over carpet. The smell of her husband's cologne. She pulled the purple up over her head.

"Hey," came a voice from the doorway.

"Hey." The son's voice was deeper, even, than his dad's. And heavier.

"Honey, we'd love for you to come out. Just eat a little dinner, 'kay? And then watch the movie with us. Maybe? No big production. Just be with us."

So, so tired. And so emptied, clean out. All this pressure to be happy. Please. If you could let me be alone.

Her oldest son made a sudden move. His voice came from above her, now. "Alright. I'm just . . . I'm going to change things here." There was ballast in that voice now, a clip on each consonant. "Mom. *Mom*? Get. Up. And. Turn. It. Around."

She pulled the purple from her face. She rolled completely over, from left to right, opened her eyes, and found she was looking right into the knees of two men in jeans. Then the son knelt. His eyes met hers. He looked right into her. She'd never seen this look, at least not from him. The earnestness and resolve. The deliberateness.

"'Kay, I'm not going to add any drama here, but you know, um, this *is* my last Christmas with you all, you know? This is *it*." He pounded a fist into the carpet and shook his head.

Was he trembling? What was the stiffness in his lower lip? In his chin?

"And so I want us to celebrate and have the Spirit. So will you please come out and be with us? Now? Mom?"

He took her hand, which gesture was a bit odd, but not too odd right then, and she let him take it. She felt each of his calluses from dribbling balls and pummeling drums.

"Come on." Now he was whispering so low she could hardly hear him. "Come on in here with me."

The gesture, a tug, unlocked something in her bones and she moved, almost effortlessly, letting the purple wrap crumple to the floor as she trailed her son and her husband down the hall, into the light, the noise, the company of her family. The other three children looked at her, stopped tinkering and quibbling, and went quiet. A suppressed or hesitant grin and, "Hi . . . Mom!" came from the youngest child, who wriggled his nose under the round little red frames of his glasses.

"Okay. Everyone?" The son holding his mother's hand announced in the middle of the room, "We need to have a prayer. We're going to turn things around here. So . . . we need to pray together. Right now. So come on. We've got to kneel."

It was the prayer of a full-grown man. His mother—and everyone—felt its substance settle on their shoulders. They knelt for a moment in silence. But not that resistant, withholding kind of silence. This was the silence of soft awe, and like the invisible bending-swelling of the arc of a rainbow, it did indeed turn things around.

"Please . . ." the mother said, "I am so sorry," and she looked around the circle. "It's just been too much . . . again . . . and I needed to get some . . . distance. It's not you, it's— "

"No, Mom," the daughter said then cleared her throat, "it's a lot, and we sometimes don't know when we've made stuff hard for you, and—"

"Or when we're bad—" said the six-year-old, who, the mom now noticed, had stars and candy canes drawn in neon marker all over his cheeks, chin, forehead, and forearms.

"No, you're not bad," the mother countered, as the innocent flamboyance of round red-rimmed glasses and temporary Christmas tattoos urged up into her throat a flash flood of regret and tenderness, "and this is not any-one's *fault* . . ."

As the mother spoke, her words disgorged a whole swamp of apologies, into which all the children and the husband now waded with their own apologies.

Then they embraced, got off their knees . . . and embraced again.

The ten-year-old son, eyes darting as if with guilt, put his arms around his mother's waist and asked, "You want me to scrub the stars and candy canes off him?" She shook her head and squeezed his shoulders, then watched him scuffle off with the youngest child at his side, turn back once, his eyebrows raised to be sure he'd understood—the body painting's okay, then—and then trot down the hall, acting The Protectorate to his little brother, who skips alongside him, blonde bowl cut bouncing.

Before long, there was laughter, ruckus, and the King's Singers decking every hall with fa-la-la-la-las.

Later that evening, the mother and her oldest son sat next to each other, legs stretched out, shoulder-to-shoulder, nestled deep into the soft brown overstuffed sofa. He, between spoonfuls of ice cream straight from the container, lip-synced Jimmy Stewart. She, while watching that son in her peripherals, scanned the life encircling her.

Dad brought in trays of homemade eggnog. Daughter wore a new light blue fleece bathrobe and flannel pajamas on which miniature pink snowmen and reindeer danced amid snowflakes. The middle son reassembled a Lego figurine while the youngest held a pillow up under his chin, a chin that sported, like a fluorescent target, a neon gold felt tip marker star planted smack dab in the center.

That Christmas Eve, the family clustered in the plush comfort of sofa and solidarity, just like they had every Christmas Eve for as long as they could remember. With mouths edged in eggnog, and with eyes groggy or wide, they nuzzled. All six of them. And they followed (or at times mirrored) the black-and-white sweetness of their favorite holiday film, "It's A Wonderful Life."

That Last Noel, life was just that: wonderful.

The First Christmas Without Him. The Second Christmas Without Him. The Third and The Fourth and The Fifth . . .

Peering into the long tunnel of Christmases that are yet to be without Parker, our family has kept to the ritual of watching "It's a Wonderful Life." I have held onto this holiday ritual even when so diminished and devastated by death that all I could do was hold back tears with one arm around my ribcage and the other around my family's shoulders.

That first Christmas after Parker died, though sliced to the bone by the scythe of sudden loss, I felt nothing like the depressive slump I'd felt the last Christmas when our boy had been alive. Oh, I was distressed, even despairing. At times, I was even quietly, privately deranged with pain. And a couple of times, I whispered that I was afraid we wouldn't make it, meaning that our marriage, our sanity, or our very hearts might fail.

But we sat together and we watched the film. And we've watched it every Christmas since. This movie—a classic about the sacredness of each imperfect human life, the triumph of family and community, the intervention of celestial beings—has become a symbol of our decision to live, even thrive, instead of utterly drowning in grief.

For me, living onward with loss has depended to a great extent on the deliberate and repeated choice to fight back the torpidity of despair. Plunging into the depths of despondency was the greatest temptation I have ever resisted in my life. While I had no suicidal thoughts—how could I ever abandon my loved ones, and especially in a time like this?—I simply wanted life to go away. Forever. When the character of George Bailey weeps that frenzied, feral cry on the frozen bridge, I understand and I weep with him.

To resist the cold, icy drag of despair, I learned over time that I needed three things: steadiness, illumination, and as much love as the world and heaven could offer or I could dredge up to give.

Steadiness. In early grief, almost all of my physical energy was devoured by the task of remaining steady and keeping my family steady. With no extra capacity for physical exertion, I slowed down as never before. I walked, talked, and even breathed at a different pace than had been my normal hyper-drive. I lacked the wherewithal for those old patterns of excess. What is more essential, though, I had no need for them. In fact, they repelled me. Grief overwrote my usual frantic scramble from distraction to distraction—however worthy those distractions might have been—and replaced that speed with heavy-duty Zen. Corporeally, I felt greatly weakened—like recovering from major invasive surgery—but that fragility allowed me to become very spiritually focused. Like this, my spiritual antennae were stretched to full extension. And it was in that steadiness that I found the knowledge and meaning I needed in order to live what on the outset seemed an unlivable life, a life bereft of our eldest. Thereafter, I made a deliberate effort to devote myself to single-mindedness. By steadying myself through frequent and focused mediation and prayer, I resisted the gravitational pull of despair and distraction, so common in today's loud, frenetic, and sometimes abusively demanding world.

Illumination. Retreat alone was not my sole response to grief. At a certain point in my experience—many months after my son's death and after as long a time of concentrated meditation and searching prayer—I felt a clear spiritual impression. It told me that if I stayed holed up much longer in the nautilus of grief, if I resisted engaging in life, if I folded myself over my heart into a work of emotional origami, if I crammed myself into a footlocker of loss buried under the boulder-slate-and-ash landslide of anguish,

I might never emerge at all. And even if one day I did come out, much else might have died in the meantime. I had a choice: I could remain cut off from others and become grief's slave, or I could extend myself toward others and remain grief's student. The former choice would bring atrophy and sorrow, the latter, growth and joy. I took small, significant steps to connect with others, accept their gestures of service, and to serve them.

Love. This service—some rendered, much received—opened up floodgates of warmth that counterbalanced the icy river of despair. Like George Bailey, I was rescued by the realization of love rushing in from all sides: for and from God; for and from family; for and from friends and even strangers. The flow of loving-kindness coaxed me out of despair, led me through that tension between resisting and reengaging, between self-protection and service, between fearing and trusting, between loss and living onward with love.

So as simplistic as this might sound, the First Noel, the Last Noel and all the Noels that will follow are tales about learning love. For me, while my love for my son has been grief's reason, it has been that same force of love that has proved grief's rescue. As wrote Leo Tolstoy, "Only people who are capable of loving strongly can also suffer great sorrow, but this same necessity of loving serves to counteract their grief and heals them."

If this is what "healing" feels like, then I suppose I am its rehabilitating patient. I can with quiet confidence say today something I could never have imagined on the outset: It has been love, the decision to open up to the possibility of it, and the deliberate choice to receive and to share it—again and again and in spite of certain risk—that has brought me off of that bridge overlooking despair and back to life. Into a fragile, imperfect, (and sometimes terrifying) but also a miraculous, sweet, and yes, even a wonderful life.

HUMILITY AND SUBMISSION

WHEN YOU HAVE to be the one to tell the doctor
To unplug your dying child's respirator—
That's when you truly come to understand
That life is always about making choices.
You speak the necessary, devastating words
And you go on—
Into a different, unimaginable future.
Eventually you stop feeling like you are bleeding inside.

But the bruises remain—
Invisible and unfelt
Until you brush up against a memory
And suddenly feel the familiar pain take your breath away.

You learn to take comfort in knowing the bleeding will stop again;
Your breathing will return to normal
And you will go on—
Facing life's imperfect choices
And finding beauty among the brokenness.

—Kay Talbot, "Choices," *What Forever Means after the Death of a Child*

LOSE YOUR LIFE and you will save it. Submit to death, the death of your ambitions and favourite wishes. . . . Submit with every fibre of your being, and you will find eternal life. Keep back nothing. Nothing that you have not given away will ever be really yours. Nothing in you that has not died will ever be raised from the dead. Look out for yourself, and you will find in the long run only hatred, loneliness, despair, rage, ruin, and decay. But look to Christ and you will find Him, and, with Him, everything else thrown in.

—C. S. Lewis, *Mere Christianity*

HE HELD NO dream worth waking; so he said,
   He who stands now on death's triumphal steep,
   Awakened out of life wherein we sleep
And dream of what he knows and sees, being dead.
But never death for him was dark or dread:
   "Look forth," he bade the soul, and fear not. Weep,
   All ye that trust not in his truth, and keep
Vain memory's vision of a vanished head
As all that lives of all that once was he
Save that which lightens from his word; but we,
   Who, seeing the sunset-colored waters roll,
Yet know the sun subdued not of the sea,
   Nor weep nor doubt that still the spirit is whole,
   And life and death but shadows of the soul.

—Algernon Charles Swinburne, "On the Death of Robert Browning," *The Poems of Algernon Charles Swinburne*

THE LORD IS nigh unto them that are of a broken heart; and saveth such as be of a contrite spirit.

—Psalms 34:18

WHAT ELSE CAN we learn from a story in which we come to accept death as a fellow traveler?

One thing might be our willingness to live with the experience of not-knowing, of living in between, which is often so alien to us; we like to insist that we are (or should be) in control of every moment of our lives. William James, in his *Varieties of Religious Experience*, translated the German concept, *Zerrissenheit* as "torn-to-pieces-hood." At some time in our lives—if not before our impending death—we will be in this place of torn-to-pieces-hood . . . this place where the stories fall apart and where, thus, nothing makes sense any longer. We can resist with all our might, we can clamber and clamor for meaning; or we can accept that some things are beyond our control, that it is the nature of all human lives that they should end. And while we cannot know for certain what is going to happen, we can gather together to support the dying and the bereaved and offer a gospel of hope . . . that God is moving in the midst of suffering.

—Greg Garrett, *Stories From the Edge*

THE SORROW FOR the dead is the only sorrow from which we refuse to be divorced. Every other wound we seek to heal—every other affliction to forget; but this wound we consider it a duty to keep open—this affliction we cherish and brood over in solitude. Where is the mother who would willingly forget the infant that perished like a blossom from her arms, though every recollection is a pang? Where is the child that would willingly forget the most tender of parents, though to remember be but to lament? Who, even in the hour of agony, would forget the friend over whom he mourns? Who, even when the tomb is closing upon the remains of her he most loved, when he feels his heart, as it were, crushed in the closing of its portal, would accept of consolation that must be bought by forgetfulness? No, the love which survives the tomb is one of the noblest attributes of the soul. If it has its woes, it has likewise its delights; and when the overwhelming burst of grief is calmed into the gentle tear of recollection, when the sudden anguish and the convulsive agony over the present ruins of all that we most loved are softened away in pensive meditation on all that it was in the days of its loveliness—who would root out such a sorrow from the heart? Though it may sometimes throw a passing cloud over the bright hour of gaiety, or spread a deeper sadness over the hour of gloom, yet who would exchange it even for the song of pleasure, or the burst of revelry? No, there is a voice from the tomb sweeter than song. There is a remembrance of the dead to which we turn even from the charms of the living. Oh, the grave! The grave! It buries every error—covers every defect—extinguishes every resentment! From its peaceful bosom spring none but fond regrets and tender recollections.

—Washington Irving, *The Complete Works of Washington Irving*

NOTHING IS LEFT or lost—nothing of good,
Or lovely; but whatever its first springs
Has drawn from God, returns to him again;
That only, which 'twere misery to retain
Is taken from you, which to keep were loss;
Only the scum, the refuse, and the dross
Are borne away into the grave of things:
Meanwhile whatever gifts from Heaven descend,
Thither again have flowed,
To the receptacle of all things good,
From whom they come, and unto whom they tend,
Who is the First and Last, the Author and the End.

Therefore be strong, be strong,
Ye that remain, nor fruitlessly revolve,
Darkling the riddles that ye cannot solve,
But do the works that unto you belong;
Believing that for every mystery,
For all the death, the darkness, and the curse,
Of this dim universe,
Needs a solution full of love must be:

And that the way whereby ye may attain
Nearest to this, is not through broodings vain
And half-rebellious—questionings of God;
But by a patient seeking to fulfil
The purpose of his everlasting Will,
Treading the path which lowly men have trod.

—Richard Chenevix Trench, *Poems*

SOME ATTRIBUTE HAD departed from her, the permanence of which had been essential to keep her a woman. Such is frequently the fate, and such the stern development, of the feminine character and person, when the woman has encountered, and lived through, an experience of peculiar severity. If she be all tenderness, she will die. If she survive, the tenderness will either be crushed out of her, or—and the outward semblance is the same—crushed so deeply into her heart that it can never show itself more.

—Nathaniel Hawthorne, *The Scarlet Letter*

TODAY, I WHO was weak as a mother,
I bend to your feet before your open skies.
I feel myself enlightened in my bitter sadness
by a better outlook on the universe.

Lord, I realize that Man is crazy
if he dares complain;
I've stopped accusing, I've stopped cursing,
but let me weep!

Alas! let the tears run down from my eyes,
since you have made Men for this!
Let me lean over this cold stone

and say to my child: Do you feel that I am here?
Let me speak to her, bent over her remains,
in the evening when all is still,
as if, reopening her celestial eyes in her night,
this angel could hear me!

—Victor Hugo, "I will see that instant until I die"

IT IS THE secret of the world that all things subsist and do not
die, but only retire a little from sight and afterwards return again. . . .
Nothing is dead: men feign themselves dead, and endure mock funerals
and mournful obituaries, and there they stand looking out of the
window, sound and well, in some new strange disguise. Jesus is not
dead: he is very well alive: nor John, nor Paul, nor Mahomet, nor
Aristotle; at times we believe we have seen them all, and could
easily tell the names under which they go.

—Ralph Waldo Emerson, "All Return Again," *The Works of Ralph Waldo Emerson*

AT THIS HOUR life seems blinding, devastating. Yet it is a measure of our dis-
cipleship of Christ that even sorely grievous hours have yielded enlightenment, a
budding knowledge of self and others, and ennoblement. When we search ourselves, it is no mystery that good, the purifying force of godliness, may arise out of
affliction. (Looking back we may wonder whether anything we really prize comes
without it.)

This should caution us in judging what is and what is not a blessing in life.

—Truman Madsen, *Eternal Man*

FACING THE DISTANT landscape, I prayed to God: "Why are you doing this to
me? Why is it that when I'm close to you, sorrow and love fill my heart?" And these

words immediately came to me; "I'm breaking your heart so you know what my heart feels like." In my mind I immediately thought of Simeon's words to Mary: " . . . a sword shall pierce your own soul too" (Luke 2:35 NRSV). In that moment I realized that the two greatest lovers of history both had broken hearts. It was as if God were saying to me, "You can't love as I love until your heart is broken. Only a heart that has been broken by love can love with my love."

—Gregory Floyd, *A Grief Unveiled*

I DO NOT believe that sheer suffering teaches. If suffering alone taught, all the world would be wise, since everyone suffers. To suffering must be added mourning, understanding, patience, love, openness and the willingness to remain vulnerable.

—Anne Morrow Lindbergh, "Lindbergh Nightmare"

THE AWFUL TRAGEDY of this life, as of the next, is not suffering. It is "suffering in vain." Or worse, it is suffering that could have been the elixir of nobility, transforming us into a godliness beyond description which, instead, has become a poison of bitterness and alienation.

But this is equally certain: From the smoldering rubble of our lives, stricken and agonized though they be, there can arise, through Christ, an incredible shining joy, a joy in the image of Christ who is the image of God who overcame all things.

—Truman Madsen, *Eternal Man*

"WHAT DO WE do with our pain so that it becomes meaningful and not just pointless empty suffering? How can we turn all the painful experiences of our lives into birth pangs or into growing pains?" We may not ever understand why we suffer or be able to control the forces that cause suffering, but we can have a lot to say about what the suffering does to us, and what sort of people we become because of it. Pain makes some people bitter and envious. It makes others sensitive and compassionate.

It is the result . . . of pain that makes some experiences of pain meaningful and others empty and destructive.

—Harold Kushner, When Bad Things Happen To Good People

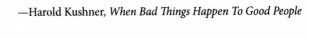

WHEN CORY DIED, I grew more in one year than I did in my fifty previous years because I submitted my will to God. Our strength is in the Lord, and our submission to His will brings joy and peace. When I think of my son in the mortal sense, I miss him so deeply. When I think of him spiritually, I know that he is doing his work as I am doing my work. As birth is to mortality, so likewise is death to immortality and eternal life.

—Edward Pinegar, quoted Grieving: The Pain and the Promise

I HAVE BEEN the mother of seven children, the most beautiful and most loved of whom lies buried near my Cincinnati residence. It was at his dying bed and at his grave that I learned what a poor slave mother may feel when her child is torn away from her. In those depths of sorrow which seemed to me immeasurable, it was my only prayer to God that such anguish might not be suffered in vain. There were circumstances about his death of such peculiar bitterness, of what seemed almost cruel suffering, that I felt I could never be consoled for it, unless this crushing of my own heart might enable me to work out some great good to others.

I allude to this here because I have often felt that much that is in that book ("Uncle Tom") had its root in the awful scenes and bitter sorrow of that summer. It has left now, I trust, no trace on my mind except a deep compassion for the sorrowful, especially for mothers who are separated from their children.

—Harriet Beecher Stowe, The Life of Harriet Beecher Stowe

A DREAM

A MONTH BEFORE Parker's accident, I had a dream. I can pinpoint the week because I was sleeping in our Paris bedroom surrounded by moving boxes already stacked against the walls in anticipation of the movers coming. I awoke to find my pillow damp with tears and sweat, and I lay cramped in the fetal position on my side, one arm stretched out of my bed.

A sickly, nauseated sensation followed me to the kitchen, where I told Dalton and Luc about the dream over breakfast. I repeated what I'd seen as I drove them across town to drop them off at their school gates, and later also told Randall about it in detail. I knew instinctively that this dream was unlike other dreams, and for reasons I could not have understood at the time, I needed witnesses of what I had seen in the cinema of my mind. The dream was so poignant, in fact, that I wrote it down, and mulled it over for days. Then with all the disruption of our move to Munich, I hardly thought of it at all. But it came back to me in sharp, frame-by-frame detail in those first days of *After*.

It is a summertime of the direct-vertical-sun sort. The sky is scorching white-blue, and it is very warm—dry, parching. I am standing on the gravelly shore of a swift river. A blond and sturdy toddler boy of about two—is it Dalton? Luc? Parker?—is being swept out of my reach by the gushing water. The boy floats on the surface of the water then dips underneath it again and again, so I have a hard time identifying him, but I know beyond doubt that he is my son. I grasp for him from the shore, but he is moving too quickly downstream, the whole time on his back, his bright eyes wide in panic, his left arm reaching up from the water. He is wearing little light blue swimming shorts.

I take off after him running, racing the current, trying to stay alongside my boy who dips and floats on the surface of the water. The banks of the river are part grass, part gravel spotted with shrubbery, and as I stumble desperately along, I see ahead that the river will soon pass under a bridge— narrow, with cement embankments. Terror slices through me as I realize that the child, who is always just beyond the touch of my fingertips, will inevitably pass under that bridge. I won't be able to see him while he is under there. There is only a small space between the water and the underside of the bridge. It is dark. *He could get stuck*, I reason with my racing self. *I'll need to jump in and try to rescue him. Will I do that? When will I do that? And where? Or do I hope and wait and trust that I will see him when he washes out on the other side?*

I stumble and run, grope and sob, calling to my son to reach higher for my hand, but his little arms cannot compete with the furious current. His eyes are wild, frenzied, his mouth open as if to cry out for me. I am barking out to the skies like an animal—"Oh, God! God, help! Reach, reach! Higher! Hiiigher! *Oh, God help me!*"—barking as I see that my boy might hit a rock here or a jutting branch there, and then this dark passage ahead and how the body will wash under it. *Should I jump in right now? Can I grab him? Is there any way I can save him before that bridge?*

Too late.

He's swept into the dark tunnel. Sprinting, panting, and crying, I scream to the empty skies for help, then lean to peer under the bridge for a glimpse of my boy, but the crashing rush of water swallows up all sound, and there is no one to hear me anyway.

I scramble down an embankment from where the water was churning in the culvert and passed under the bridge. Water gushes out of the tunnel through a large round opening like a huge open mouth then plunges a few meters into a lagoon. Yet I hear no rush of water, no smacking against rocks, only the sound of my heart pounding in my ears. This is a dead end.

Catching my breath with my sight riveted on the tumbling water, I wait. The sun crackles on my sweating skin as I then feverishly scan the surface of the lagoon, watching for anything to bob up. I watch for a very long, cruel moment. The taut, smooth skin of this strange pool of water shimmers, untouched by any sign of the earlier turmoil and rough current.

Silence hangs in the heat. I circle the pool. The sun throbs, a humming sentinel guarding a cornflower-blue sky, hissing through wavelets of summer heat rising off the glassy pond. Time passes. An hour? Hours? It is a time out of time. It is forever. Still no sign of life. Just a pool reflecting the clouds.

And a mother, quavering and breathless, waiting on the shore. Her eyes are still wide with expectation, her whole heaving torso infused with adrenalin. Then, slow-moving, like the water itself—listless, pulseless—her hope begins to melt. She tries to refocus—is there something she missed, couldn't see?—and her brows twitch once, before her eyelids slide down, hiding the absence that her eyes see but her spirit cannot, cannot, *cannot* comprehend.

The leaden weight of nothingness descends, enclosing her like a tomb. First, it presses on the crown of her head. Then on her shoulders. Then the nape of her neck. Then her will, which folds limply. Her knees follow, buckling, and the brittle waist-high weeds go down with her as she kneels on the ground. In the landscape she could be mistaken for a rock, hardly moving, barely breathing, just this side of alive. Until she lifts two hands, hiding her eyes, profile sinking, downward, inward, heartward, beneath the full-blown sun, whose round reflection floats on the water like a white world.

ENLARGEMENT AND REFINEMENT

GRIEF DRIVES MEN to serious reflection, sharpens the understanding, and softens the heart.

—John Adams, *The Writings of Thomas Jefferson*

TO SPARE ONESELF from grief at all cost can be achieved only at the price of total detachment, which excludes the ability to experience happiness.

—Erich Fromm, quoted in *Telling It Like It Is*

TRULY, IT IS in darkness that one finds the light, so when we are in sorrow, then this light is nearest of all to us.

—Meister Eckhart, quoted in *Blessings*

GRIEF ALONE CAN teach us what is man.

—Lytton Bulwer, quoted in *A Dictionary of Quotations from the English Poets*

FIRE TESTS GOLD, suffering tests brave men.

—Seneca

[TO BE A hero means] not withdrawing from the world when you realize how horrible it is, but seeing that this horror is simply the foreground of a wonder. . . . It wouldn't be life if there weren't temporality involved, which is sorrow—loss, loss, loss. You've both to say yes to life and see it as magnificent this way; for this is surely the way God intended it.

—Joseph Campbell, quoted in *Stories From the Edge*

IF THE INTERNAL griefs of every man could be read, written on his forehead, how many who now excite envy would appear to be the objects of pity?

—Metastasio

A MAN MUST create the world
of which he is the center.
This can be a masterwork:
The painting of an artist,
The piece of a cabinetmaker,
The field of a peasant,
The symphony of a composer;
The page of a writer.
It can be a family.
And when tragedy comes,
as it will, we must take this
suffering into our hands
and, through will power,

transform it into a fruit
that will nourish us
As we begin life again.
This is the fragile miracle
Hidden within us all!

—David Duncan, quoted in *Grieving*

LET DEATH BE daily before your eyes, and you will never entertain any abject thought, nor too eagerly covet anything.

—Epictetus, quoted in *A Dictionary of Thoughts*

HOLDING TRUE TO our sacred knowledge is not just a tidy way to pass through the fire; it is the only way through.

For our faith to be measured, we must pass through trials that offer no sight of deliverance. Satan hopes we will despair and give up on God. He hopes we will let go of what we know. If our faith is strong only under small loads, it is not fully grown. If we have confidence in God only during the good times, we are foolish.

> *Then Job . . . fell down upon the ground, and worshipped, and said, . . .*
> *the Lord gave, the Lord hath taken away; blessed be the name of the Lord.*
> *In all this Job sinned not, nor charged God foolishly.*

Faith in the full degree does not foolishly accuse God. It insists on his goodness, wisdom and power. It is tenacious and firm. A fullness of faith knows that suffering somehow makes sense, that God must disguise his hand during our probation, that suffering is a fleeting detail in eternity, and that someday we will see the big map that explains the path we were treading.

The faithful know that doubt can cancel joy, but pain cannot.

—Wayne E. Brickey, *Making Sense of Suffering*

FOR YEARS AND years we've gathered in to this church to affirm our belief, because we knew the day would come when faith was the only thing that could get us through.

Well, now the day is here. And we will survive the grief, and the questions that do not have answers. We will survive by leaning into our faith. If you don't have enough yourself, then lean into the faith of the church. But don't dare try to grieve without believing the heavenly Father has received Casey into his eternal arms, or you will never survive the loss.

Not only does our decision to believe in the grace of God get us through death, it also allows us to give thanks for the three precious weeks we had with Casey. Again, this is a choice, and maybe one of the most heroic choices you can be asked to make. But it's the only way you're going to survive. If you choose to resent the loss, your heart will eventually turn dark and you will be unable to love anything in life. But if, in time, you get to the place of choosing to give thanks for the gifts Casey brought into our lives, you will discover that some of his childlike tenderness has been left behind in your own heart.

—M. Craig Barnes, quoted in *This Incomplete One*

THOSE WHO GRIEVE are well qualified to become our teachers. They have stood at the very threshold of life, and they understand the true meaning of love. They have a vision and awareness that far surpasses those whose lives have never been pierced with deep pain and suffering. They speak to us honestly and courageously from the heart of the refiner's fire. They understand the importance of values and priorities. They are deeply sensitive. They will no longer trust in superficial answers or well-worn cliché's. They guard against those who are afraid of their pain and too uncomfortable to communicate in an authentic way. They are impatient with those who have learned to use their faith in life after death as a reason to avoid doing the work of grief, or those who believe grief is unnecessary in the presence of faith.

—DeAnna Edwards, *Grieving*

TRULY I AM living life to the fullest. I've made a way for the pain and the full life to co-exist. You can have both. It's like going to a party with a toothache. The real healing is when you accept that the pain is always there. It has changed the way I define myself. Formerly I might have called myself a journalist, or a mother; now, first and foremost, I'm a bereaved parent. That's what I feel is the most important and prominent part of who I am.

—Veronica, interviewed in *When the Bough Breaks*

I WILL GO, I will go carry my crown of fading leaves
To my father's garden where flowers live again;
I will spread out at length my kneeling soul:
My father has secret ways to conquer pain.

I will go, I will go tell him, at least with my tears
"See, I have suffered . . ." He will look at me,
And under my changed face, my charmless pallor,
Because he is my father, he will recognize me.

He will say, "It is you then, dear sad soul!
Is the ground slipping beneath your lost feet?
Dear soul, I am God: be troubled no more;
Behold your home, behold my heart, come in!"

O mercy! O kindness! O holy refuge! O father!
Your child who was weeping you have heard!
I have reached you already since I await you
And since you possess already all that I have lost.

You do not reject the flower no longer fair,
That crime of earth is forgiven in heaven.
You will not curse your unfaithful child,
Not for having sold nothing, but for having given all.

—Marceline Desbordes-Valmore, "The Leafless Garland"

IT IS IMPORTANT to be faithful to the memory of those we love. Living shut away in misery is not being faithful. We must not allow ourselves to be destroyed by the past, but to remain faithful to it by making it serve as a springboard. For life is in progress toward the future. One must trust in whatever comes. We must continue to plough our furrow, straight and deep as they would have done themselves, as you would have done with them. For them. To be faithful to those who have died is to live as they would have lived, to make them live in us.

—Martin Gray, quoted in *Grieving*

GREAT GRIEF IS a divine and terrible radiance which transfigures the wretched.

—Victor Hugo, *Les Misérables*

THE SUN HIDES not the ocean, which is the dark side of this earth, and which is two thirds of this earth. So, therefore, that mortal man who hath more of joy than sorrow in him, that mortal man cannot be true—not true, or undeveloped. With books the same. The truest of all men was the Man of Sorrows, and the truest of all books is Solomon's, and Ecclesiastes is the fine hammered steel of woe.

—Herman Melville, *Moby-Dick*

WITH GRIEVING, JUST as you undergo a physical and psychological tearing down and building up, you also experience a parallel process of spiritual destruction and rebirth. If you can withstand the storm, if you can weather the destruction, and even embrace the confusion, it is possible to eventually emerge with a renewed, stronger faith.

—Ashley Prend, quoted in *What Forever Means after the Death of a Child*

JOY IS NOT the absence of pain. Joy is the presence of God. Tragedy can increase our joy and increase our faith.

—DeAnna Edwards, *Grieving*

MELANIE, STANLEY, STUART, and Michelle were the best things that ever happened to me. Even in their short lives, they exceeded any hopes I could have had for them. Yes, I know I have to go forward now. By marrying and bringing these two girls into the world, that's what I'm choosing to do. . . .

And even now I still feel like hell is only a step away. But I choose not to step into it.

—Christine McFadden, interviewed in *Oprah Magazine*

HE WHO LEARNS must suffer.
And even in our sleep
pain that cannot forget falls
drop by drop upon the heart,
and in our own despair,
against our will,
comes wisdom to us
by the awful grace of God.

—Aeschylus, quoted in "People & Events"

THE DEATH OF a dear friend . . . which seemed nothing but privation, somewhat later assumes the aspect of a guide or genius; for it commonly operates revolutions in our way of life, terminates an epoch of infancy or of youth which was waiting to be closed, breaks up a wonted occupation, or a household, or a style of living, and allows the formation of new ones more friendly to the growth of character. . . . And the man or woman who would have remained a sunny garden-flower, with no room for its roots and too much sunshine for its head, by the falling of the walls and the neglect of the gardener, is made the banian of the forest yielding shade and fruit to wide neighbourhoods of men.

—Ralph Waldo Emerson, *The Works of Ralph Waldo Emerson*

SUFFERING IS A time to reeducate our hopes, our savoring reflexes. It offers us an elevated spot above the landscape, a rare view, a chance at real wisdom. . . .

To learn from adversity, we need to slow down, kneel down, listen carefully, and consult the sacred books. . . .

If we consider well, without haste or self-pity, the Father's mind will at length whisper to ours. We will see past the outward. We will be settled, even in the smallest holdings and poorest fortunes. We will know that an outward loss opens the door to inner gain.

—Wayne E. Brickey, *Making Sense of Suffering*

PART V

LIGHT, LOVE, AND LIFE OVER DEATH

REMEMBERING, CONNECTEDNESS, AND CONTINUING THE BOND

AFRICANS HAVE A proverb: "*Owu antweri obaako mforo.*" A rough translation is "The ladder of death is not climbed by only one person." For Africa, death traditionally is "not an individual affair" but "binds up relationships in society, revitalizing the living and underscoring their sense of community." The death of a villager becomes an opportunity to "give concrete expression to community solidarity." The emphasis on the communal is often observed in Africa-American communities as well, and not surprisingly African Americans are more likely that most other Americans to describe a continued relationship with a deceased loved one.

—George Bonanno, *The Other Side of Sadness*

WHEN WE ARE apart, we give those we love places in our thoughts and prayers. We remember them. We speak of them with others. We shape our lives in terms of commitments and covenants with them. We share their interests and concerns. We model our actions and characters on theirs. We think of and appreciate how we and our lives are different for knowing them.

—Thomas Attig, *How We Grieve*

ONLY THIS EVENING I saw again low in the sky
The evening star, at the beginning of winter, the star
That in spring will crown every western horizon,
Again . . . as if it came back, as if life came back,
Not in a later son, a different daughter, another place,
But as if evening found us young, still young,
Still walking in a present of our own.

—Wallace Stevens, "Martial Cadenza," *The Collected Poems of Wallace Stevens*

IN MANY PLACES the family of a child who dies, and the child's friends, not only know why the child died and where he is but can check up on how he's doing, ritually offer him gifts and blessings, and continue to play a role in his life after death.

Imagine how it might be for us if we could follow our children's progress in some other world. Would it change how we miss them? Would it affect how we grieve? Would it help us heal? I think it would.

—Sukie Miller, *Finding Hope When A Child Dies*

WHEN I REMEMBER bygone days
I think how evening follows morn;
So many I loved were not yet dead,
So many I love were not yet born.

—Ogden Nash, "The Middle," quoted in *Albertus C. Van Raalte*

THE CENTRAL CHALLENGE as we grieve is learning to love in a new way, to love someone in separation, at least as long as we walk this earth. Nothing is more difficult. Nothing is more important. Nothing is more rewarding.

—Thomas Attig, *How We Grieve*

***

THEY SHALL GROW not old, as we that are left grow old:
Age shall not weary them, nor the years condemn.
At the going down of the sun and in the morning,
We will remember them.

—Laurence Binyon, "For the Fallen," quoted in *The Musical Times*

***

I **THINK NO** matter where you stray,
That I shall go with you a way.
Though you may wander sweeter lands,
You will not forget my hands,
Nor yet the way I held my head
Nor the tremulous things I said.

You will still see me, small and white
And smiling, in the secret night,
And feel my arms about you when
The day comes fluttering back again.
I think, no matter where you be,
You'll hold me in your memory
And keep my image there without me,
By telling later loves about me.

—Dorothy Parker, "But Not Forgotten," quoted in *I'll Go No More A-Roving*

***

AS [CO-MOURNERS] WE help to normalize this loss when we convey to parents that the goal is not to "detach" from or "let go" of their child, but to acknowledge the reality of the child's physical death while also building new connections to the child's spirit.

—Kay Talbot, *What Forever Means After the Death of a Child*

HE WHO HAS gone, so we but cherish his memory, abides with us, more potent, nay, more present than the living man.

—Antoine de Saint-Exupery, *Le Petit Prince*

FAREWELL TO THEE! but not farewell
To all my fondest thoughts of Thee:
Within my heart they still shall dwell;
And they shall cheer and comfort me.

Life seems more sweet that Thou didst live,
And men more true Thou wert one:
Nothing is lost that Thou didst give,
Nothing destroyed that Thou hast done.

—Anne Brontë, "Farewell," quoted in *Anne Brontë: The Other One*

NOTHING CAN FILL the gap when we are away from those we love, and it would be wrong to try and find anything. We must simply hold out and win through. That sounds very hard at first, but at the same time it is a great consolation, since leaving the gap unfilled preserves the bond between us. It is nonsense to say that God fills the gap. He does not fill it, but keeps it empty so that our communion with another may be kept alive, even at the cost of pain.

—Dietrich Bonhoeffer, quoted in *Never Far from Home*

IN CULTURES IN which life is a continuum and time is not something you run out of or use up, death does not signify the irreconcilable end of all life and all experience. Death is more an event, a space, a separation, followed usually by a resting period . . . and then new life. And this cycle is unending.

—Sukie Miller, *Finding Hope When a Child Dies*

THAT SUCH HAVE died enables Us
The tranquiller to die;
That Such have lived,
Certificate for immortality.

—Emily Dickinson, *The Poems of Emily Dickinson*

ON THE DAY of my death when my coffin is going by,
don't imagine that I have any pain about leaving this world.

Don't weep for me, and don't say, "How terrible! What a pity!"
For you will fall into the error of being deceived by the Devil,
and that would be a pity!

When you see my funeral, don't say, "Parting and separation!"
For me, that is the time for union and meeting.

When you entrust me to the grave, don't say,
"Good-bye! Farewell!" for the grave is only a curtain for
the gathering in Paradise.

When you see the going down, notice the coming up. Why should
there be loss because of the setting of the sun and moon?

It seems like setting to you, but it is rising. The tomb seems like a
prison, but it is the liberation of the soul.

What seed ever went down into the earth that didn't grow back up?
So, for you, why is there this doubt about the human "seed"?

What bucket ever went down and didn't come up full? Why
should there be any lamenting for the Joseph of the soul
because of the well?

When you have closed your mouth on this side, open it on that side,
for your shouts of joy will be in the Sky beyond place and time.

—Jelal ad Din Rumi, "It seems like setting to you, but it is rising"

═══════════════

THE LIVING AND the dead are not separated from each other by time and space.
As far as the Celts are concerned, the otherworld and this world overlap and
interpenetrate.

—J. Ó Ríordáin, quoted in *Stories from the Edge*

═══════════════

THERE IS NO death. Only a change of worlds.

—Chief Seattle

═══════════════

IT IS A bit like a fading light. It grows dim but never goes out, never, not completely
anyway. I find that enormously reassuring. I used to worry that someday the light
would disappear—that I would forget, and then I would really have lost Claire. I
know, now, that doesn't happen. It can't. There is always a little flicker there. It is a
bit like the small glowing embers you see after a fire dies down. I carry that around
with me, that little ember, and if I need to, if I want to have Claire next to me, I blow
on it, ever so gently, and it glows bright again.

—Karen Everly, interviewed in *The Other Side of Sadness*

#8

BASKETBALL WAS PARKER'S oxygen. Friendship was his sunlight. God was his soil. He dumptrucked loads of energy into all things that were a fusion of ball, friends, and God. For example, this is the social network profile he wrote about himself:

> *About me: Hey, my name is Parker, I live in Paris, this is my 8th yr here. I speak French, Norwegian, and English. I love basketball and volleyball, hanging out with friends, tearing up a drum set. I love listening to music! I also love my family, I love talking to ppl. I'm a really easy person to talk to because I'm laid back and talk a lot. I love my church, I believe in my religion, [and] I follow it as best I can. I try to be the best friend I can be.*

> *Who I'd like to meet: God, Jesus, and 7 NBA basketball players*

> *Heroes: my family, a few of my friends, the president of my church and a few other church leaders, Jesus Christ, and a few basketball players*

The same year he wrote that profile (his second-to-last year of high school at the American School of Paris) one of his "bros," as he called his teammates, was a kid named Dan. Dan was a great ballplayer who sharpened his game after school in the gymnasium with Parker running the court, practicing layups, shooting from the free-throw line, and slam-dunking. We have footage the two took of themselves—the panting and the squeakity-squeaking on rubber soles along the waxed floor, bursting with testosteroney bellows, "Pass it here, LeBron!" (Dan's alias), or "Go back, baaaack Kobe!" (Parker's alias).

Dan joked with Parker that no white Mormon boy was ever going to equal Kobe in either vertical jumping or overall coolness, but this didn't keep Parker from idolizing Bryant a bit. Parker had Kobe's pictures on his bedroom wall, and even his number eight on both his basketball and volleyball uniforms.

"Eight, Mom. Like the symbol for infinity, but awake instead of on its side sleeping. And taller." Parker told me this when I asked its significance while laundering his jersey after their team won the international basketball championship. We have a great picture of Parker and Dan holding the massive shining trophy together high over their heads. You could, by studying that photo, almost make out their booming and whooping shouts-into-the-air. They came from a place beneath those taut-muscled necks ridged with protruding veins, from inside those bodies pumping with lifeblood and a fierce force of spirit, from joy at their invincible brotherhood, which erupted in that moment into one ecstatic, explosive bloom.

When Dan got news that Parker had not survived his coma, he was wild with anguish and anger. Then he felt detached, dulled to life. He grappled with figuring out what it all meant, this idiotic living and dying thing, and, more specifically, what it was supposed to mean for him. What matters now? Who is safe, anyway? And who cares?

After some false starts, Dan found his passion again, and poured it into establishing a basketball academy in Kenya named Dankind Academy. Its aim was to grow strong players, players with characteristics that, the academy's official trailer explained, should reflect those of a certain promising player named Parker Bradford—open-minded, accepting, a loyal friend, and exemplary team player, whose high aims included sacrificing himself for others. Dan was on his way to building an organization that would build up young Kenyans, who in turn would build up Kenya.

We kept loose track of how Dankind Academy was growing. Through various channels we got cursory details of what was happening in Dan's life and with his dream. But for a spell, we didn't get news at all. Until we received the following letter.

> Dear Bradford family,
> It has been a while since I have been in touch with you and a while since I have posted on Parker's Facebook wall, but when you hear this story you will understand why and how things have

actually turned out and fallen into place for my business, the Dankind Basketball Academy, in a way I can hardly believe or describe.

As you know, I have been in Nairobi for the last six months for what has turned out to be a great first season for the Academy. The original idea was that I bring players back to France, to a town close to my home, and have them train on a daily basis here. But the two-year budget to make this happen was originally around €500 thousand. That cost and problems with Visas made those plans impossible.

So I tried to make things happen in England. But the same obstacles arose. In the end I took two trips to Nairobi where I was going all over the place to find good players, safe courts to train on, and preferably accommodations close by. After two trips to Kenya during which I was desperately juggling options and trying to battle through all sorts of corruption and overpricing, I managed to find a six-bedroom house where we were told that we could use the gym at the nearby sports centre twice a day at a low price. I was happy that things looked like they were going to work out, and the annual budget dropped to what I felt would maybe be reasonable for a year.

Things looked great as I knew I was able to have my very own team registered in the Nairobi Basketball Association and have fourteen boys living in-house, providing them with two meals a day plus a light breakfast. We would be training at a decent court with a coach who was doing an amazing job volunteering for us. We could practice twice a day, had money for transportation to and from games, and all within the €36 thousand budget. The future looked bright.

Right after we got into a practice routine, however, the sports centre began to try and squeeze us for more money and were suddenly uncooperative with us. They started giving away our court time to anyone who was willing to pay more for short-term events. They did this a few times without even consulting with us. We were so disappointed and lost our second-ever game during a week where the players couldn't practice nearly as much as they wanted or I expected.

Buying beds, sheets, pillows, and everything else we needed for the house the same week pushed me all the way up to my monthly limit on my credit card. I had been keeping to my weekly limit of withdrawing €300 a week, which was a tight budget for all I was trying to accomplish for all our players, and hit my rock bottom moment on a Wednesday when I was basically stuck without a way to pay for food for the rest of the week or transport to the next game on the upcoming weekend.

At this point, I was hoping that Dan was going to ask us if we would be in a position to fund a few months or so of Dankind Academy, that he'd maybe already wrung his parents dry, that this would be a way of continuing a tribute to Parker. Mentally, I was already writing out a check, glad that Dan felt comfortable asking us for help.

But that wasn't why he was writing. I kept reading.

Up until this point where things looked pretty hopeless, I had always made my withdrawals in Nairobi centre just before our games on the weekend. Those withdrawals had to last for the whole week. Now I was forced to take out money around the area where the players and I lived. I had never done that before, and had no idea where to go and receive money from France through Western Union from my parents who were going to bail me out of the predicament. (Love you mum and dad!)

One of my players, a giant of a guy named Lino, told me he knew where the closest bank was, maybe a mile away from the house we were all staying in and said he would take me there. As we walked and talked, he tried to show sympathy. I made sure he knew that I was fully aware that the problem with "getting money from France" was a "western issue," and reminded him (and myself) that the whole reason I came to Africa was because I knew how much worse people had it here, and I wanted to help make a difference in young lives using my passion for basketball.

You know how Parker and I lived for basketball, how our years playing together and then being team co-captains side-by-side, and winning the championship together were highlights of our lives. In all this work with my Academy, I've been thinking of him, my friend who was more like a brother, and how his shortened life made a difference. In spite of all these difficulties I was facing, I wanted to do the same.

Here I was, walking alongside Lino. He was a refugee from the longest civil war in the last century and started off life fleeing his homeland to then be displaced into a refugee camp in Kakuma before coming to Nairobi. He knew what real troubles were. So I stayed upbeat. I told him this funding thing was a simple problem to solve, but I needed him to back me up to solve our training situation. I was worried that I had rented the house close to the sports centre and now it looked like we couldn't even train there, which basically defeated the whole purpose of coming to Africa in the first place. Then I looked over at Lino, and told him I could never imagine being in his shoes, and the horrors he and his people had seen. But he was such a good-hearted and happy person, so respectful and well mannered. It seemed natural that I share with him the story of my brother Parker, my Mormon Kobe, and how losing him was the most tragic and life-altering thing that had ever happened to me.

Lino was respectful as I talked about the video I posted about Parker on YouTube and explained how even though I was unsure about the future of our training, I was happy that I had found a group of players that were not only tall and super athletic, but had great hearts and attitudes and would live up to the goal of the Academy, which is to produce role models just like Parker. Lino told me that Parker would be proud of what I was doing and was surely watching down on us. For me, this was something. You know I've grown up without going to church and not being of any religious group, but I thought this "watching down" idea sounded great, and if there is a heaven, Parker is there and I hope he does enjoy watching my little, humble Kenyan basketball Academy practice and play.

Here is where things get insane, even strange and maybe unbelievable. Literally, right then as Lino and I are walking down this kind of trashy, junky street filled with deep potholes everywhere, as opposite a setting from Paris as you're going to find—just as Lino and I finished talking about Parker, all of a sudden we saw a parking lot in front of a building to our right. There was a groomed garden all around the car park. The grass was pristine. The building was gorgeous. There were plants perfectly arranged all around, too. The place looked like a small bit of heaven. And right there in the parking lot, very basic, with no rims or nets, stood two basketball stands.

This was the middle of the week and there was nobody around on the streets or near the building but the two of us, and we walked closer, down to the front gate. That's where I saw the sign for the first time: The Church of Jesus Christ and Latter-Day Saints. I was so shocked, I think I gasped, and explained to Lino that that title was the full version of Parker's Mormon church. If he ever would have made a visit to Kenya, I said to Lino, this is definitely the church he would have gone to on Sundays.

Like I said, that was strange enough. As I walked to the bank (which happens to be maybe a hundred meters away from the church), I made a decision that I would go and see whether training on these two hoops could possibly be an option for us in the future. I picked up the money from Western Union and decided that on the approaching Saturday when my bankcard limit would be renewed and I could take out another €300 I would return to the same bank and see if anyone was around at the church. Maybe someone would help me.

On Saturday, the gate to the church was open and so was the side entry. So I thought I might as well pop my head in and see if I could talk to anyone about the courts. The first person I met was sitting down all alone. And he was wearing a Kobe Bryant jersey—not a #24 jersey like Kobe wears right now, but the yellow one with the #8. Just like the one Parker wore all the time when "The Black Mamba" was our favorite player.

I could not believe what I was seeing. And it turned out that this Kobe #8 guy I'd stumbled onto was the very person who had ordered the baskets in the first place. He explained to me that there had been problems with people using the court and smoking and drinking there after they were done, and so the church had decided to take off the baskets because those who were using them were disrespecting the wishes of the church and its purpose. Quickly, I explained the whole idea of Dankind Academy—high personal standards, honesty, hard work, politeness, all those things I associate with Parker—and then Kobe #8 explained that unfortunately he had been waiting for the "bishop," I think it was, all morning and that he hadn't shown up. Could I come back the next day?

I left the church that Saturday thinking I would have to wait a whole week to see the bishop to ask about using this court for training, but once again just as I had finished telling myself I would just have to be patient and stay on this lead, I walked straight into two missionaries on the street. They were both from the US. It was like they just appeared or something—right there on my path. We three talked for ages, and I explained everything to them about the Academy and even about Parker. They gave me their phone number as well as the bishop's. So by the end of the next week when I thought I would still be waiting to see the bishop, I had already talked with him about using the courts and he had given me the keys to the church.

Given. Me. The. Keys.

Dankind Academy is now using the parking lot and the baskets from Monday to Saturday as much as we need to. Things have gone from strength to strength since then despite all the other obstacles that come up day to day. We have added four brand new baskets to the court and put basketball court lines down on the parking lot/court area, too. The boys practice morning and afternoon at the courts five to six days a week depending on our weekend games. It's been a string of miracles. How else can I describe it?

Lino had said that Parker was looking down on us. He'd been so matter-of-fact and nonchalant. And now I literally cannot help but think about Parker every single day and every time I enter that court right in front of his church. I feel like I am saying hello to him opening the gate, and every time I leave I feel like I am saying goodbye, just like when the two of us would practice together at school. And we've all decided on the team that since Parker is looking down on us, it's better that we are outside. That way, he has a good view.

He'd be happy, I think, knowing that we're playing at his church, living life the way he did, being passionate about basketball, and are with good teammates who are committed to working hard every day. He's happy, too, that Dankind won the regional championship here in Kenya, and that we all held that big trophy above our heads. So Parker could see.

MINISTERS AND MENTORS

THE DEAD ARE invisible, not absent.

—Augustine of Hippo, "The dead are invisible"

THIRTEEN YEARS AGO I lost a brother, and with his spirit I converse daily and hourly in the spirit, and see him in my remembrance, in the regions of my imagination. I hear his advice, and even now write from his dictate.

—William Blake, quoted in *The Heart of Grief*

MOSTLY, THOUGH, WE were, in some way, together. She was not (to my knowledge or perception) with me in ghostly form, although I later came to think she had been perhaps. But in a not-at-all mystical sense she lived, she was vivid and alive, in me. Our love continued.

—Sheldon Van Auken, *A Severe Mercy*

DYING PATIENTS, YOUNG and old, experience that they become aware of the presence of beings who surround them, and who help them. Young children often refer to them as their playmates. The churches have called them guardian angels. Most researchers would call them guides. It is not important what label we give them, but it is important to know that every single human being from the moment of birth until the moment when we make the transition and end this physical existence, is in the presence of these guides or guardian angels who will wait for us and help us in the transition form life to life after death. Also, we will always be met by those who preceded us in death who we have loved.

—Elizabeth Kübler-Ross, *On Life After Death*

AT ONE POINT I talked to an Interfaith Chaplain about this. The Chaplain had lost her teenage son in a pedestrian/auto accident close to her home—a fateful spot that she had to often drive by. She told me that she began to think about that spot not as an area of destruction but as a holy place, even a sanctuary. That made me realize that this stretch of road was the last place where you took a breath on your own; it was the last place where you had any conscious awareness; it was the place where you began your passage into the next world. It truly is a holy site for me. I like to think that after you were ejected from your car and came to rest on the ground, that you were not alone. I feel that before the paramedics and police arrived, you were in the company of eternal beings. I hope they encircled you and sustained you; I pray that they surrounded you during that awful time. I think that there were divine beings around you while the mortal beings were attempting to save your life. When I think about it that way, I realize that the spot where you came to rest in the middle of the busy freeway is most surely hallowed ground.

—Ellen Knell, *Letters to Erica*

THIS OTHER WORLD is not way off in the sky some place, but that it is superimposed upon the world in which we live. That other world is simply on a higher, or, at least, a different frequency than we on earth occupy. And the line of demarcation becomes, under certain circumstances, so thin that there can be a vibration, or the sense of a presence, so that we know those whom we have loved and lost are not far from us.

—Norman Vincent Peale, quoted in *Beyond Death's Door*

BUT, O SARAH! if the dead can come back to this earth and flit unseen around those they loved, I shall always be near you; in the garish day and in the darkest night . . . always, always, and if there be a soft breeze upon your cheek, it shall be my breath, or the cool air fans your throbbing temple, it shall be my spirit passing by.

Sarah do not mourn me dead; think I am gone and wait for thee, for we shall meet again.

—Sullivan Ballou, quoted in *The American Civil War*

THE OLD HOUSE
Is full of ghosts, dear ghosts on stair and landing,
Ghosts in chamber and hall; garden and walk
Are marvellous with ghosts, where so much love
Dwelt for a little while and made such music,
Before it too was taken by the tide
That takes us all, of time's receding music.
Oh, all is music! All has been turned to music!
All that is vanished has been turned to music!
And these familiar rafters, that have known
The child, the young man and the man, now shelter
The aging man, who lies here, listening, listening—
All night, in a half dream, I have lain here listening.

—John Hall Wheelock, "Night Thoughts in Age," *Modern Verse in English*

I AM SURE that this whole planet is surrounded by spirits, by saints, by our ances-tors, and that they see what is happening and they almost beg you, "Why don't you ask me to help you? Because I can help you only if you ask; if you are closed I cannot penetrate."

—Robert Muller, "I am sure that this whole planet is surrounded by spirits"

[AS A SEVEN-YEAR-OLD], I saw and remember my mother leaning over the head of the coffin and kissing him. . . . All life changed for me; everything from then on was different. In most everything I did the memory of the image of my father was present. When I remembered him his clear physical image came up before me; I could see him as clearly as if he were present.

—Mahonri Young, quoted in *Song of Joys*

AND THOUGH THE Lord give you the bread of adversity, and the water of afflic-tion, yet shall not thy teachers be removed into a corner any more, but thine eyes shall see thy teachers: And thine ears shall hear a word behind thee, saying, This is the way, walk ye in it, when ye turn to the right hand, and when ye turn to the left.

—Isaiah 30:20–21

THE TALE OF TWO PARKERS

THIS IS THE tale of two Parkers. This is also by extension the tale of two freak events that yanked two families onto two unforeseen, and shadowy trajectories. This tale tells how the invisible and visible realms—we'll call them heaven and earth—interpenetrate. How we are not destined to flail in our agonies alone. How our most noble human qualities are revealed when we extend ourselves toward those in distress and need, and this, more than any other thing, is a measure of our humanity.

———

Big Parker is my firstborn. On July 20, 2007, he was eighteen years and five months old to the day. He was also lying in a deep coma caused by having been oxygen deprived for too long when he was knocked unconscious underwater after twice reentering a lethal whirlpool trying to save a college classmate who was drowning. A week from the exact hour of his death, we stood, drooped and trembling over his casket. Then watched his promising life go into the dark earth.

Little Parker is the son of John and Renée. He and his twin sister were conceived a few months after Big Parker's funeral, which Renée attended, having flown to Utah from her home in Paris, which is where we Halls and Bradfords had lived and loved each other. I still remember when we were visiting Paris after Big Parker's funeral, and Renée whispered to me, her eyes glinting, that she was expecting. "Twins," she added, as she dipped her head so that her blonde hair fell covering half of her face, "and if one is a boy, we are thinking of naming him Parker." She swept her finger along the edge of her hair, tucking a lock behind her ear, "If that is—" she then stopped herself, lifting her eyebrows as if to apologize and request permission, "If that is. . . alright with you?"

Twins Parker and Penelope were the prized babies to their three older princess sisters, who kept things at a rollicking clip with spontaneous dance-a-thons, picnics in the local parks, and frequent excursions to Euro Disney. Which happens to be exactly where they were on February 20, on what would have been Big Parker's twentieth birthday. And that was the day Little Parker (just eight months old) contracted pneumococcal meningitis.

When I got the phone call in Munich that Little Parker was in a medically induced coma and "probably would not make it another day," I caught the next plane to Paris. Folding and refolding the waxy white airplane napkin, I couldn't block out possible scenes of an ashen-faced Renée folding up baby boy clothes to be boxed or given away; I tried to suppress the impossible notion of my boy's name being a curse; I foresaw the fragility that would invade and potentially reduce these mighty parents; I narrated to myself the story of loss Renée would yearn to tell, and I feared all the ears that wouldn't want to hear it, that scary but sacred story of the phantom child.

At France's premier children's hospital, cloaked in paper gowns, masks, and gloves, Renée and I entered the isolation booth where Little Parker lay motionless, his swollen head and listless body wrapped in gauze and sterile cotton, the hospital personnel avoiding eye contact while attempting light conversation. It was, to me, a scene of unspeakable but crashing familiarity. The volume of my pleading inner dialogue with God and with Big Parker—"Make him live! Strong brain! Strong lungs, strong, strong!!"—was so loud, I was sure the staff would ask me—s'il vous plait!—to keep my thoughts down.

From that weeklong coma Parker did return to life. But it was not a strong life. Cerebral meningitis had ravaged his system leaving him virtually deaf, hydrocephalic, convulsive, shunted, and cut and sewn so many times his head looked like a Spirograph drawing. He was gravely compromised neurologically, his gravitational vector was shot, he was droopy and unresponsive, and he had to be fit with cochlear implants in order to retrieve any hearing. (John and Renée and their four girls under age seven began teaching themselves sign language—both in English and in French.)

Over the two years that followed, Renée and I exchanged a volume of e-mails, sharing our days and tracking our boys. We wrote to each other of heaven's severe teaching methods, the wonder of small joys, the isolation and irony that mark major loss, the slicing and bruising contours of grief's landscape, the deepening spiritual experiences hardly transferable by written word, and our love, hope, yearning, and passion for our Parkers. We recognized only after our different losses that our sons actually never were all ours. They were, before all else, God's.

In none of these exchanges was the increased presence of the Spirit— and of spirits—in our lives more powerfully shared than in this email from Renée, describing a happening during their family's summer stateside vacation:

> We arrived late on a Sunday night at my parents' home in Southern California. We put the kids to bed, and John fell exhausted into bed well after midnight. I stayed up a couple more hours, tooling around as I always do whenever I grab the rare silent moment.
>
> At precisely 6:22 a.m. I awoke to repeated, panicked, unrecognizable screams. They were neither coming from where we'd put the twins to sleep, nor from where the older girls were fast asleep upstairs. They ripped me out of bed, these high-pitched, panicked screams for help, and I wandered quickly through the dark and into the kitchen where I met my mother, who was also awakened by the terrifying, continued screams. We knew all our children were sound asleep. Puzzlement growing to panic, we wondered, Is it the neighbors? Maybe it's a—
>
> Then I saw something out of the corner of my eye through the dining room window. A child, floating in the pool. It was Parker, screaming, thank God, face up, floating on his back.
>
> Shrieking and half crying, racing but unable to move quickly enough, we ran to rescue him. His limbs were not flailing or thrashing; he was not bobbing in and out of the water. His body was perfectly calm and nearly still. But he was screaming—a shrieking, frenzied, repeated plea for help.
>
> He had screamed for several minutes by the time I'd become alert enough to get out of bed, traverse the length of the house to the kitchen, and wonder aloud with my mom, all before we finally found him.
>
> Melissa, you know my little boy does not know how to swim. He

does not know how to float. How many two-year-olds do, even the healthy ones? The week previous I'd even noticed that with Parker's balance issues and unusual dispersion of weight due to his hydrocephaly, he actually tended to end up on his face while in the water much more frequently than other children. Even the life jackets designed to force children onto their backs actually forced Parker to his front. Supervising him meant we were physically holding part of him all the time we were anywhere near water.

My two-year-old son can barely stand, let alone walk. Yet he somehow climbed out of his crib and crawled through the garage, opened and passed through a second door from the garage, headed down the side yard and discovered the pool, opened a closed gate, and decided to get into the water. All at 6 o'clock in the morning. How could this child navigate his way there, through a dark garage and into dark waters?

Had he not screamed (this deaf boy who, without his cochlear implant, is mute), we would not have found him for at least one hour when the older girls woke up asking if they could swim, or an hour later than that, when Penelope would have awakened and seen Parker's empty crib. Instead, there he lay—cold, fatigued, and limp for an hour in our arms before he warmed up.

It was then I remembered that the night before, at 2 a.m., I'd knelt to pray. I had prayed earnestly for more inspiration regarding Parker and his care. I had prayed that something significant would happen the next day, something to signify to me that God was still mindful of me. Me, his aching daughter. And my baby. His baby. Our sick, growing baby.

I don't know what to think beyond these facts: That God heard and answered my prayers a little too quickly and a lot too literally for me. That there are clearly angels watching over us, over this boy, and I am so infinitely indebted to them. That miracles happen every day. That we have already seen miracles with this boy, and that I fully expect to see more. That a loving Father not only hears prayers—aching prayers of a mother with a growing boy—but that He answers them too.

I know, too, that in spite of all precautions and vaccinations and closed doors and gates—in spite of all I want to do and can do—I am, in the end, not the one in charge here.

Melissa, can I ask this next thing? Forgive me if it cuts you wide open. Do you think your drowned son was there holding mine up from drowning?

━━━━━━━━

I hoped to illustrate with this story how the invisible and visible realms—I wrote that we'd call them heaven and earth—interpenetrate. In writing that, I wasn't pressing for the perfect poetic conclusion to this tale. I wasn't winding up for a neatly bundled yarn about this Parker's arms holding up that other Parker's body.

Although I smile softly, dip my head, and ask, *well, why not?*

What I meant by the interpenetrating realms refers to but also goes beyond what or who saved a little boy from drowning. This story I have shared points to a bigger question than what happened in those predawn hours when an entire household slept and a hydrocephalic infant who could barely crawl made it through a dark garage and a locked gate and into a pool, entered the water, and remained floating perfectly on his back while he, deaf and virtually mute, screamed frantically yet without thrashing and until he was rescued.

The bigger question this tale points to is about meaning. Renée enumerated the many meanings the tale held for her. But what might the story mean for us?

The story of our Big and Little Parkers suggests to me that there are realities that lie outside of our mundane and mortally confined comprehension, things that we might, holding tightly to preconceived notions, dismiss as simply strange or inexplicable. What can we do about them, after all? They are, as we sometimes call them, "beyond us."

But if for a moment we allow our worldview to stretch enough to include the unseen or incorporeal realm, if we look into the "places where life's carapace is cracked," as Huston Smith puts it, "through its chinks [to] catch glimpses of a world beyond," maybe then we might find something of great value. Something crucial. Or paradigm inverting. Or cosmology blowing.

In addition to those questions of deep spiritual meaning, I think this tale provides a potent metaphor. It is a metaphor about our frail and fleeting human existence, about the nature of loss and grief, and about what we can do to be the saving arms for those drowning in sorrow.

There will be those, like Little Parker, who, through bizarre turns of irony, misfortune, and viral strains, almost die but do not, yet are left with other losses. Their suffering and their family's grief rise in panicked cries like those of an infant floating helplessly on his back in cold water. They need arms to cradle and rescue them.

And there will be others. Like Big Parker, there are those, who, due to brutally cruel twists, a hidden whirlpool, and a blow to the skull while underwater, will die. Their family's grief rises in purpled shrieks like the ones Parker himself tried to voice as he was pulled underwater again and again by the suction of an icy meat grinder. Those bereaved, too, they need arms.

When the cries that sail to the skies carve the long piercing arc of "Why?"—when one falls ill and another remains well, or when one dies and another does not—that is when our sustaining arms are probably needed the most. The "Why?" is a cried question that can only be answered by a weeping God. And I believe that, with His own tears—the first tears shed at any and all human suffering—He offers a silent prelude to His answer to the "Why?"

If someone is drowning in the glacial waves of grief, why wait for his voice to grow hoarse and his limbs to lose blood and his will to wane while he "gets over it"? Or why step away, awaiting angels to swoop in and scoop them up? It is our arms that must reach to succor, our arms that must mediate God's love. And when the waves close over whoever is sinking, writes reverend and activist William Sloane Coffin, "God's heart [is] the first of all our hearts to break."

In light of that, then, we have part of the answer to the cry of "Why?" It is that none of us knows enough to claim anything was God's will, and that the rest of the answer to that cry will somehow and sometime be realized in the arms of love. That love, continues Coffin, "not only begets love, it transmits strength." Indeed, our tears like our arms, when shared in love, emanate the very strength of God, which can bear every last drowning one of us.

PRESSING FORWARD
AND ENDURING WELL

I'VE GOT TO admit to you that now I sense that I'm becoming something different because of having been given the gift of endurance. I must confess to you that life is more precious to me today than it was before this episode. I must confess to you that I had taken life for granted pretty much until Laura Lue got sick. Life had been very, very good to me. I had never been significantly crossed by tragedy. And therefore there was a tendency in me to simply up and take for granted this incredible gift of aliveness. But I'll never do that again. Having sensed how powerless I was to hold on to her life, having sensed that I could do so little for someone I loved so much, has made me that much more anxious to take every day as the gift that it is, and not to take for granted the people that I touch and I love, but to look on them as a kind of windfall, a kind of grace, and a kind of gift. I know with assurance that I have become a different person because I had to endure something I wasn't given the grace for changing.

—John Claypool, *This Incomplete One*

THERE ALWAYS COMES, I think, a sort of peak in suffering at which either you win over your pain or your pain wins over you, according as to whether you can, or cannot, call up that extra ounce of endurance that helps you to break through the circle of yourself and do the hitherto impossible. That extra ounce carries you through *le dernier quart d' heure*. Psychologists have a name for it, I believe. Christians call it the Grace of God.

—Elizabeth Goudge, *The Castle on the Hill*

TO APPOINT UNTO them that mourn in Zion, to give them beauty for ashes, the oil of joy for mourning, the garment of praise for the spirit of heaviness; that they might be called trees of righteousness, the planting of the Lord, that he might be glorified.

—Isaiah 61:3

PEACE, MY HEART, let the time for the parting be sweet.
Let it not be a death but completeness.
Let love melt into memory and pain into songs.
Let the flight through the sky end in the folding of the wings over the nest.
Let the last touch of your hands be gentle like the flower of the night.
Stand still, O Beautiful End, for a moment, and say your last words in silence.
I bow to you and hold up my lamp to light you on your way.

—Rabindranath Tagore, *Works of Rabindranath Tagore*

SORROW LOOKS BACK, Worry looks around, Faith looks up.

—Ralph Waldo Emerson

THE THING I didn't understand about the death of someone who has been part of us or whom we have dearly loved is that there is no going back to normal. We have just cracked open and begun a new existence. In a matter of hours the survivors have metamorphosized into different creatures, never to be the same.

That moment pushed me to a crossroad of my beliefs. Would I be angry and bitter and shake my fist at God, my body or whatever else I could think of? Would I wallow in the pity and anger that I cycled between all day long? Or would I choose faith? Would I believe that a Father in Heaven—a parent who loved his children as much, even more, than I loved mine—had my best interests at heart? Would I believe that he knew me better than I knew myself and would allow me the experience of losing a child to make me a stronger, greater, more compassionate person?

I sat on my back porch one cold evening a month or so after leaving the hospital. I knew that the choice needed to be made. What would it be? Anger or faith? It had been distilled to two options.

I chose faith. I choose faith.

—Hildie Westenhaver, *Beehvive and Birdsnest*

I SUPPOSE ALL of us hover between two ways of regarding death, which appear to be in hopeless contradiction with each other. First there is the familiar and instinctive recoil from it as embodying the supreme and irrevocable disaster. . . .

But, then, there is another aspect altogether which death can wear for us. It is that which first comes to us, perhaps, as we look down upon the quiet face, so cold and white, of one who has been very near and dear to us. There it lies in possession of its own secret. It knows it all. So we seem to feel. And what the face says in its sweet silence to us as a last message from one whom we loved is:

> *Death is nothing at all. It does not count. I have only slipped away into the next room. Nothing has happened. Everything remains exactly as it was. I am I, and you are you, and the old life that we lived so fondly together is untouched, unchanged. Whatever we were to each other, that we are still. Call me by the old familiar name. Speak of me in the easy way which you always used. Put no difference into your tone. Wear no forced air of solemnity or sorrow. Laugh as we always laughed at the little jokes that we enjoyed together. Play, smile, think of me, pray for me. Let my name be ever the household word that it always was. Let it be spoken without an effort, without the ghost of a shadow upon it. Life means all that it ever meant. It is the same as*

it ever was. There is absolute and unbroken continuity. What is this death but a negligible accident? Why should I be out of mind because I am out of sight? I am but waiting for you, for an interval, somewhere very near, just around the corner. All is well. Nothing is hurt; nothing is lost. One brief moment and all will be as it was before. How we shall laugh at the trouble of parting when we meet again!

So the face speaks. Surely while we speak there is a smile flitting over it; a smile as of gentle fun at the trick played us by seeming death.

—Henry Scott Holland, "I have only slipped away into the next room"

THE CHILD WAS a gift. The grief does not smother the gratitude. And death . . . is not the end. We grieve, but not as those who have no hope. Yet none says that since death is not the end, we should not grieve. Though grief does not smother hope, neither does hope smother grief.

—Nicholas Wolterstorff, quoted in *This Incomplete One*

JOY AND SORROW are inseparable . . . together they come and when one sits alone with you . . . remember that the other is asleep upon your bed.

—Kahlil Gibran

IT IS THE giving part I miss, the feeling of giving to Jesse without expectation of anything in return. And now that's how I experience Jesse in the fullest way, in the giving. By giving, I don't mean to charities. . . . I mean the giving of myself to others in less tangible ways, the sympathetic ear, the small thoughtful remembrance, the acknowledgement of other people's joys and sorrows. That's exactly what I don't want to do. I want to stay inside and be alone. I want to wander the rooms of my house blankly, like a confused spirit trapped between worlds. But I can't find Jesse that way. . . .

To be present in this world, the world without Jesse, that's the hardest thing. But it's the only way to find him.

—Leone, *Jesse*

———

THEN SAID MARTHA unto Jesus, Lord, if thou hadst been here, my brother had not died. But I know, that even now, whatsoever thou wilt ask of God, God will give it thee. Jesus saith unto her, Thy brother shall rise again. Martha saith unto him, I know that he shall rise again in the resurrection at the last day. Jesus said unto her, I am the resurrection and the life: he that believeth in me, though he were dead, yet shall he live: And whosoever liveth and believeth in me shall never die. Believest thou this? She saith unto him, Yea, Lord: I believe that thou art the Christ, the Son of God, which should come unto the world.

—John 11:21-27

———

THE TEST COMES when everything that is dear to us slips away—our home and those we love, our body and its many ways of living, our mind and its caring thoughts—and there is absolutely nothing left to hold on to. It is then that one must have the faith to surrender to a loving Lord, to believe that he will not allow us to fall into a cruel and bottomless canyon, but will bring us to the safe home which he has prepared for us.

—Henri Nouwen, *In Memoriam*

———

MY FOOT HATH held his steps, his way have I kept, and not declined. Neither have I gone back from the commandment of his lips: I have esteemed the words of his mouth more than my necessary food. . . .

Till I die I will not remove mine integrity from me.

—Job 23:11,12; 27:5

———

WE CAN'T PRAY that [God] will make our lives free of problems, this won't happen, and it is probably just as well. We can't ask Him to make us and those we love immune to disease, because He can't do that. We can't ask him to weave a magic spell around us so that bad things will only happen to other people, and never to us. . . . But people who pray for courage, for strength to bear the unbearable, for the grace to remember what they have left instead of what they have lost, very often find their prayers answered. They discover that they have more strength, more courage than they ever knew themselves to have. . . . Their prayers helped them tap the hidden reserves of faith and courage which were not available to them before.

—Harold Kushner, *When Bad Things Happen to Good People*

THE ONLY RELIGIOUS way to think of death is as part and parcel of life; to regard it, with the understanding and with the emotions, as the inviolable condition of life.

—Thomas Mann, quoted in *Philosophy and the Self*

DEATH BE NOT proud, though some have called thee
Mighty and dreadfull, for, thou art not soe,
For, those, whom thou think'st, thou dost overthrow,
Die not, poore death, nor yet canst thou kill mee;
From rest and sleepe, which but thy pictures bee,
Much pleasure, then from thee, much more must flow,
And soonest our best men with thee doe goe,
Rest of their bones, and soules deliverie.
Thou art slave to Fate, Chance, kings, and desperate men,
And dost with poyson, warre, and sicknesse dwell,
And poppie, or charmes can make us sleepe as well,
And better then thy stroake; why swell'st thou then?

One short sleepe past, wee wake eternally,
And death shall be no more, Death, thou shalt die.

—John Donne, "Death Be Not Proud," quoted in The Metaphysical Poets

---

WE ARE SOMETIMES required to trust without understanding. Except this much we can understand: whatever has come upon a person is not random. The Lord has allowed it and will give us grace to bear it and benefit from it for our advancement. And when he is calling us to pass through that which we call afflictions, trials, temptations, and difficulties, did we possess the light of the Spirit, we would consider this the greatest blessing that could be bestowed upon us.

—M. Catherine Thomas, Selected Writings of M. Catherine Thomas

---

THE NEARER I approach the end, the clearer I hear around me the immortal symphonies of the worlds which invite me. It is marvelous yet simple. . . . For half a century I have been writing my thoughts in prose, verse, history, drama, romance, tradition, satire, ode, song—I have tried all; but I feel that I have not said the thousandth part of what is in me. When I go down to the grave I can say, like so many others, "I have finished my day's work," but I cannot say, "I have finished my life's work"; my day's work will begin the next morning. The tomb is not a blind alley. It is a thoroughfare. It closes in the twilight to open in the dawn. My work is only beginning. My work is hardly above its foundation. I would gladly see it mounting and mounting forever. The thirst for the infinite proves infinity.

—Victor Hugo, quoted in The Conservative

NONE OF US knows for certain how long we'll be here. On Steve's better days, even in the last year, he embarked upon projects and elicited promises from his friends at Apple to finish them. Some boat builders in the Netherlands have a gorgeous stainless steel hull ready to be covered with the finishing wood. His three daughters remain unmarried, his two youngest still girls, and he'd wanted to walk them down the aisle as he'd walked me the day of my wedding.

We all—in the end—die in medias res. In the middle of a story. Of many stories.

—Mona Simpson, "A Sister's Eulogy for Steve Jobs"

THERE IS A great directing head of things and people—a supreme being who looks after the destinies of the world. I have faith in a supreme being, and all my thoughts are regarding the life after death—where the soul goes, what form it takes and its relations to those now living.

I am convinced that the body is made up of entities which are intelligent. When one cuts his finger, I believe it is the intelligence of those entities that heals the wound. When one is sick, it is the intelligence of these entities that brings convalescence.

You know that there are living cells in the body so tiny that the microscope cannot show them at all. The entity that gives life and motion to the human body is finer still and lies infinitely beyond the reach of our finest scientific instruments. When the entity deserts the body, the body is like a ship without a rudder—deserted, motionless and dead.

—Thomas Edison, "Edison Says Soul Survives," *The Spokesman Review* online

IF YOU WOULD indeed behold the spirit of death, open your heart wide unto the body of life.

For life and death are one, even as the river and the sea are one.

In the depth of your hopes and desires lies your silent knowledge of the beyond;

And like seeds dreaming beneath the snow your heart dreams of spring.

Trust the dreams, for in them is hidden the gate to eternity.

Your fear of death is but the trembling of the shepherd when he stands before the king whose hand is to be laid upon him in honour.

Is the shepherd not joyful beneath his trembling, that he shall wear the mark of the king?

Yet is he not more mindful of his trembling?

For what is it to die but to stand naked in the wind and to melt into the sun?

And what is to cease breathing, but to free the breath from its restless tides, that it may rise and expand and seek God unencumbered?

Only when you drink from the river of silence shall you indeed sing. And when you have reached the mountain top, then you shall begin to climb.

And when the earth shall claim your limbs, then shall you truly dance.

—Khalil Gibran, *The Prophet*

YOU WHO WEEP, come to this God, for he weeps.
You who suffer, come to him, for he cures.
You who tremble, come to him, for he smiles.
You who pass, come to him, for he remains.

—Victor Hugo, "Written at the Foot of a Crucifix," *Les Contemplations*

I DON'T THINK we need to be afraid of life. Our hearts are very frail, and there are places where the road is very steep and very lonely. But we have a wonderful God. And as Paul puts it, what can separate us from his love? Not death, he says immediately, pushing that aside at once as the most obvious of all impossibilities. No, not death. For I, standing here in the roaring of the Jordan, cold to the heart with its dreadful chill and very conscious of the terrors of its rushing, I can call back to you who, one day in your time, will have to cross it: Be of good cheer, my friend, for I feel the bottom and it is sound.

—Arthur Henry Gossip, quoted in *The Incomplete One*

I AM STANDING upon the seashore. A ship at my side spreads her white sails to the morning breeze and starts for the blue ocean. She is an object of beauty and strength. I stand and watch her until at length she hangs like a speck of white cloud just where the sea and sky come to mingle with each other.

Then someone at my side says, "There, she is gone!"

"Gone where?"

Gone from my sight. That is all. She is just as large in mast and hull and spar as she was when she left my side and she is just as able to bear her load of living freight to her destined port.

Her diminished size is in me, not in her.

And just at the moment when someone at my side says, "There, she is gone!" there are other eyes watching her coming, and other voices ready to take up the glad shout, "Here she comes!"

And that is dying.

—Henry Van Dyke, quoted in *Can I Walk You Home?*

IF THE GOD who revealed life to us, and whose only desire is to bring us to life, loved us so much that he wanted to experience with us the total absurdity of death, then— yes, then there must be hope; then there must be something more than death; then there must be a promise that is not fulfilled in our short existence in this world; then leaving behind the ones you love, the flowers and the trees, the mountains and the oceans, the beauty of art and music, and all the exuberant gifts of life cannot be just the destruction and cruel end of all things; then indeed we have to wait for the third day.

—Henri Nouwen, *A Shared Sorrow*

NO PAIN THAT we suffer, no trial that we experience is wasted. It ministers to our education, to the development of such qualities as patience, faith, fortitude, and humility. All that we suffer and all that we endure, especially when we endure it patiently, builds up our characters, purifies our hearts, expands our souls, and makes us more tender and charitable, more worthy to be called children of God . . . and it is through sorrow and suffering, toil and tribulation, that we gain the education that we come here to acquire and which will make us more like our Father . . . in heaven.

—Orson F. Whitney, quoted in *Faith Precedes the Miracle*

SON, I AM the Lord, who gives strength in the time of tribulation. Come to me when it is not well with thee.

Stand firmly, and be of good courage: comfort will come to thee in its proper season. Wait for me, wait, I will come and cure thee.

Let not therefore thy heart be troubled . . . believe in me, and trust in my mercy. When thou thinkest I am far from thee, I am often nearest to thee. . . . All is not lost, when anything falls out otherwise than thou wouldst have it. Thou must not judge according to thy present feeling.

—Thomas à Kempis, "Come to me when it is not well with thee"

━━━━━━━━━━━
━━━━━━━━━━━

LIFE IS RATHER a state of embryo, a preparation for life; a man is not completely born till he has passed through death.

—Benjamin Franklin, quoted in *A Dictionary of Thoughts*

━━━━━━━━━━━
━━━━━━━━━━━

THOSE WHO ARE near me do not know that you are nearer to me than they are
Those who speak to me do not know that my heart is full with your unspoken words
Those who crowd in my path do not know that I am walking alone with you
They who love me do not know that their love brings you to my heart.

—Rabindranath Tagore, "Those who are near me do not know"

━━━━━━━━━━━
━━━━━━━━━━━

AH MY DEAR angry Lord
Since thou dost love, yet strike;
Cast down, yet help afford;
Sure I will do the like.
I will complain, yet praise;
I will bewail, approve:
And all my sour-sweet days
I will lament, and love.

—George Herbert, "Bitter-Sweet," *The Country Parson*

BRIDGE TO ELYSIUM

ONLY A BRIEF walk over a bridge spanning a river, and you are in Elysium.

If the performance in the Théâtre des Champs-Élysées (the Theater of the Elysian Fields) begins tonight at 8 o'clock, I can still finish my last spoonful of soup at 7:35 while repeating last-minute bedtime instructions to Parker while Claire shoves a crayon and a crumpled parental consent form into my one free hand. Luc, our youngest, a dripping escapee from bathland, races wet and naked through the kitchen, while Dalton, nearly eleven years old, recites Victor Hugo's *"Demain dès l'aube"* in front of our entryway mirror. I whisper to Randall to check his pockets for change to give to the theater ushers and I check my own pockets for tickets, two of them, which I then wave through the air with a flourish. We blow kisses and shut behind us the doors to that whole wonderfully ordinary world.

Crossing from our home on the left bank of the Seine over the Pont de l'Alma to the theater on the right bank, we talk in quick clips, our conversation shedding the world behind us and anticipating the world ahead.

"So Handel really conducted the *Messiah* in English?" Randall asks me, reaching to take my hand. "In Covent Garden? Just months before he died?"

"I'm pretty sure, uh-huh. You put detergent in the dishwasher?"

"Mm-hmm." We lose each other's hands in the crowd as we cross at the light. I catch up:

"You *sure* these are tonight's tickets?" I hold them to my eyes, checking the print under the lamplight.

"Gotta be. Can you walk a teeny bit faster in those heels?"

"Try-ing . . . You *did* turn on the dishwasher, right?"

At 7:50 sharp we pass through the crowded theater lobby and take the stairs two at a time so that by 7:55 we slide into our crimson velvet seats with time enough to gaze up at the art deco ceiling and frescoes. My breathing slows down. My pulse settles. The house lights recede. The surrounding murmurs muffle, then ebb to complete silence. This suspended moment is a time-lapse blossoming, and I sink deep into its heat-filled whorl, lush petals of the sublime unfolding right against my skin.

There was a time when my husband and I made frequent journeys to that Elysian netherworld. Salient among them all is this very evening. On the program was Beethoven's *Ninth Symphony* and the stage was crowded with more than three hundred performers from virtually the entire world. The final chorus of Schiller's text of "Ode to Joy" began musically as it does textually, with a beautiful spark of "Joy! Joy!" igniting a surge that flamed into full-blown musical fireworks:

> *Joy, beautiful spark of the Gods*
> *Daughter of Elysium,*
> *We enter, fire-imbibed*
> *Heavenly, thy sanctuary.*
> *(Schiller 115–119)*

The entire theater rang with full orchestra and choir and with something else that went beyond sound waves, and on the final note, the otherwise urbane Parisian audience shot to its feet, roaring, stomping stilettos in ecstasy. People threw flowers onto the stage and arms and tickets and programs into the air while ovations thundered, flooding the hall like an ocean of joy itself.

During our walk home that night, instead of chirpy conversation we carried a silent, resonant heft held tightly in our hand-in-hand stagger over the Seine. In place of a long, grinning sigh, there was a kind of humming dumbfoundedness rippled with awe and reverence. A sense, even, of urgency and import.

We paused in the shadows between the glow of street lamps lining the bridge. There we stood, speechless on the Pont de l'Alma, the river flowing beneath us, its inky course pulsing with a glinting pelt of silver. Its flow teased that beauty from our grip, and we felt it slipping. *This, too*—the thought came unbidden—*will end.* How many more times, we asked each other, would we be able to stand just like this: together, safe, watching the river glide noiselessly under our feet, the sublime still pearling on our spirits the way sweat beads on the upper lip?

We tiptoed across the darkened threshold of our apartment. All was well: food in fridge, water in pipes, heat in radiators. Beethoven still rang in our ears, peace hung in the air. And despite the fact that no detergent was in the dishwasher, and that it had never been turned on in the first place, everything felt right in the world.

The three younger children were long since in bed. The one in charge, eighteen-year-old Parker, was still working, facing the bluish light of the computer screen, hunched over a psychology class project.

"Freud," he mumbled, acknowledging our parental checking-in.

I gave half a chuckle. "Know what his name means?"

Right palm spread against his brow, Parker propped up his exhausted head.

"Uh, let's see. Boring?"

"*Joy.* Joy boy Sigmund *Freud*! '*Freude*' means joy. You drop the 'eh' at the end."

"Okay. And oxymoron is what *that* means." (At this late hour he was visibly unimpressed with Freud.) "You drop the 'oxy' at the start."

Smiling, I kissed the back of my eldest son's head and whistled Beethoven as I kicked off my heels. Randall loosened his tie. We hung our coats, tossed the tickets, and went to bed in a world that felt part Elysian Field perfection, part garden variety quotidian, but both parts a completion—a whole, overflowing with abundance. And what abundance: All six of us under one roof. All of us together. *All* of us. *Together.* In the moment, that reality felt self-evident, more the standard mental checklist than the miraculous. But as I pulled the blanket over my shoulder, that knowledge returned: *This, too, will end.*

"Ode to Joy," and the following months for which Beethoven seemed the soundtrack, made for a benevolent prefiguring. So heightened was that time, in fact, that I wrote about it to family and friends. Part of our family's 2006 Christmas letter:

> *What stirs me most about this year's journey with its countless goings-out and comings-back, is that every last one of us has actually come back. Dressed in his school's sports warm-ups, Parker lugged himself and his carry-on suitcase through our apartment*

door just a few days ago and, recognizing as never before his safe return from another away game as the marvel it was, I took this man-sized son in my arms and held him there a nice long while. He'd just been gone a couple of days, but we'd missed him more than usual. Why? Because while he was gone, our family had been jarred by the news that a young man, the son of our good friends—a boy with whom our own son had played basketball— had been killed. Only months into his service as a missionary for our church, he'd been dragged under the wheels of a train.

Parker takes trains. Every day of his life he takes them, hopping casually from one Metro line to the other, or loading himself and his teammates onto high-speed commuters heading out of France for international sports competitions.

And now, by some quirk of fate I cannot fathom and will not accept, I have my son. And my friend does not have hers. How one step can change everything.

For months my focus was opened from pesky minutiae to the big picture, tightened, too, from billowing, bellowing distractions to the small. A young man's fatal step had changed me. Or so I thought.

During that year, our last year in Paris, I was reflective, deeply in tune with leavings and losses of every kind. But my friend's loss was only vicarious for me. Soon enough, I was back to the surface of surfacey things.

Our last year in Paris. Sounds like a chick flick, no way befitting the stark reality that lay in store for our family. We would never again know our family as intact—life as whole. We would never again experience the world as continual, the next hour as a given. And we would never again refer to that year as "our last year in Paris." In one split second, it would become The Last Year.

We would bury Parker.

―――――――――

Watching through the chapel window, I tried to follow a single snowflake as it wafted to earth. A makeshift quartet of young men was beaming, eyebrows raised, attempting the prelude, "Joy to the World." I hunched into my heart, trying to disappear into a nautilus of isolation and nausea. There was, even—and sometimes especially—at church, no escape from words that sailed white-hot skewers through my chest. Fewer than five months from implosion, and we were still very much the walking dead. We were, nonetheless, faithfully holding on, all five of us. (*Five of us.* The words felt blasphemous, even when I only thought them. Heaven knows I could not speak them.)

And I could not sing the word *joy*. It seemed a mockery to me. Joy to *this* world? This world whose crust is "soaked with the tears of the suffering"? Where there are trap doors and booby traps, out-of-the-clear-blue-sky terminal diagnoses, crushing train wheels, hidden whirlpools? This perilous, unpredictably violent minefield of a world where, with one step (like the fatal step of my friend's son, like the fatal step of my own son), that which we rely on—the solid, foreseeable—vanishes right out from under our feet? No wonder C. S. Lewis wrote that grief feels so much like fear. There is a decidedly vertiginous sensation that overtakes you when grief is most acute. It is like standing in an elevator on the fifty-eighth floor when, without warning, all the cables snap. That free falling, falling, *falling.*

Falling against an inert sky, the snow outside the window kept its perfunctory rhythm, dispassionate as a player piano scroll. I tried to count flakes through a glaze of tears as the congregation prepared for the Sacrament with the hymn, "He Died, The Great Redeemer Died." The text at any other previous time in my life would have felt exclamatory, hopeful. Now, I couldn't even make it through the first two shocking syllables.

In the air around me, voices swirled listlessly:

"And Israel's Daughters wept around."

At once, I am elsewhere. In front of my mind's eye is my daughter, collapsed on her knees at the side of an ICU gurney. A battered animal bray gurgles out of her throat as her brother's life support is turned off, its swoosh silenced.

"A thousand drops of precious blood."

I see myself shivering, nose to my comatose son's ear, whispering, then kissing the seven ugly gashes on his head. My husband's eyes are unrecognizably stark as he carefully folds a new white tissue and dabs the blood that leaks from his child's swollen eyes.

"Here's love and grief beyond degree."

An ICU nurse—young, maybe six months pregnant—is bracing herself against a corner wall as we emerge from those last moments. Stumbling into the hallway, we droop into the arms of waiting family and friends, then over someone's shoulder I notice this nurse and see she is wearing royal blue scrubs, the same color as the curtains that hung in Parker's bedroom in Paris. I also see she is crying.

"The Lord of glory died for men."

Back in my chapel pew. A sprightly soprano, our chorister, was audible above the congregation's plodding drone, and especially when she came to the word I could not speak: *died.* I winced, then raised my eyes only to see that she was smiling. Broadly. In a jerk that surprised me as much as Randall, I was up and moving. Scooted first past him, then past my questioning children, out of the pew and straight to the door as voices sang, *"But lo! What sudden joys were heard!"*

Out of the chapel. Out of the building. Onto the street. Into the cold. I needed air. I needed answers. How *joy?* After the razor-sharp edge of experience, how would there ever again be something as floppy as joy? The snowflakes caught in my eyelashes and my shoes skidded on ice, but all I felt was hot sorrow surging through me like lava, clearing the landscape of my body. Life, I felt my viscera insisting, would herewith be void of joy. Let the naïve and the unscathed *do* joy. Let them have their jaunty, jocular joy. Their joking, lighter-than-air joy. Their back-slapping, mint-julep-sipping, broadly-smiling joy. But the experienced, the bereaved? We who know better and see the world as it really is: reeling in personal and widespread terror, seething in wickedness, spinning off its axis?

Joy?

No. I could not—would not—bring myself to it.

———

My total inability to acknowledge joy months after Parker's death made it hard for me to understand why, in the earliest and most chaotic days of grief, I had still felt a profound security—a hint of joy—alongside the searing, crippling agony. I felt this at the funeral, for instance. Several of Parker's friends had traveled from their different countries of origin to the site of his services. At one point during the viewing, I noticed that these friends were clustered in a corner. They were draped on each other, holding each other up, weeping, shoulders shaking.

I broke from the reception line and, in one spontaneous gesture, took them into a circle where, with our arms around one another's shoulders, we bowed our heads. Then I prayed. I prayed out loud that our Father in Heaven and their friend Parker would calm and guide each of them, and that God's presence would surround them and hold them up. Just like our circle. I cannot recall in detail all that poured out of me along with my tears, but when I ended—and this I do recall in every detail—I looked them each in the eye and said, "No fear. *No fear.*"

A strange thing to say. Better on a skateboarder's T-shirt than on the lips of a grief-stricken mother. But in that moment, I clearly saw the risk of them choking with fear, of them panicking at the prospect of living in a frightening world where random things like Parker's death happen. I saw how any one of them could easily curl up in bitterness or despair and end up like Freud himself, who grumbled, "What good to us is a long life, if it is difficult and barren of joys, and if it is so full of misery that we can only welcome death as a deliverer?" So I repeated to them (and to myself) the same message Parker's spirit and certainly other encircling spirits had been repeating to me from the first minutes of terror: "No fear. *No fear.*"

Now, some months later, as snow continued to bury the world out there, I was suffocating under the weight of heartache so anvil-heavy it was crushing any resolve I had to be fearless, to allow for joy, to engage in life. I was learning that it's one thing to feel fearlessness and resolve when held up, arm around shoulder, in a huddle of loving friends or when encircled by angelic attendants. It's quite another thing to grope after resolve when you are isolated and you only have one place to turn: the icy tiles of your kitchen floor, where you crawl on your hands and knees in the middle of many a blue-black winter predawn.

Those unsympathetic kitchen tiles. The farthest point from where everyone else might be sleeping, where I could stumble and close myself off. I would wrestle, in chilly nighttime isolation, with God and with all those angels who I felt had abandoned me. Kneeling in my pajamas, I sometimes railed. *This is enough,* I heard myself hiss through gritted teeth. *We cannot do this much longer. Look at these children, so confused, so alone. Look at my husband, down thirty-five pounds, gaunt, broken.* And in case heaven could not hear me or doubted my cause, I sometimes (always) pounded my fists. Pummeled those impassive tiles.

Angels heard me. Or better, I heard them. When my knees and fists grew sore, I took the family scriptures from the kitchen counter, sat cross-legged, and began searching in the darkness with my pen light for answers in those pages. The angels I found there visited the appallingly destitute in the loneliest crevices of isolation, desperation, and darkness. When they visited, they often chanted the same salutation: "Fear not." As I imagine it, they sang in muted harmonies, their warm light rippling through frozen hearts. With that simple two-syllable reassurance, things would start vibrating. Sheep would stop chewing their cud. Cattle would stop lowing. Folks would be sore amazed. A cold kitchen floor would become a heat-filled sanctuary.

Why, of all the things angels could choose to say—of all the things Parker could say to his grieving mother—why these two words, "Fear not"? I learned, over weeks and months of intense spiritual tutorial, that the reasons go far beyond vague encouragement. Heavenly emissaries are more than cheerleaders who urge with, "C'mon guys, you can do it." And their words go far beyond mere placation, "There, there. We come in peace. Don't worry. Be happy."

"Fear not" is a divine injunction straight from God. God Himself, whose sufferings outstrip all the accumulated sufferings of the infinitude of creation, greets us with those words. "Fear not," he says to Abram, Isaac, Jacob, Joshua, Daniel, Joseph, Zacharias, Simon, and scores of others. Angels—messengers from God—are instructed, before anything else, to drive out fear in this trembling, suffering, and from any mortal perspective, justifiably frightened world. "Fear not," whole house of Israel. "Fear not," all humankind. More than a pep talk, more than a pat on the head, "fear not" is a warning directed *at* fear—an exorcism, even. "Fear not" is God's steely, conquering command: "Fear, be not! Fear, be gone!"

To exorcise fear, God floods the darkness of this world with His blazing presence. And wherever His presence is, not only can fear not remain, but confidence, peace, contentment, wholeness, strength, and light—all cousins of joy—can flourish. Does the pain of loss disappear? No. Does my yearning for my son cease? No. Not in the least. But what does happen is that alongside—or better, from within—the pain and yearning comes a sense of being lovingly upheld by God. The terrifying free-fall of fear ends, just in time, in His hands. Then, eyes squeezed tightly shut in preparation for impact, we realize with a gasp that those hands have been only a few inches ahead of our whole, dizzying descent. Indeed, those hands have descended below all things. They bear the marks to prove it. And so, still splayed flat and panting, we slowly open our view to this pellucid truth: Yes, we really can trust God with our lives.

And what is joy for me now, some years from my zero point? It is still, for me, a lurching, to-and-fro thing. This, because as soon as joy softens my heart, I am most sharply aware of my son's absence. Surprised by joy in that Wordsworthian sense, I find myself mourning anew, straining my eyes through the unfurling shadowiness of years ahead where, over and over again, I see only the echoing presence of his absence. And it is immense.

For that immense absence, the most powerful antidote I have experienced is seeking God's increased presence; for in the Father's presence, I find both the "peace that passeth all understanding" as well as *my son's* presence. Both that Father and this son have been clearly manifested to me by ever-multiplying proofs in ever-multiplying instances where prayers have been answered in precise detail. Guidance in its jot-and-tittle specificity has been given. Strength—emotional, mental, and physical—has come from hidden wells I never could have imagined existed. As a result, I can say, as does Job, that, "now mine eye seeth thee." Although loss was initially blinding—for so very long I could see nothing but loss—with experiences that solidified my trust in God, the same loss cleared my ability to perceive sacred subtleties. Like a blind person's heightened senses of hearing and touch, I was capable of discerning subtle spiritual messages. The blinding effect of loss helped me see different dimensions, bigger realities. "*I morti verze i oci ai vivi*," the ancient Romans recited as part of their burial rites:

"The dead open the eyes of the living."

With newly-opened eyes, the living are able to see that "joy is not the absence of pain. Joy is the presence of God. Tragedy can increase our joy and increase our faith." This verity sheds new light on an often-quoted passage of scripture, which reads, "Then shall thy confidence wax strong in the presence of God." (see Doctrine and Covenants 121:45) With a simple reslanting in emphasis and a slight reordering of words, the verse holds a rather different meaning: "Then shall thy confidence *in the presence of God* wax strong." This sort of muscular confidence in the fact that God is present—and not passively, but passionately and personally—in our lives, banishes fear, limits pain, and enlarges our capacity to receive and radiate joy.

My confidence in God grew when I stockpiled spiritual experiences that evidenced the continued presence of my son. They were serial, verifiable, some too sacred to share, some shared with others. In fact, such experiences continue to this day. Some came as outright gifts. Others, through long and careful study and willingness to risk sharing myself and my son's story with people who would listen. Every time I did, I learned that something within me ignited and expanded, telling me what is true: *Parker lives.* God was gently and patiently drawing me toward Him and toward greater confidence in His presence, His own *and* my son's.

This is presence bigger than absence. This is the nature of intimate knowing, the fount of fearlessness. This is the Atonement at work. This is life after death. This is the wellspring of my evolving joy.

An ancient writer named Alma typifies the most highly evolved sort of joy: "There could be nothing so exquisite and so bitter as were my pains," he writes. "Yet . . . on the other hand, there can be nothing so exquisite and sweet as was my joy." These words point to a joy that is not unfettered, sparkling joie de vivre, that carbonated giddiness or the caffeine-jolt of temporal amusements or artificial stimuli. Deep joy, in fact, has little if anything to do with bubbles that dance to the surface. Joy, like that of which wise minds write and of the sort I sense now, is profound reverence mixed with sweeping gratitude. It is, for me, synonymous with worship. It has height, depth, timbre, and texture unlike anything I knew before I knew sorrow of similar proportions. This joy is accompanied not by laughter, but often by tears, although genuine joy is not merely emotion. One could say that genuine joy eclipses and goes beyond—below and above—mere emotion, connecting with a timeless, cosmic, teeming chorus of creation that is constantly worshipping God.

How appropriate, then, that Beethoven's "Ode to Joy" reaches its highest note, its musical summit, when the lyric reaches its highest philosophical truth: "Above the starry canopy / A loving Father must dwell." It is God's presence that stimulates divine joy; it is our faith in His presence that sustains such joy.

====

The last year was not my last time in Paris. On visits there, I have stopped with my husband on the Pont de l'Alma—at about the ninth lamppost, which marks mid-bridge. There, the two of us mid-lifers scan the panorama from the left bank and then to the right, trying to take in the expanse around us, the magnificence of where we stand in the moment. There has been so much. There will be much more. Standing in what I call the "present tension," everything seems to melt into one eternal round. My husband checks his watch. We pick up our speed and make it to the Théâtre des Champs-Élysées in time to take the stairs thoughtfully, one-by-one, to our seats. There, I sink in, look up, and wait for . . . for whatever comes next.

As house lights fade, my mind illumines. I am newly aware of where I am sitting: the Elysian Fields. Greek mythology's underworld. Here, I recall, Hades, in a cruel sleight-of-hand, kidnapped and kept Demeter's daughter Persephone, and throughout a full year, the grief-tormented mother searched wildly for her child. In symbiotic mourning, all nature shut down. Then came the exhilarating moment of the mother-child reunion where all creation, like the mother, exulted in joy. Daughter and mother, like the earth, returned instantaneously to life. Of all rites in ancient Greece, those of the cult of Demeter, annual rituals called the Mysteries, are considered the most important and sacred. They mark the mother's descent in loss and grief, her search, and her eventual ascent into a new existence. Historians claim the Greeks concluded these initiatory rites with tremendous, music-filled, joy-drenched festivities.

One foot in imagined Elysium and the other leaving its Parisian counterpart, I cross over the Seine toward the left bank with my husband. We climb the stairs to the apartment (which now belongs to another family of six; their oldest son sleeps behind the same royal blue curtain as did ours), and I stand wordlessly outside the building's entryway that his full-grown body filled with squared shoulders, burgeoning presence. Through that all, I hear the wise voice of another Alma—this time it is the father of the younger, who wrote earlier—advising, "This life is the time to prepare to meet God." It seems both of the Almas and the Pont de l'Alma express that one leveling truth: It's only a bridge span over a river. Soon enough, you will be in Elysium.

The sounds of this city recede so that I think I hear something else. A faint descant, warm but lofty, comes to my heart's listening ear. It is angels. "Fear not."

I think I know those lyrics.

Walking through the calm of late evening, I pause below my son's window, waiting for the next word. It is coming. Slowly.

"Joy."

I know that voice. It has deepened and taken on a burnish since the days it came from behind that royal blue curtain.

"Joy," he repeats, as if inviting harmony.

"To the world."

With my son, I might just be able to hum along.

APPENDIX 1

SUGGESTIONS FOR MOURNING WITH AND COMFORTING OTHERS

It's hard to know what to do or say to someone who has lost a loved one, hard to know how to help. This list from several different sources should help you understand what really helps but also what really hurts.

TO DO AND SAY

- "I love you."
- "You are not alone. I am with you."
- "I remember when . . ." and not fearing to saying the deceased's name and talk about him or her.
- Come quietly, without expectations.
- Stay as long as you sense you are welcome.
- Do not ask if you can help. Just help.
- Help in practical ways.
- If you feel shocked, awkward, without words, devastated, nervous . . . say so.
- Listen first. No speeches needed.
- Come back. And back again. Bring food, help, and quiet wisdom.
- Share some special music.
- A gentle, communicative touch.

- An hour or more of your time, just listening.
- Regular e-mails or texts, short but reassuring.
- Warm food in your best dishes. You can also simply wash the dishes piling in the sink.
- Remember the bereaved around holidays, birthdays, and the anniversary of the death (dates which can be especially painful).
- Suggest establishing an annual marking of the deceased's birth and/or death date.
- Join in a service project done in the deceased's memory.
- Send a handwritten card.
- Send any photos you have of the deceased.
- Plant trees or flowers in the deceased's memory.
- Arrange memorial services at school, work, church, clubs, etc.
- Establish a scholarship or fund in the deceased's honor.
- Suggest others who are similarly bereaved with whom the survivors might take up contact.
- Compose music or write poetry or create any other artistic rendition in memory of the deceased.
- Care for the physical needs of the home, car, yard, or laundry.
- Care for other family members, especially children, in the first several weeks and as long as it takes.
- Give a special notebook for the bereaved to record thoughts, scriptures, dreams, and impressions.
- Offer literature that builds strength and courage.
- Inspirational addresses through Internet or other sources.
- Avoid rowdiness or irreverence in the bereaved's presence.
- Suggest going on a walk in nature together.
- And all of the above *for a much longer duration of time* that you have previously thought, remember: grief always outlasts conventional comfort.

NOT TO DO OR SAY

Please, don't ask me if I'm over it yet.
I'll never be over it.
Please, don't tell me she's in a better place.
She isn't with me.
Please, don't say at least she isn't suffering.
I haven't come to terms with why she had to suffer at all.
Please, don't tell me you know how I feel
Unless you have lost a child.
Please, don't ask me if I feel better.
Bereavement isn't a condition that clears up.
Please, don't tell me at least you had her for so many years.
What year would you choose for your child to die?
Please, don't tell me God never gives us more than we can bear.
Please, just tell me you are sorry.
Please, just say you remember my child, if you do.
Please, just let me talk about my child.
Please, mention my child's name.
Please, just let me cry.

—Rita Moran "Please, don't ask me if I'm over it yet"

- "I understand just how you feel."
- "Something a lot worse than that happened to me."
- "He lived a long life. He was ready to go."
- "Aren't you over the death of your loved one yet?"
- "God took him."
- "God needed (or wanted) her."
- "God gave you this trial to make you stronger."
- "It's God's will."
- "God doesn't give us more than we can bear."
- "If you have enough faith, she will get well."
- "He is much better off in heaven. He is happier there."
- "Because your child took his own life, you will never be together in the eternities."
- "There is a reason for everything."

- "Count your blessings."
- "Only the good die young."
- "Your loved one is freed from this terrible world."
- "You have an angel in heaven."
- "She has only been transferred to a new mission."
- "Keep the faith."
- "Put it behind you and get on with your life."
- "Time will heal everything."
- "Be strong, keep your chin up."
- "Get over it, move on."
- "There are worse things that could have happened."
- "Let me get you out of this funk."
- "Don't let your children see you being weak."
- "Don't wallow in self-pity."
- "Don't cry, you'll see him again."
- "Don't cry, you make things worse."
- "Don't cry, you'll hold your deceased back from progressing."

The following list of suggestions is taken from a book that, though written as a children's fable, is intended for all ages. I have found its wisdom sound and universal.

- Grief is a process you go through as you adjust to the loss of anything or anyone important in your life.
- The loss of a job, divorce, a move, death of someone you love, or a change in health status are just a few of the situations that can cause grief.
- Grief is both physically and emotionally exhausting. It is irrational and unpredictable and can shake your very foundation.
- The amount of "work" your grief requires will depend on your life experiences, the type of loss, and whatever else you have on your plate at the time.
- A sudden, unexpected loss is usually more traumatic, more disruptive, and requires more time to adjust to.
- If your loss occurred through violence, expect that all the normal grief reactions will be exaggerated.
- You may lose trust in your own ability to make decisions and/or trust others.
- Assumptions about fairness, life order, and religious beliefs are often challenged.
- Smells can bring back memories of a loss and a fresh wave of grief.
- Seasons, with their colors and climate, can also take you back to that moment in time when your world stood still.
- You may sense you have no control in your life.
- Being at work may provide relief from your grief, but as soon as you get in the car and start driving home you may find your grief come flooding back.
- You may find that you are incapable of functioning in the work environment for a short while.
- Because grief is distracting it also means you are more accident prone.
- The object of grieving is not to get over the loss or recover from the loss but to get through the loss.
- Over the years you will look back and discover that this grief keeps teaching you new things about life. Your understanding of life will just keep going deeper.

—Pat Schweibert and Chuck DeKLyen, *Tear Soup*

APPENDIX 2

For more information about Melissa Dalton-Bradford and other stories related to *On Loss and Living Onward*, please visit the book's facebook page at https://www.facebook.com/lossandlivingonward.

SUGGESTED READING LIST

90 Minutes in Heaven by Don Piper and Cecil Murphey

After My Son's Suicide by Darla Isackson

After the Death of a Child: Living with Loss Through the Years by Ann K. Finkbeiner

All These Things Shall Give Thee Experience by Neal A. Maxwell

The Art of Being a Healing Presence by James E. Miller and Susan C. Cutshall

The Bereaved Parent by Harriet Sarnoff Schiff

Bereavement: Studies of Grief in Adult Life by Colin Murrary Parkes

Beyond Endurance: When a Child Dies by Ronald J. Knapp

Beyond Tears: Living After Losing a Child by Ellen Mitchell

The Birth That We Call Death by Paul H. Dunn

Blue Nights by Joan Didion

The Broken Heart by Bruce C. Hafen

A Broken Heart Still Beats: After Your Child Dies by Anne McCracken and Mary Semel.

Comfort: A Journey Through Grief by Ann Hood

Continuing Bonds: New Understandings of Grief by Dennis Klass, Phyllis R. Silverman, and Steven L. Nickman

Dance With Them by Kathryn Lynard Soper

An Exact Replica of a Figment of my Imagination by Elizabeth McCracken

The Fall of Freddie the Leaf: A Story of Life for All Ages by Leo Buscaglia

First You Die by Marie Levine

For They Shall Be Comforted by Alma B. Burton and Clea M. Burton

For They Shall Be Comforted by Camille Call Whiting

The Gateway We Call Death by Russell M. Nelson

Glimpses Beyond Death's Door by Brent L. Top and Wendy C. Top

Glimpses of Heaven: True Stories of Hope & Peace at the End of Life's Journey by Trudy Harris

Global Mom by Melissa Dalton-Bradford

The God Who Weeps by Terryl Givens and Fiona Givens

A Grace Disguised by Gerald Sittser

A Grief Observed by C. S. Lewis

A Grief Un-Veiled: One Father's Journey Through the Death of a Child by Gregory Floyd

The Grieving Garden: Living With the Death of a Child by Suzanne Redfern and Susan K. Gilbert

Grieving: The Pain and the Promise by Deanna Edwards

The Heart of Grief: Death and the Search for Lasting Love by Thomas Attig

Here If You Need Me by Kate Braestrup

Holding On To Hope by Nancy Guthrie

How to Survive the Loss of a Child by Catherine M. Sanders

How We Grieve: Relearning the World by Thomas Attig

Jesus Wept by Joyce Ashton and Dennis Ashton

Joy Cometh in the Morning by Fran C. Hafen

Kayak Morning: Reflections on Love, Grief, and Small Boats by Roger Rosenblatt

Lament For a Son by Nicholas Wolterstorff

Life After the Death of My Son by Dennis L. Apple

The Life Beyond by Robert L. Millet and Joseph Fielding McConkie

Life Lessons by David Kessler and Elisabeth Kübler-Ross

The Long Goodbye by Meghan O'Rourke

Making Toast by Roger Rosenblatt

Man's Search for Meaning by Viktor E. Frankl

Meaning Reconstruction & the Experience of Loss by Robert A. Neimeyer

Not My Will, but Thine by Neal A. Maxwell

Nothing Was the Same by Kay Redfield Jamison

On Grief and Grieving by Elisabeth Kübler-Ross and David Kessler

On Life After Death by Elisabeth Kübler-Ross

The Other Side of Sadness by George A. Bonanno

Paula by Isabel Allende

Proof of Heaven by Eben Alexander

Refuge: An Unnatural History of Family and Place by Terry Tempest Williams

A Severe Mercy by Sheldon Vanauken

Spirit World Manifestations by Joseph Heinerman

Stories From the Edge by Greg Garrett

Tear Soup by Pat Schwiebert and Chuck DeKlyen

The Truth About Grief by Ruth Davis Konigsberg

The Tunnel and the Light: Essential Insights on Living and Dying by Elisabeth
    Kübler-Ross

They Saw Beyond Death by Arvin S. Gibson

This Incomplete One by Michael D. Bush

Turn My Mourning Into Dancing by Henri Nouwen

Visits From Beyond the Veil by Marlene Bateman Sullivan

What Forever Means After the Death of a Child by Kay Talbot

When a Bough Breaks by Judith R. Bernsetin

When Bad Things Happen to Good People by Harold S. Kushner

Working It Through by Elisabeth Kübler-Ross

The Worst Loss: How Families Heal from the Death of a Child by Barbara D. Rosof

The Wounded Healer by Henri J. M. Nouwen

Written in Bones by Robert Bahn

The Year of Magical Thinking by Joan Didion

ACKNOWLEDGEMENTS

BORN TO DIE, all of us are born to grieve. And what can we possibly do with all of this grief? In the chorus of voices gathered in these pages, I hope you have found the whisperings of hope that from all this grief new life can in fact be regenerated; that a whole community can be forged from cinders; and that our losses, more than our gains, are what link us as humans. I feel a galvanized interconnectedness with the many who helped my family live onward after the loss of our son. Many of those same people gave their talents, wisdom, and support so that I could compile and complete this volume. I'm humbled every time I think of their influence, and I want to thank some of them openly here.

Never will I find the words to sufficiently convey my love for my husband, Randall. He has been my constant, my oxygen, my part. Together, we have wept until we were hoarse, but we have also re-learned how to laugh until our eyes dripped tears. In both states—crushed by sorrow or filled with joy—we have held together and held one another upright. Randall, better than anyone alive, knew how painful but imperative the writing of this book has been, so he insisted I keep at it by buying me my swivel chair, my new laptop and gadgets, and by managing our family while I headed off on book tours and lecture series.

Randall's loving example has been mirrored by our three magnificent living children, Claire, Dalton, and Luc, without whose sweetness and strength I never would have survived our loss, lived onward with purpose, or written about it all. It is a holy privilege to be their mother. I praise them each for transforming pain into deeper faith, brighter joy, and broader compassion. I also thank my good parents, David and Donna Dalton; my brother, Aaron, whose exacting mind has sieved through my writing and made it finer; and my sisters Alison and Hilary, who continue to teach me about other losses that elude the printed page.

My friends are indispensible. I did not know just how indispensible, however, until I was isolated in a new geography and paralyzed by acute, early grief. Our email exchanges across thousands of miles were like lifelines, and contain, I'm convinced, some of the wisest counsel and most loving prose in print. Sharlee Mullins Glenn has been a brilliant ray of hope shining through the years and through these pages, has coaxed me out of my cramped self-critic's corner, either pointing me toward or literally escorting me to publishers and editors, and has offered encouragement as well as editorial service as a pure act of love. Jacque Adcock White has been a powerhouse of counsel and support, and has been generous with her many gifts. Michelle R. Lehnardt, multi-talented friend, has accompanied me from my very first blog post to my first video trailer (which she filmed) for my first book, and to the most recent trailer for this book, shot with her signature sensitivity and artistry. She also orchestrated a grief roundtable and other speaking engagements centered on loss and its aftermath. Maja Busche Wensel has been a tower of strength and a source for understanding other forms of grief. Bonnie Jean Beesley has been an engine of practical unflappability, the embodiment of wise discretion, and a source of spiritual authenticity. Kristiina Harrison Sorensen has offered solid editorial feedback and the kind of soul-warming compassion you could sink into all the way up to your chin. Kimberly Clarke Carlile, valued friend, has taught me life-altering lessons while also championing my writing as if it were her own. Diane Neff Schwartz has been a vital sounding board and sharer in sorrow and fortitude. Vesna S. Higham, who for a full year called me in Munich every Thursday morning at 5:00 a.m. Saskatchewan time, modeled the kind of sacrifice and patience inspired co-mourning requires. My Singapore sisters from backgrounds as diverse and energy as palpable as that unique city-state enveloped me in their care and gave me daily energy to complete this project. And Lauren Price Roux, my mighty Swiss sister, has proven to me that differences are the complementary surfaces upon which the spark of soulmate-hood can be struck. As my writings have approached print, she has carried my bags, lifted my morale, challenged my acquiescence, and loved all of my beloveds.

To Neylan McBaine I am deeply indebted for interviewing me for the Mormon

Women Project and for encouraging my speaking engagements on topics addressed in this book. Aaron Hubbard ("Mr. H.") assumed a central role in our family immediately after we lost Parker, and that centrality has remained, blessing us all. Daniel Peers-Hoegen, from "#8", has made us, and his friend Parker very proud. Susan Tiberghien has been a sage and generous mentor from the first time I met her at the wonderful Geneva Writer's Group, which she established and leads with her husband, Pierre-Yves. Laura Welch facilitated my Harvard lectures, for which I am grateful. To the many who attended those lectures and others on the content of this volume—from Singapore to Paris to Munich to Geneva to New England and the Rockies of the US—I have been awed, instructed, and enriched by their input. There is loss everywhere we turn, it seems, but survivors are proof that where loss is there also is life—pockmarked and potholed, imperfect and lurching, but beautiful and dense with meaning, and worth our limping continuance.

A wagon train of bereaved friends and family members has gathered annually for the Parker Fairbourne Bradford July Hike and Charity event. We thank all of them past, present, and future, especially the families of John and Renée Hall, Dean and Lisa Garlick, Jeff and Cheri Earl, Bruce and Patsy Brereton, and Randy and Julie Reneer, all of whom carry their own stories of loss. Much admiration and gratitude go to fellow-hiker Ellen Knell specifically, whose beautiful "Letters to Erica" feature among the quotes in this collection. I also thank Mark and Julie Magleby for their wise and insightful correspondence. Other bereaved mothers have tutored me: Andrea Rediske, Tammy Barker Sandstrom, Courtney Cope, Lana Kemp Smith, Leisa Firth, and Emi Dalton Edgley. May this book reflect something of all these stories of grief, and honor these survivors' ongoing relationships and fortitude in spite of heartbreak.

A team of editors has surmounted another terrain at least as demanding as our annual Rockies hike: the mountain range of bibliographic source-checking an anthology like this requires. The earliest drafts were organized and sanitized by Michele Preisendorf, Sharlee Glenn, and Jessie Christensen. Angela S. Hallstrom offered editing insights for "Bridge to Elysium." Ashley Isaacson Woolley applied her keen mind and pure heart to do the major editing of all the essays but "Tale of Two Parkers." I will always consider Ashley's one-year sojourn in Geneva a windfall for me personally and a meant-to-be for this volume.

I wish to thank the crew at Familius, beginning with Aimee Hancock, who sought legal permissions for my hundreds of pages of quotes, including the dozens that, sadly, could not make it to print here. Maggie Jensen Wickes kept her sweetness and good humor while working long, tedious hours with microscope and tweezers, editing the whole final manuscript. David Miles created an exquisite cover and handsome layout. And Christopher Robbins, CEO, applied his vision, level-headedness and acquaintance with grief to shepherd this volume along in a timely and pleasant manner.

And now to my literary (if not literal) community of grief experts. I humbly thank authors Nicholas Wolterstorff, William Sloane Coffin, Henry Nouwen, Thomas Merton, Joan Didion, Roger Rosenblatt, Kate Braestrup, Ann Morrow Lindbergh, Gerald Sittser, C. S. Lewis, Samuel Clemens, William Wordsworth, Henry Longfellow, Alfred Tennyson, W. H. Auden, Emily Dickinson, Victor Hugo, Shakespeare, Aeschylus, the writer(s) of the Psalms, and above all, the writer(s) of the Book of Job. Their writings buoyed me up when I was so alone in those first bleak "monastery" months of early-onset grief. Their truths have rung in my heart and head ever since.

In contrast to that last name-specific list of people who helped with well-placed words, I must also recognize the nameless many who tried, fumbled, recovered, and then usually apologized for never finding the right words to help us. Their sincere speechlessness touches me still. Parisian taxi drivers. Egyptian tour guides. Indonesian massage therapists. Malaysian moving teams. Utahn dry cleaners. Idahoan ICU nurses and life flight personnel. Pennsylvanian elementary school teachers. New York City policemen. German dental hygienists. French music instructors. Swiss door-to-door sales people. Singaporean Sunday School children. Westerners. Easterners. Strangers. Intimates. Every last one rendered wordless by the sighed story of one young man's death.

To him, my Parker, lastly, I acknowledge my eternal debt and continued commitment to live a life worthy of his loving last act and ultimate sacrifice.

March, 2014

Prangins, Switzerland

BIBLIOGRAPHY

Aeschylus. "People & Events: RFK and Tragedy." pbs.org. Last modified July 1, 2004, pbs.org. http://www.pbs.org/wgbh/amex/rfk/peopleevents/e_grief.html.

à Kempis, Thomas. "Come to me when it is not well with thee." *Consolatio*. Last modified January 13, 2006. http://www.consolatio.com/2006/01/come_to_me_when.html.

Allingham, William. *The Wadsworth Anthology of Poetry*. Edited by Jay Parini. Boston: Thompson Wadsworth, 2006.

Andersen, Hans Christian. *The Little Mermaid*. Denmark: C. A. Reitzel, 1837.

Apple, Dennis L. *Life After the Death of My Son: What I'm Learning*. Kansas City, MO: Beacon Hill Press, 2008.

Ashton, Joyce and Dennis. *Jesus Wept: Understanding and Enduring Loss*. Springville, UT: Cedar Fort, 2001.

Attig, Thomas. *The Heart of Grief: Death and the Search for Lasting Love*. New York City: Oxford University Press, 2000.

———. *How We Grieve: Relearning the World*. New York City: Oxford University Press, 1996.

Augustine, "Saint Augustine: I wondered that other men should live when he was dead." *Consolatio*. Last modified January 31, 2005. http://www.consolatio.com/2005/01/saint_augustine.html.

———. "Augustine of Hippo: The dead are invisible." *Consolatio*. Last modified April 24, 2005, http://www.consolatio.com/2005/04/the_dead_are_in.html.

Baker, Mary L. "Master the Tempest is Raging," *Hymns of the Church of Jesus Christ of Latter-day Saints*, 105. Salt Lake City, UT: The Church of Jesus Christ of Latter-day Saints, 1985.

Barnes, Julian. "Pure Story." *Flaubert's Parrot*. New York City: Vintage Books, 1984.

Baudelaire, Charles. "Baudelaire: The dark gulf where my heart has fallen." *Consolatio*. Last modified October 8, 2007. http://www.consolatio.com/2007/10/baudelaire.html.

Bernstein, Judith R. *When the Bough Breaks: Forever After the Death of a Son or*

Daughter. Kansas City, MO: Andrews McMeel Publishing, LLC, 1998.

Berry, William. *The Art of the Commonplace: The Agrarian Essays.* Berkeley, CA: Counterpoint. 2002.

Blake, William. *The Poetical Works of William Blake.* Edited by Edwin J. Ellis, London: Chatto & Willis, 1906.

Bohn, Henry George. *A Dictionary of Quotations from the English Poets.* London: George Bell and Sons, 1881.

Bonanno, George A. "Grief and Bereavement During the Holidays: What Can Science Tell Us." Psychology Today. December 9, 2009. http://www.psychology-today.com/blog/thriving-in-the-face-trauma/200912/grief-and-bereavement-during-the-holidays-what-can-science-t

———. *The Other Side of Sadness: What the New Science of Bereavement Tells Us About Life After Loss.* Philadelphia, PA: Basic Books, 2009.

Booty, John E., ed. *John Donne: Selections from Divine Poems, Sermons, Devotions, and Prayers.* Mahwah, NJ: Paulist Press, 1990.

Boswell, James. *The Life of Samuel Johnson, LL. D.* New York City: E. P. Dutton and Co, 1913.

Bowden, Paul. *Telling It Like It Is: A Book of Quotations.* Smashwords, April 15, 2011. Google ebook.

Braestrup, Kate. *Here If You Need Me: A True Story.* New York City: Little, Brown and Company, 2007.

Brickey, Wayne E. *Making Sense of Suffering.* Salt Lake City, UT: Deseret Book, 2001.

Browning, Elizabeth Barrett. *The Poetical Works of Elizabeth Barrett Browning.* Vol. 3. London: Smith, Elder, and Co., 1890.

Brownley, Margaret. *Grieving God's Way.* Enumclaw, WA: WinePress Publishing, 2004.

Brundtland, Gro Harlem. *Dramatiske År.* Norway: Gyldendal Norsk Foldag ASA, 1998.

Byron, Lord George Gordon and Thomas Moore. "The Tear." *The Poetical Works of Lord Byron.* Philadelphia, PA: William T. Amies, 1878.

Bush, Michael D., ed. *This Incomplete One: Words Occasioned by the Death of a Young Person.* Grand Rapids, MI: Eerdmans, 2006.

Cameron, Julia. *Blessings: Prayers and Declarations for a Heartful Life.* New York City: Putnam, 1998.

Card, Orson Scott. "When joy, grief share the same day." The Village. Last modified August 28, 2008. http://www.nauvoo.com/mormontimes/columns/2008-08-28.html.

Carter, Robert Ayres. *I'll Go No More A-Roving: More Memories of a Writer's Life: 1976–1983.* Bloomington, IN: AuthorHouse, 2011.

Cecil, David, and Allen Tate. *Modern Verse in English.* Great Britain: Eyre and Spottiswood, 1958.

Clapton, Eric. *Clapton: The Autobiography*. New York City: Broadway Books, 2007.

Coffin, William Sloane. *The Collected Sermons of William Sloane Coffin: The River-side Years*. Vol 2. London: Westminster John Knox Press, 2008

Darwin, Charles. *The Life and Letters of Charles Darwin: Including an Autobi-ographical Chapter*. Edited by Francis Darwin. New York City: Appleton and Co., 1896.

———. *The Expression of the Emotions in Man and Animals*. United Kingdom: John Murray, 1872.

Davis, Norma S. *A Song of Joys: The Biography of Mahonri Mackintosh Young—Sculptor, Painter, Etcher*. Provo, UT: M. Seth, and Maurine D. Horne Center for the Study of Art, 1999.

Dayton, Tian. *Emotional Sobriety: From Relationship Trauma to Resilience and Balance*. Deerfield Beach, FL: Health Communications, 2007.

Desbordes-Valmore, Marceline. "The Leafless Garland." Last modified January 5, 2005. *Consolatio*. http://www.consolatio.com/2005/01/the_leafless_ga.html.

de Lamartine, Alphonse. Goodreads.com. Accessed November 15, 2013. https://www.goodreads.com/quotes/41585-grief-and-sadness-knits-two-hearts-in-closer-bonds-that

de Saint-Exupery, Antoine. *Le Petit Prince (The Little Prince)*. Hertfordshire, UK: Wordsworth Editions Limited, 1995.

de Todi, Jacopone. "And It Made Me Silent." *Consolatio*. Last modified January 25, 2005. http://www.consolatio.com/2005/01/and_it_made_me_.html.

de Unamuno, Miguel. *Tragic Sense of Life*. Hamburg, Germany: Tredition Classics. 2012.

Dickens, Charles. *Great Expectations*. United Kingdom: Chapman & Hall, 1861.

Dickinson, Emily. *The Poems of Emily Dickinson: Including Variant Readings Criti-cally Compared with All Known Manuscripts*. Cambridge, MA: Harvard Univer-sity Press, 1998.

———. *The Poems of Emily Dickinson*. Edited by Ralph William Franklin. Cam-bridge, MA: First Harvard University Press, 2005.

Didion, Joan. *Blue Nights*. New York City: Alfred A. Knopf, 2001.

———. *The Year of Magical Thinking*. New York City: Alfred A. Knopf, 2005.

———. "When everything changes." *New York Magazine*, October 2, 2005.

Dumas, Alexander. *The Count of Monte Cristo*. Berkeley, CA: Mundus Publishing. 1988.

Edel, Leon (ed.). *Henry James: Selected Letters*. Cambridge, MA: Harvard Univer-sity Press. 1987.

Edison, Thomas. "Edison Says Soul Survives." *The Spokesman Review*. August 11, 1923. http://news.google.com/newspapers?nid=1314&dat=19230811&id=9uZ-VAAAAIBAJ&sjid=weEDAAAAIBAJ&pg=5821,5193615.

Edwards, DeAnna. *Grieving: The Pain and the Promise*. American Fork, UT:

Covenant Communications, 1989.

Edwards, Tryon, ed. *A Dictionary of Thoughts: Being a Cyclopedia of Laconic Quotations*. Detroit, MI: F. B. Dickerson Co., 1908.

Eliot, George. *The Mill on the Floss*. Boston: Ginn and Company. 1914.

Emerson, Ralph Waldo. *The Works of Ralph Waldo Emerson*. Vol. 2. London: Macmillan and Co., 1882.

———. Goodreads.com. Accessed March 1, 2014. https://www.goodreads.com/quotes/511854-sorrow-looks-back-worry-looks-around-faith-looks-up.

Ericsson, Stephanie. *Companion Through the Darkness: Inner Dialogues on Grief.* New York City: HarperCollins, 1998.

Euripedes. In Craufurd Tait Ramagein. *Great Thoughts from Classic Authors*. New York City: John B. Alden, 1891.

Finkbeiner, Ann K. *After the Death of a Child*. Baltimore, MA: The Johns Hopkins University Press, 1998.

Floyd, Gregory. *A Grief Unveiled: One Father's Journey Through the Death of a Child*. Brewster, MA: Paraclete Press, 1999.

Frankl, Viktor. *Man's Search for Meaning.* New York City: Simon and Schuster, 1963.

Gardner, Helen. *The Metaphysical Poets*. New York City: Penguin, 1972.

Garrett, Greg. *Stories from the Edge: A Theology of Grief.* Louisville, KY: Westminster John Knox Press, 2008.

Geary, James. *Geary's Guide to the World's Great Aphorists*. New York City: Bloomberry, 2007.

Geller, Eileen. "The St. Thomas Guide to Surviving Grief: Including the 'Take a Bath' Cure for what ails you," Consoling Grace, 2006, http://www.consoling-grace.com/griefsupportthomas.html.

Gibran, Khahil. *The Prophet*. New York City: Alfred A. Knopf, 1923.

———. Goodreads.com. Accessed Decemeber 15, 2014. https://www.goodreads.com/quotes/780-joy-and-sorrow-are-inseparable-together-they-come.

Goodwin, Doris Kearns. *Team of Rivals: The Political Genius of Abraham Lincoln*. New York City: Simon and Schuster, 2005.

Goudge, Elizabeth. *The Castle on the Hill*. Mattituck, NY: Amereon Limited. 1976.

Hale, Dorothy J. *The Novel: An Anthology of Criticism and Theory 1900–2000*. Malden, MA: Blackwell, 2006.

Hannan, Mairead and Paul Kelly. *One Night the Moon*. Film. Performed by Kaarin Fairfax. Directed by Rachel Perkins. MusicArtsDance Films, 2001.

Hawthorne, Nathaniel. *The Scarlet Letter*. New York City: Simon and Schuster. 2004.

Herbert, George. "The Flower." In Francis T. Palgrave *Book of Sacred Song*. Oxford: Clarendon Press, 1890.

Herbert, George, and John Wall. *The Country Parson; The Temple*. Mahwah, NJ: Paulist Press, 1981.

Holland, Henry Scott. "I have only slipped away into the next room." *Consolatio*. Last modified February 8, 2005. http://www.consolatio.com/2005/02/i_have_only_sli.html.

Hopkins, Gerard Manley. *Gerard Manley Hopkins: The Critical Heritage*. Edited by Gerald Roberts. New York City: Routledge, 2000.

Horchler, Joani N. and Robin R. Morris. "The Death of a Child—The Grief of Parents: A Lifetime Journey." *He@lth*. Last modified September 21, 2010. http://www.athealth.com/consumer/disorders/parentalgrief.html.

Hugo, Victor. "Ecrit au bas d'un crucifix." Translated by Melissa Bradford-Dalton. *Les Contemplations, Book 3*, 1856.

———. *Les Misérables*. New York City: Dodd, Mead and Co., 1862.

———. "I will see that instant until I die." *Consolatio*. Last modified January 20, 2005. http://www.consolatio.com/on_the_death_of_a_child/page/3/.

———. "Tomorrow, as soon as it is dawn," *Consolatio*. Last modified February 1, 2005. http://www.consolatio.com/2005/02/tomorrow_as_soo.html.

———. "Veni, Vidi, Vixi; I came, I saw, I lived," *Consolatio*. Last modified December 1, 2006. http://www.consolatio.com/on_the_death_of_a_child/page/3/.

Hurston, Zora Neale. *Their Eyes Were Watching God: A Novel*. New York City: First Perennial Library, 1990.

Irving, Washington. *The Complete Works of Washington Irving in One Volume*. Paris: Baudry's European Library, 1834.

Jacobson, Jeanne M., Elton J. Bruins, and Larry J. Wagenaar, eds. *Albertus C. Van Raalte: Dutch Leader and American Patriot*. Holland, MI: Hope College, 1996.

Jonson, Ben. *The Broadview Anthology of Poetry*. Edited by Herbert Rosengarten and Amanda Goldrick-Jones. Ontario, Canada: Broadview Press, 2009.

Joyce, James. *Dubliners*. Berkeley, CA: Mundus Publishing. 1926.

Keith, John, attr. "How Firm a Foundation." *Hymns of the Church of Jesus Christ of Latter-day Saints*, 85. Salt Lake City, UT: The Church of Jesus Christ of Latter-day Saints, 1985.

Keller, Julia. "The Marshall plane crash, remembered thirty years later: 'It's always with you,'" *Consolatio*. Last modified December 11, 2006.http://www.consolatio.com/2006/12/the_marshall_pl.html.

Kelley, Melissa M. *Grief: Contemporary Theory and the Practice of Ministry*. Minneapolis, MN: Fortress Press, 2010.

Kimball, Spencer W. *Faith Precedes the Miracle*. Salt Lake City, UT: Deseret Book Company, 1972.

King, Stephen. *Different Seasons*. New York City: Signet, 1982.

Knell, Ellen. *Letters to Erica*. Unpublished manuscript, last modified February 28, 2014. Microsoft Word file.

Knapp, Ronald J. *Beyond Endurance*. Bloomington, IN: Rondald Kapp, 2005.

Kübler-Ross, Elisabeth. *Death: The Final Stage of Growth*. New York City:

Touchstone, 1986.

Kübler-Ross, Elisabeth. *On Life After Death*. Berkeley, CA: Celestial Arts, 1991

Kushner, Harold. *When Bad Things Happen to Good People*. New York City: Anchor Books, 2004.

Laërtius, Diogenes. Goodreads.com. Accessed March 1, 2014. https://www.goodreads.com/quotes/204685-we-have-two-ears-and-only-one-tongue-in-order

Lama, Dalai and Howard C. Cutler. *The Art of Happiness in a Troubled World*. New York City: Doubleday, 2009.

Langland, Elizabeth. *Anne Brontë: The Other One*. Totowa, NJ: Barnes and Noble, 1989.

Leone, Marianne. "A Mother's Grief—Without Time Limits." *The Boston Globe*. September 8, 2010. http://www.boston.com/community/moms/article/2010/09/08/a_mothers_grief__without_time_limits/.

———. *Knowing Jesse: A Mother's Story of Grief, Grace, and Everyday Bliss*. New York City: Simon & Schuster, 2010.

Lessing, Doris. "Grief like a weight of cold pain." *Consolatio*. Last modified July 21, 2008. http://www.consolatio.com/2008/07/doris-lessing-g.html.

Lewis, C. S. *A Grief Observed*. San Francisco: HarperCollins, 2001.

———. *The Problem of Pain*. San Fransisco: HarperCollins. 1994.

———. *Mere Christianity*. New York City: HarperCollins, 2001.

Lindbergh, Anne Morrow. *Hour of Gold, Hour of Lead: Diaries and Letters 1929–1932*. New York City: Harcourt, Brace, Jovanovich, 1973.

———. "Lindbergh Nightmare," *Time*. February 5, 1973.

Lincoln, Abraham. *Collected Works of Abraham Lincoln*. New Brunswick, NJ: Rutgers University Press, 1953.

Lindemann, Erich. "Symptomatology and Management of Acute Grief." *The American Journal of Psychiatry* 151:6 (June 1944).

Linn, Erin. *150 Facts About Grieving Children*. Incline Village, NV: Publisher's Mark, 1990.

Lipscomb, Andrew Adgate and Albert Ellery Bergh, eds. *The Writings of Thomas Jefferson*. 1907. (ebook)

Longfellow, Henry Wadsworth. *The Poetical Works of Henry Wadsworth Longfellow*. Vol. 3. New York City: Houghton Mifflin, 1886.

———. *The Works of Henry Wadsworth Longfellow*. Boston: Houghton Mifflin, 1886.

MacDonald, George. *Phantastes*. United Kingdom: Smith, Elder & Co., 1858.

Madsen, Truman. *Eternal Man*. Salt Lake City, UT: Shadow Mountain, 1966.

Mahfouz, Naguib. *Palace Walk*. Translated by William M. Hutchins and Olive Kenny. New York City: Doubleday, 1990.

Marrocco, Nancy. *A Promise in the Storm: Grieving and Dying with Hope*. Winona, MN: St. Mary's Press, 1997.

Maule, John C. *The Friend: A Religious and Literary Journal.* Vol. 56, no. 4. July 5, 1912.

McCarthy, Cormac. *All the Pretty Horses.* New York City: Alfred A. Knopf, 1992.

McCracken, Anne and Mary Semel. *A Broken Heart Still Beats: After Your Child Dies.* Center City, MN: Hazelden, 1998.

McGrath, Charles. "An Interview with Jim Harrison: Pleasures of the Hard-Worn Life." *New York Times.* January 25, 2007. http://www.nytimes.com/2007/01/25/books/25harr.html?pagewanted=all.

Medea, Benjamin, and Jodie Evans. "A Nation Rocked to Sleep." *Stop the Next War Now: Effective Responses to Violence and Terrorism.* Maui, HI: Inner Ocean Publishing, 2005.

Melville, Herman. *Moby Dick.* New York City: Harper and Brothers, 1851.

Mendelson, Edward, ed. *W. H. Auden: Collected Poems.* New York City: Modern Library, 2007.

Merton, Thomas. *New Seeds of Contemplation.* New York City: New Directions, 2007.

Metastasio, *Giga Quotes.* Last modified May 1, 2011. http://www.giga-usa.com/quotes/authors/metastasio_a001.htm.

Millay, Edna St. Vincent. *The Selected Poetry of Edna St. Vincent Millay.* Stillwell, KS: Digisreads.com Publishing, 2005.

Miller, Henry. *Tropic of Cancer.* New York City: Grove Press, Inc., 1961.

Miller, Sukie. *Finding Hope When A Child Dies: What Other Cultures Can Teach Us.* New York City: Fireside, 1999.

Mitchell, Ellen, Carol Barkin, Audrey Cohen, Lorenza Colletti, Barbara Eisenberg, Barbara J. Goldstein, Madelaine Perry Kasden, Phyllis Devine, Ariella Long, and Rita Volpe. *Beyond Tears: Living After Losing a Child.* New York City: St. Martin's, 2004.

Monaghan, Patricia. *The Red-Haired Girl from the Bog: The Landscape of Celtic Myth and Spirit.* Novato, CA: New World Library, 2003.

Moran, Rita. "Please, don't ask me if I'm over it yet." *Consolatio.* Last modified October 2, 2006. http://www.consolatio.com/2006/10/please_dont_ask.html.

Morris, Gary, ed. *To My Soul Mate: Words to Share with the Love of a Lifetime.* Boulder, CO: Blue Mountain Press, 2006.

Morton, Julius Sterling. *The Conservative.* Vol. 3, no. 21. November 29, 1900.

Muir, Kate. *Left Bank.* New York City: Penguin, 2006.

Müller, Robert. "I am sure that this whole planet is surrounded by spirits." *Consolatio.* Last modified February 22, 2006. http://www.consolatio.com/2006/02/i_am_sure_that_.html

Nicholi, Armand M. Jr. *The Question of God: C.S. Lewis and Sigmund Freud Debate the Meaning of God, Love, Sex and the Meaning of Life.* New York City: Simon and Schuster, 2002.

Norris, Kathleen. *Amazing Grace.* New York City: Riverhead Books, 1998.

Nouwen, Henri. *Eternal Seasons.* Notre Dame, IN: Ave Maria Press, 2004.

———. *A Sorrow Shared.* Notre Dame, IN: Ave Maria Press, 1980.

———. *Turn My Mourning into Dancing.* Nashville, TN: Thomas Nelson, Inc, 2001.

———. *The Wounded Healer: Ministry in Contemporary Society.* New York City: Doubleday, 1979.

———. *In Memoriam.* Notre Dame, IN: Ave Maria Press, Inc., 1980

Nouwen, Henri J. M. Goodreads.com. Accessed March 1, 2014. https://www.goodreads.com/author/quotes/4837.Henri_J_M_Nouwen

Nye, Naomi Shihab. "Kindness." http://www.panhala.net/Archive/Kindness.html.

Ó hÉigeartaigh, Pádraig. "My sorrow, Donncha." *Consolatio.* Last modified March 10, 2005, http://www.consolatio.com/2005/03/my_sorrow_donnc.html.

Olsen, Christopher J. *The American Civil War: A Hands-on History.* New York City: Macmillan, 2007.

"Oprah Talks to Christine McFadden." Oprah.com. May 2007. http://www.oprah.com/omagazine/Oprah-Interviews-Christine-McFadden/10.

Organ, Troy Wilson. *Philosophy and the Self: East and West.* Ontario, Canada: Associated University Presses, 1987.

Owen. Goronwy. "Goronwy Owen: Elegy for his daughter Ellen." *Consolatio.* Last modified March 14, 2005. http://www.consolatio.com/2005/03/elegy_for_his_d.html.

Plautus, Titus Maccius. QuotationsBook.com. Accessed January 10, 2014. http://quotationsbook.com/quote/1852/.

Prose, Francine. "Hell's Angels." *Live Your Best Life: A Treasury of Wisdom, Wit, Advice, Interviews, and Inspiration from O, the Opra Magazine.* Birmingham, AL: Oxmoor House Inc., 2005.

Quindlen, Anna. "Public & Private: Life After Death." *New York Times.* May 4, 1994. http://www.nytimes.com/1994/05/04/opinion/public-private-life-after-death.html.

Ravitch, Diane, ed. *The American Reader: Words That Moved a Nation.* New York City: HarperCollins, 200.

Rilke, Rainer Maria. *Say Hello to Your Very Own Book of Quotes.* Quotationsbook.com. (ebook).

———. *Letters to a Young Poet.* Frankfurt am Main, Germany: Penguin Books. 1933.

Rollinat, Maurice. "Maurice Rollinat: The doe mourns her fawn." Last modified November 18, 2006. *Consolatio.* http://www.consolatio.com/2006/11/rollinat_the_do.html.

Rosenblatt, Roger. *Kayak Morning: Reflections on Love, Grief, and Small Boats.* New York City: HarperCollins Publishers, 2012.

Rossi, Melody. *May I Walk You Home? Sharing Christ's Love with the Dying.*

Bloomington, MN: Bethany House, 2007.

Rumi, Jelal ad Din. "Rumi: It seems like setting to you, but it is rising." *Consolatio.* Last modified April 29, 2005. http://www.consolatio.com/2005/04/ghazal_911. html.

Salter, Stephanie. "The Myth of Managing Grief." *San Francisco Chronicle.* April 7, 2002. http://www.sfgate.com/cgi-bin/article.cgi?f=/c/a/2000 /04/07/ED89714. DTL.

Sanders, Catherine. *How to Survive the Loss of a Child: Filling the Emptiness and Rebuilding.* New York City: Three Rivers Press, 1998.

Schiff, Harriet Sarnoff. *The Bereaved Parent.* New York City: Crown Publishers, 1977.

Schiller, Friedrich. "An Die Freude." *Schiller Gedichte.* Stuttgart, Germany: Phaidon Verlag, 1982.

Schweibert, Pat and Chuch DeKlyen. *Tear Soup: A Recipe for Healing After Loss.* Portland, OR: Grief Watch, 1999.

Scovel, Carl. *Never Far from Home: Stories from the Radio Pulpit.* Boston, MA: Skinnerhouse, 2004.

Seattle, Chief. Goodreads.com. Accessed February 1, 2014. https://www.goodreads. com/quotes/776489-there-is-no-death-only-a-change-of.

Seneca. Goodreads.com. Accessed February 1, 2014. https://www.goodreads.com/ quotes/672798-fire-tests-gold-suffering-tests-brave-men.

Shakespeare, William. *The Riverside Shakespeare.* Edited by G. Blakemore Evans. Boston: Houghton Mifflin Co., 1974.

Silverman, Phyllis R. *Never Too Young To Know: Death in Children's Lives.* New York City: Oxford University Press, 2000.

Silverman, Phyllis R. and Madelyn Kelly. *A Parent's Guide to Raising Grieving Children: Rebuilding Your Family After the Death of a Loved One.* New York City: Oxford, 2009.

Simpson, Mona. "A Sister's Eulogy for Steve Jobs." *New York Times.* October 30, 2011. http://www.nytimes.com/2011/10/30/opinion/mona-simpsons-eulogy-for-steve-jobs.html?pagewanted=all.

Simsic, Wayne. *Cries of the Heart: Praying Our Losses.* Winona, MN: Saint Mary's Press, 1994.

Sittser, Gerald L. *A Grace Disguised: How the Soul Grows Through Loss.* Grand Rapids, MI: Zondervan, 2004.

Smith, Huston. *Why Religion Matters.* New York City: Harper Collins Publishers Inc., 2001

Smith, Joseph F. "Conference Report, April 1916"; see also *Gospel Doctrine.* 5th ed. Salt Lake City, UT: Deseret Book Company, Inc., 1939.

Smollett, Tobias, John Morley, William F. Fleming, and Oliver Herbrand Gordon Leigh, eds. *The Works of Voltaire.* New York City: E. R. Dumont, 1901.

Soper, Kathryn Lynard. "My Grief Observed." *Dance with Them*. Orem, UT: Segullah Books, 2010.

Stevens, Wallace. *The Collected Poems of Wallace Stevens*. New York City: Vintage, 1990.

Stone, Jon R. *The Routledge Dictionary of Latin Quotations: The Illiterati's Guide to Latin Maxims, Mottoes, Proverbs, and Sayings*. New York City: Routledge, 2005.

Stowe, Harriet Beecher. *Uncle Tom's Cabin*. Oxford: Oxford University Press. 1852.

Tagore, Rabindranath. "Tagore: Those who are near me do not know." *Consolatio*. Last modified January 20, 2005. http://www.consolatio.com/2005/01/those_who_are_n.html.

———. *Works of Rabindranath Tagore*. MobileReference. 2010. (google ebook)

Talbot, Kay. *What Forever Means after the Death of a Child: Transcending the Trauma, Living with the Loss*. New York City: Brunner-Routledge, 2002.

Tennyson, Alfred Lord. *The Poetical Works of Alfred Lord Tennyson*. New York City: Thomas Y. Crowell and Co., 1900.

The Book of Mormon: Another Testament of Jesus Christ. Trans. Joseph Smith, Jr. Salt Lake City, UT: The Church of Jesus Christ of Latter-Day Saints, 1981.

The Doctrine and Covenants. Salt Lake City, UT: The Church of Jesus Christ of Latter-day Saints, 1921.

The Musical Times. Vol. LVII, January to December 1916. New York City: H. W. Gray Co., 1916. (ebook)

Tileston, Mary Wilder. *Daily Strength for Daily Needs*. Indo-European Publishing, 2012.

Tolkien, J. R. R. *The Return of the King*. England: George Allen & Unwin, 1955.

Masters, Edgar Lee. *The Second Book of Modern Verse: A Selection from the Work of Contemporaneous American Poets*. Edited by Jessie Belle Rittenhouse. New York City: Houghton Mifflin, 1920.

Thomas, Catherine M. *Light in the Wilderness: Explorations in the Spiritual Life*. Edited by Linda Hunter Adams and Gary P. Gillum. Provo, UT: Amalphi Publishing, 2008.

———. *Selected Writings of M. Catherine Thomas*. Provo, UT: Amalphi Publishing, 2007.

Top, Brent. *Beyond Death's Door*. Salt Lake City, UT: Bookcraft, 1993.

Totten, Noah. "Mary Jane Coleman: I know he did not lie corset stiff." *Consolatio*. Last modified September 11, 2006. http://www.consolatio.com/page/22/.

Trench, Richard Chenevix. *Poems*. New York City: Redfield, 1856.

Twain, Mark. "Mark Twain after the death of his wife: I am a man without a country." Last modified April 28, 2008. *Consolatio*. http://www.consolatio.com/2008/04/mark-twain-afte.html.

———. *What is Man and Other Essays*. New York City: Harper and Brothers, 1917.

Vanauken, Sheldon. *A Severe Mercy*. New York City: HarperCollins e-books, 1980.

Watts, Isaac. "He Died! The Great Redeemer Died." *Hymns of the Church of Jesus Christ of Latter-day Saints*, 192. Salt Lake City, UT: The Church of Jesus Christ of Latter-day Saints, 1985.

Westenhaver, Jennie. *Beehive and Birdnest* (blog). http://www.beehiveandbirdsnest.com/category/serious.

Whitmore, Susan. "Susan Whitmore: You're never going to have your normal life back, but it doesn't mean it won't be a good life." *Consolatio*. Last modified December 27, 2007. http://www.consolatio.com/2007/12/susan-whitmore.html.

Wilde, Oscar. *De Profundis*. London: Methuen and Co., 1908.

Wolterstorff, Nicholas. *Lament for a Son*. Grand Rapids, MI: Eerdmans, 1987.

———. "Rights and Wrongs, an Interview with Nicholas Wolterstorff." http://www.religion-online.org/showarticle.asp?title=3533.

Wordsworth, William. "The Affliction of Margaret." *The Complete Poetical Works of William Wordsworth*. New York City: Macmillan and Co., 1893.

Wordsworth, William. "Surprised By Joy." Poetryfoudation.org, 2014.

Wortman, Camille. "Getting Through the Holidays: Advice from the Bereaved." PBS.org, Grief and Loss Blog. http://www.pbs.org/thisemotionallife/blogs/getting-through-holidays-advice-bereaved.

ABOUT THE AUTHOR

MELISSA DALTON-BRADFORD IS a writer, independent scholar, world citizen, and mother. She holds a BA in German and an MA in comparative literature, both from Brigham Young University. She speaks, reads, and writes fluent German, French, and Norwegian; is conversant in Mandarin; and has taught language, humanities, and writing on the university level. Bradford has performed professionally as a soprano soloist and actress in the US, Scandinavia, Central Europe, and South East Asia. She and her husband raised their family of four children in Hong Kong, Vienna, Oslo, Paris, Munich, Singapore, and Geneva.

ABOUT FAMILIUS

Welcome to a place where mothers are celebrated, not compared. Where heart is at the center of our families, and family at the center of our homes. Where boo boos are still kissed, cake beaters are still licked, and mistakes are still okay. Welcome to a place where books—and family—are beautiful. Familius: a book publisher dedicated to helping families be happy.

Visit Our Website: www.familius.com

Our website is a different kind of place. Get inspired, read articles, discover books, watch videos, connect with our family experts, download books and apps and audiobooks, and along the way, discover how values and happy family life go together.

Join Our Family

There are lots of ways to connect with us! Subscribe to our newsletters at www.familius.com to receive uplifting daily inspiration, essays from our Pater Familius, a free ebook every month, and the first word on special discounts and Familius news.

Become an Expert

Familius authors and other established writers interested in helping families be happy are invited to join our family and contribute online content. If you have something important to say on the family, join our expert community by applying at:

www.familius.com/apply-to-become-a-familius-expert

Get Bulk Discounts

If you feel a few friends and family might benefit from what you've read, let us know and we'll be happy to provide you with quantity discounts. Simply email us at specialorders@familius.com.

Website: www.familius.com

Facebook: www.facebook.com/paterfamilius

Twitter: @familiustalk, @paterfamilius1

Pinterest: www.pinterest.com/familius

The most important work

you ever do will be within the

walls of your own home.

CPSIA information can be obtained
at www.ICGtesting.com
Printed in the USA
FFOW02n2134110817
38716FF